The Future Remembered

THE 1962 SEATTLE WORLD'S FAIR AND ITS LEGACY

Paula Becker, Alan J. Stein & The HistoryLink Staff

Also by Alan J. Stein and Paula Becker:
Alaska-Yukon-Pacific Exposition: Washington's First World's Fair

Project manager: Tom Brown
Design: Nancy Kinnear, Marie McCaffrey
Editors: Tom Brown and Priscilla Long
Copy editor and indexer: Julie Van Pelt
Photographic research: Megan Churchwell

Printed and bound in China by C & C Offset Printing
First printing: October 2011

16 15 14 13 12 11 5 4 3 2 1

A HistoryLink book

Published by Seattle Center Foundation in association with
HistoryInk/HistoryLink.org

HistoryLink.org

seattle center
foundation

next
50
SEATTLE CENTER 2012

HistoryLink.org, the online encyclopedia of Washington state history

ISBN 9780615469409
Library of Congress Control Number: 2011926584

The paper used in this publication meets the minimum requirements of
American National Standard for Information Sciences—Permanence of
Paper for Printed Library Materials, ANSI Z39.48-1984.∞

front cover Century 21 Exposition foresaw a sleek, bright,
promising Tomorrow.

front cover flap The Bubbleator, shown here in 1963 after
relocation to the Food Circus, lifted 150 fairgoers at a time
into Century 21 Exposition's World of Tomorrow.

endpages Twenty-one 21-year-old women pose for a
publicity photo in front of the Coliseum construction on
April 21, 1961.

facing page The fairgrounds at night.

The Future Remembered

THE 1962 SEATTLE WORLD'S FAIR AND ITS LEGACY

PAULA BECKER, ALAN J. STEIN & THE HISTORYLINK STAFF

Contents

CENTURY 21 EXPOSITION

Foreword

By Jay Rockey

opposite The Seattle World's Fair official poster promised a clean, clear, streamlined Tomorrow.

IN OCTOBER 1957, THE WORLD CHANGED. With the Soviet launch of *Sputnik* we knew the 1962 Seattle World's Fair had to be more than a "Festival of the West" or a simple anniversary celebration of the 1909 Alaska-Yukon-Pacific Exposition (A-Y-P): it had to be a fair of, for, and about the future.

We owe a great deal to the talented men and women who turned this audacious idea into a transformative event that captured the imagination of the world, introduced Seattle as a global city, and deliberately left our community a civic center that is thriving 50 years later. These community leaders created a solid core of civic culture that has radiated in multiple directions for decades, and ignited a spark of ingenuity and imagination that has helped shape our region.

As the director of public relations and advertising for the Century 21 Exposition, Inc., (Seattle World's Fair) I worked with these visionaries every day for many months. Their story lives on in these pages, a chronicle of a moment in time that captured the imagination of a community and a nation. Along with the Great Seattle Fire, the Klondike Gold Rush and the A-Y-P Exposition, the 1962 Seattle World's Fair draws a line where our collective history can be marked.

Fifty years later, Seattle Center, the vibrant civic center that is the fair's greatest legacy, is preparing to celebrate its 50th anniversary. This celebration, The Next Fifty, appropriately does more than just look back to the Seattle World's Fair: it once again ignites the creativity and vision of our community and looks toward our shared future.

Here's to the next 50 years of Seattle Center, our community, and our entire region. The future we dreamed of in 1962 has finally arrived ... or has it?

Century 21 is off and running. Come, let's dream again.

CENTURY 21 EXPOSITION — THE 1962 SEATTLE WORLD'S FAIR — was called into being by civic leaders with a vision who would not hear "No." Their dual purpose: to celebrate their city while stimulating its growth, and to create the enduring legacy of a permanent civic center, which became Seattle Center. The audacity of building a world's fair specifically to leave so much behind is stunning, still, innovative beyond the thinking of any other exposition.

The exposition could not have succeeded without the work of community leaders, city, state, and national cooperation, and the enthusiastic participation of foreign nations. Once Seattle citizens were coaxed on board, they too became a key part of the fair's success. They opened their homes to visitors, they worked on the fairgrounds, they lent support by purchasing shares in the exposition, they smiled and smiled and smiled and welcomed the world to their city during 1962.

Some fairs, like the World's Columbian Exposition of 1893 in Chicago and the 1904 Louisiana Purchase Exposition in St. Louis, marked significant historical anniversaries. The Seattle World's Fair, like New York's 1939–1940 World's Fair, whose motto was "Building the World of Tomorrow," looked forward.

Century 21 was the first exposition in 22 years to be held on American soil. It looked forward with bold audacity, literally reaching for the stars through emphasis on science, seeking to ease global tensions through emphasis on peaceful uses of space technology, and transforming 13 square blocks — 74 acres — of Seattle into what

would become a treasured resource for the city, through the late 20th century and bravely on, into the real 21st.

The Space Needle, created for the fair, became Seattle's icon, while the Monorail imagined a future that was sleek, streamlined, and bold. The foreign nations that took the fair's chance to introduce their industries and cultures to Americans forged important ties of trade and diplomacy. The performing arts and the visual arts both benefited greatly from Century 21 — seeds planted at the fair sprouted, were nurtured, and have flourished into a vibrant cultural community. The Federal Science Pavilion, a completely innovative way to teach science to the masses, became the Pacific Science Center, where that important work continues.

Seattle's citizenry in 1962 differed markedly from what would come. Population in the state of Washington in 1960 was 2,853,214, according to the 1960 federal census, with 935,014 residing in King County. Of that number, 557,087 lived in Seattle, which ranked 19th in city size nationally. Within Seattle, 91.6 percent of the population was white, 4.8 percent was black, 3.1 percent was Asian and Pacific Islander, 0.3 percent American Indian, Eskimo, and Aleut, and 0.1 percent Other. (Persons of Hispanic/Latin derivation were included in the "White" count in the 1960 census.) By comparison, the 2010 census found the state's population was 6,724,540, with nearly 30 percent living in King County and 630,320 in Seattle. No demographic breakdowns from the 2010 census were available as we went to press,

Introduction

By Paula Becker and Alan J. Stein

but in the 2000 census Seattle's population was 70.1 percent white, 8.4 percent black, 13.1 percent Asian, 1 percent American Indian and Native Alaskan, 0.05 percent Native Hawaiian and Pacific Islander, 4.5 percent persons reporting two or more races, and 5.3 percent Hispanic or Latino. Seattle ranked 23rd in city size nationally.

Hindsight makes it clear that in 1962 many enormous changes were nascent: racial and social upheaval, the rock music scene, the women's movement, the Vietnam War, the shock and outrage of political assassinations. The landmark Civil Rights Act of 1964, which banned discrimination on the basis of race and sex, was two years in the future during Century 21.

This was an era when women's work could and did influence events — but women rarely got credit for it. Being female meant you might be a beauty queen, but not an astronaut. Some American women were fighting for inclusion in the U.S. space program in 1962 — a question on which the House Space Committee would hold hearings during July 1962, and that would be answered in the negative during Century 21's final days. But even so, at a fair whose logo depicted Man in Space, women helped make history.

A decade into the real Century 21, Seattle has put its resources and talent on the global table and has often reaped the benefits. We have survived difficult times: the tense, frightening days of the Cuban Missile Crisis, which President Kennedy unveiled on October 22, 1962, the day after the fair closed; the collective grief at the president's assassination the following year; the slowly building outcry against the Vietnam War; mounting cynicism at the actions of political leaders; the growth of greed in the closing decades of the twentieth century; and the psychic and emotional body blow America experienced on September 11, 2001, have left us, 50 years hence, in the odd position of looking back nostalgically on 1962's vision of the future.

The Century 21 Exposition laid hopeful, confident, impetuous claim to that future — a future ginned up from science-fiction mystique mixed with cutting edge science, peopled with newly emerging heroes like John Glenn and other pioneers of the New Frontier. The fair's present was replete with food and fun, with entertainment that spanned the gamut from Gracie Hansen's beloved if brassy burlesque to the highest-level performing arts culture Seattle had yet enjoyed.

Seattle boosters, business leaders, elected officials, and, finally, everyday citizens branded their bold undertaking America's Space Age World's Fair — at once staking claim to the country, the magnitude of space, and the whole wide world. Never again would Seattle be discounted.

Chapter 1

Reaching for the Stars

1955–April 20, 1961

The Century 21 Exposition is conceived, gains key supporters who understand its potential to give Seattle a permanent civic center, and defines its theme as space and science in response to *Sputnik*'s launch.

The 1962 Seattle's World's Fair showcased a world of the future filled with new technology, a better understanding among nations, and most of all, a feeling of heightened hope and optimism. This at a time when fallout shelters, civil defense alerts, and duck-and-cover drills were part of everyday life. Had it not been for a shiny metal sphere no larger than a beach ball, the fair might have turned out differently. The launch of the Soviet satellite *Sputnik* on October 4, 1957, brought about major — and immediate — changes in American culture and also turned plans for the Seattle World's Fair upside down. What had started off as a simple "Festival of the West" was quickly transformed into the forward-looking Century 21 Exposition — America's Space Age World's Fair.

The fair imagined our future, yet its roots burrowed deep into the past. Seattle's first world's fair, the Alaska-Yukon-Pacific Exposition, was held in 1909 to celebrate the tremendous growth and development the 1897 Klondike Gold Rush had brought to Washington.

WASHINGTON'S FIRST WORLD'S FAIR The A-Y-P ran from June 1, 1909, to October 16, 1909, and drew more than 3.7 million people. This cornerstone event in Seattle's history had a lasting effect on those who attended. Al Rochester was one of them.

opposite One of John Graham & Company's preliminary concept drawings for Century 21 Exposition design.

previous page Proud Washingtonians helped advertise by adorning their car bumpers with Century 21's fluorescent sticker.

Hired at age 13 to slice bread in a food concession on the fairgrounds, Al was provided with a pass giving him access for the entire fair period. The concession failed after only a few weeks but the lad, pass in hand, made coming to the A-Y-P his passionate vocation all summer long. Al Rochester must have seen it all: the gloriously landscaped grounds; the majestic Federal Government Building stuffed with thousands of important American artifacts; the Manufactures Building, where he could watch demonstrations of everything from carpet weaving to salmon canning; the Alaska Building, with its display of gold under armed guard; the Hawaii Building, where ukulele players strolled and samples of fresh pineapple were offered; and of course the Paystreak, A-Y-P's carnival midway, where he sometimes earned a few pennies drumming up crowds for the exotic performances.

In 1944, young Al, by then the well-respected local businessman Alfred R. Rochester, was elected to the Seattle City Council, a position he held until 1956. Two world wars and the atomic bomb separated Seattle from 1909 and the A-Y-P, but Al Rochester was one person who remembered the fair — how grand it had been for him and how successful for the city. As city councilman, Al Rochester became the spark between the fair many had nearly forgotten and the fair no one would ever forget.

ONE MORE ROUND The story of how Rochester proposed the notion of a fair to mark the A-Y-P's 50th anniversary became, almost at once, the stuff of legend. It goes like this:

Rochester and a few others had the germ of an idea for a fair to mark the A-Y-P's golden anniversary. In January 1955, over martinis at the Washington Athletic Club in downtown Seattle, Rochester broached the subject with Seattle Chamber of Commerce Director Don Follett and with Ross Cunningham, a reporter for *The Seattle Times*. The three agreed that Rochester should try to gain the city council's support.

On January 31, the Seattle City Council heard the first reading of the resolution Rochester had drafted. It petitioned the state legislature to investigate the desirability and feasibility of holding a world's fair in Seattle in 1959 to mark the 50th anniversary of the A-Y-P. On February 1, somewhat mysteriously, state Senator William Goodloe, a Republican from Seattle, and other King County legislators found copies of the resolution waiting on their chairs in the state chambers. With Goodloe's immediate enthusiasm, a bill authorizing the formation of such a committee and requesting $5,000 to cover expenses was read to the state legislature — in effect, before the Seattle City Council had even formally asked for it.

The Seattle City Council formally adopted the memorial resolution on February 7. Goodloe chaired the Senate Judiciary Committee, where he had the bill assigned. The committee sent the bill to the senate floor where, on February 16, despite some resistance from Eastern Washington legislators, it passed. On February 28, after hard lobbying by Goodloe and state Senator Albert Rosellini, it passed the state house. Governor Arthur B. Langlie then signed the bill into law, creating a commission to study the feasibility of a fair.

ENTER EDDIE CARLSON Governor Langlie appointed Goodloe and Senator Andrew Wineberg as the senate representatives to the Washington World's Fair Commission. He appointed Representatives Ray L. Olsen and Donald F. McDermott from the house. He appointed Tacoma businessman Paul H. Sceva and Tacoma hotel executive Alfred Williams. Finally, to chair the commission, Langlie wisely chose Seattle businessman Edward E. "Eddie" Carlson.

Carlson, executive vice president of Western Hotels and former manager of the exclusive Rainier Club, was an inveterate civic booster, dedicated to public service. A steady, friendly, fiscally prudent leader, the 43-year-old Carlson had worked his way up the ladder on his own strong merit and knew everyone from busboys to billionaires.

ALASKA-YUKON-PACIFIC EXPOSITION

The 1909 Alaska-Yukon-Pacific Exposition stands as a crowning example of what a community can do when everyone pulls together. Millions of visitors came from around the state, the nation, and the world to view educational exhibits, stroll the lushly manicured grounds, and be entertained on the Paystreak midway, while Seattle promoted itself as a gateway to the rich resources of Alaska, the Yukon, and Asia.

When the exposition ended, the University of Washington gained a beautifully landscaped campus and much-needed new buildings. Seattle strengthened its bonds with what we now call the Pacific Rim. Profits from the A-Y-P were poured back into the community, helping groups like the Anti-Tuberculosis League and the Seaman's Institute. Most importantly, the A-Y-P gave prominence to Seattle and Washington, cementing their role on the world's stage.

The Alaska-Yukon-Pacific Exposition's grand Court of Honor culminated in a stunning view of Mount Rainier.

So busy was Carlson with his work for Western Hotels and on civic projects that, when the governor asked him to serve on the World's Fair Commission, he tried to demur. As Carlson later recalled, Langlie said, "If we can't turn to you in the private sector and have you help us with those things that we in government are supposed to do, how can we in government go ahead?" Carlson quickly came on board.

The Olympic Hotel, managed by Western Hotels, was Carlson's kingdom, and it became the incubator of the Seattle World's Fair. The World's Fair Commission held its first meeting in the Olympic's Parlor A on August 19, 1955. The commissioners discussed possible sites for the possible fair: Sand Point Naval Air Station, then still under the navy's control, and Fort Lawton (now Discovery Park), then owned by the army.

CENTERING IN Meanwhile, another group of civic boosters was busy working on a remedy for something modern that Seattle lacked but obviously needed: a city civic center where art, music, theater, and other cultural and community needs could be facilitated. These two dedicated groups of individuals, working on parallel tracks for their city's greater good, would soon come together and by their fission start a reaction of such magnitude that it still resonates today.

The committee campaigning for a civic center had been appointed by Seattle Mayor Allan Pomeroy in January 1954 and was chaired by Seattle investment banker Robert J. Block. Mayor Pomeroy told *The Seattle Times*, "Seattle's community facilities for sports, cultural activities, convention and public administration functions are most inadequate. The founders and early settlers of Seattle moved entire hills to make a city. Certainly we can solve the financial and organizational problems which a civic center would entail."

ARENA   AUDITORIUM   VETERAN'S HALL.   RECREATION FIELD

CIVIC AUDITORIUM
ARENA &
RECREATION FIELD

SEATTLE

"The auditorium building will provide a place where the citizenry of Seattle can foregather to discuss civic problems, share ideas and ideals and learn both to think together and to speak a common language. ... A city without a home or a common meeting place tends to separate into individual communities and lose all coherence and unity. ... This building should have inscribed upon its portal the words: "'I am here to serve Seattle. Use me. Spare me not.'"

SEATTLE MAYOR BERTHA LANDES, MAY 18, 1928

Small groups and individuals around the city mailed in contributions (mainly $10, $25, and occasionally $100) to support the work of the civic center committee, indicating broad grassroots support.

After a 15-month study by a team of architects, engineers, real estate salespeople, and city planners, the committee recommended the creation of a 32-acre downtown park with cultural, convention, and parking facilities, and the remodeling of the Civic Auditorium many blocks away near 4th Avenue N and Mercer Street. The suggested park site was on First Hill, east of the then-planned Tacoma-Seattle-Everett Tollway (never built, although its suggested route formed the basis for the Seattle Freeway — now Interstate 5 — when that construction commenced in 1958). Block challenged residents to have the courage to look "10, 25, and even 50 years" ahead, adding, "the question now is whether Seattle is big enough to think in terms of 1975."

COMING TOGETHER On September 6, 1955, Eddie Carlson wrote to Block, describing the World's Fair Commission. The commission wanted to "sense the desire of other related groups to such a program." It had already met with representatives of the Seattle City Council the, Washington State Advertising Commission, Greater Seattle, the Seattle Chamber of Commerce, *The Seattle Times*, and the *Seattle Post-Intelligencer*. Might Block come to lunch at the Olympic Hotel and share his thoughts with them? Block agreed, setting in motion what would become Seattle's brilliant Trojan horse: the creation of what fair director Joseph Gandy would later term "a Civic Center disguised as a World's Fair."

In December 1955, the Seattle City Council created a 39-member Civic Center Advisory Commission, which absorbed Block's committee, and instructed it to report its findings to the city council by July 1, 1956. On this commission were three representatives from the Washington World's Fair Commission: Eddie Carlson, William Goodloe, and Ray Olsen. Seattle attorney Harold S. Shefelman chaired the new body.

LOCATION, LOCATION, LOCATION By late February 1956, meanwhile, the World's Fair Commission had gathered sufficient information supporting community interest in a world's fair and had moved on to site selection. On the rainy morning of March 22, most commissioners toured the sites under consideration: Fort Lawton (both the entire site and the waterfront portion south of West Point); Sand Point Naval Air Station; Duwamish Head; First Hill (including an enlargement of the area the Block committee was considering for a performing arts center); fill land on Union Bay (owned by the University of Washington and formerly part of the A-Y-P Exposition site); and an enlarged footprint near Denny Way that included the Seattle Civic Auditorium and Ice Arena. The committee also briefly considered, then discarded, Green Lake, Woodland Park, and Newport Bay.

The commissioners winnowed their options to two sites: First Hill and the area around the Civic Auditorium and Ice Arena. After much discussion, Eddie Carlson (as quoted by the fair's official historian, Murray Morgan) summarized the juncture at which these dedicated civic leaders found themselves:

"There are two facets to this project. One is long range development for the city, and the other is to do a job as far as the world's fair is concerned. There is real justification if, out of the fair, the city and the state can get some permanent buildings. Time moves rapidly. If I were to have to make a decision as to the most important aspect of our work, I would sacrifice other things in order to get some long range benefits."

MORE THAN FAIR Governor Langlie had created the World's Fair Commission for a project whose scope was limited — assessing the viability of a single event, a world's fair that would undoubtedly boost the city for a time. But Carlson and his team were determined to seize this opportunity to broaden the project to encompass the region's continuing growth and sustained well-being.

opposite top left Seattle's Civic Auditorium, Ice Arena, and Recreation Field provided the growing city with a nucleus for culture, enjoyment, and the exchange of ideas.

lower left The brochure produced to celebrate the complex utilized Northwest Coastal Indian totem pole iconography to link the new facilities with regional history.

right Kroll's Map of Seattle shows the future fairground/Seattle Center site before demolition began.

left Student population at the Warren
Avenue School, built in 1903, peaked
in 1929 with an enrollment of 734.
Beginning in 1944, it housed a
pioneering program serving children
with cerebral palsy. Programs for
blind, partially sighted, and hearing-
impaired students were added soon
after.

right An aerial view of the future fair
site with existing buildings included
the Armory (above center), Memorial
Field (center), and the Ice Arena, Civic
Auditorium, and VFW Hall complex
(lower right corner).

"It seemed to us ridiculous that a community would undertake the expense and the effort to build a fair, and then afterwards to tear down all of the buildings. [Bringing the projects together meant] accomplishing things with a concerted, coordinated effort that you couldn't accomplish otherwise," Carlson later recalled.

A SITE FOR SORE EYES From this point on, the World's Fair Commission directed its planning toward the Civic Auditorium and Ice Arena site.

It was initially unclear which structures occupying the site might be of use. The Civic Auditorium, with its terrible acoustics and barnlike interior? The Ice Arena, beloved by generations of Seattle ice skaters? The hulking Washington State National Guard Armory that loomed over Thomas Street? The aging homes and apartment houses? Warren Avenue School, where special classes served kids with cerebral palsy, hearing impairment, and blindness? And what about the few parcels where new construction — a small hotel or business office, perhaps — had tidied up a patch of land? Could High School Memorial Stadium be made to serve? The Nile Shriners were about to break ground for their new temple over on 2nd Avenue N. How might that affect the commissioners' choice?

The civic center commission's deadline looming, Harold Shefelman's team met three or four times each week at 7:30 in the morning. The committee eventually settled on the Civic Auditorium site — partially because the World's Fair Commission had chosen it, which meant the civic center project could benefit immensely by using the site after the fair closed.

ACHIEVING CONSENSUS In September 1956, the World's Fair Commission issued its report to Governor Langlie and the 1957 legislature, recommending that a two-season "Festival of the West" be held from July through October 1960 and again in 1961. The report acknowledged that there was really not time to mount a 1959 golden anniversary celebration of the Alaska-Yukon-Pacific Exposition.

Seattle.
When the Klondike
was struck – 1896
C.L.Andrews Photo

View of Potlatch Meadows, the future fairground site, taken from the Clarence Bagley home at 2nd Avenue N and Aloha Street, 1896.

POTLATCH MEADOWS AND THE BOGUE PLAN

The site chosen for the world's fair was an area early settlers dubbed "Potlatch Meadows" in the mistaken belief that the local indigenous people held their tribal festivals there. The area's first white residents, David and Louisa Denny, simply called it "the prairie." The Denny claim was bounded to the south by what is now Denny Way, to the north by Mercer Street, to the east by 5th Avenue N, and to the west by Elliott Bay. Over time, the land was platted into smaller parcels.

In 1910, Seattle commissioned civil engineer Virgil Bogue, a colleague of the Olmsted brothers' landscape design firm, to prepare a detailed plan to guide Seattle's future development. His ambitious proposal envisioned a grand civic center complex in the recently leveled Denny Regrade, with a broad corridor leading out to a massive train station on the south shore of Lake Union — all within sight of the former Potlatch Meadows. Wary of the potential bill for Bogue's dream — which also included a rapid-transit tunnel to Kirkland and the purchase of Mercer Island as a city park — in 1912 voters rejected the plan by nearly two to one.

Carlson's report underscored the civic brilliance of marrying the incipient fair/festival to the nascent civic center, creating a site and buildings that could live beyond the fair. Calling the opportunity unique, the report stated, "The opportunity to carry this forward in concert may never happen again during several generations."

On November 6, 1956, Seattle voters approved a $7.5 million bond issue that would fund the acquisition of 28 acres of land, mostly south and west of the Civic Auditorium, as a site for the civic center; provide funds to construct a 3,500-seat concert and convention hall; build an 800-seat auditorium; make improvements to the existing Civic Auditorium; and add parking and landscaping to the campus. The civic center and world's fair were now permanently intertwined.

STATELY MANNER Statewide elections in 1956 strengthened political support for the fair. Rather than seek reelection, Langlie challenged U.S. Senator Warren G. Magnuson and lost by a landslide. Albert Rosellini, formerly King County's Democratic state senator and already a great supporter of the world's fair, won Washington's gubernatorial election.

left Ewen Dingwall, known as Ding, was the fair's first employee. His steady oversight was a major factor in Century 21's success.

middle Clayton Young orchestrated the site's transformation from city neighborhood to Seattle Center.

right Barry Upson bore increasingly important duties as the march toward the fair progressed, eventually becoming director of domestic exhibits.

below Supporters of the civic center bond that would eventually help create Seattle Center papered neighborhoods with brochures that explained the project's significance.

VOTE

YES

for a

CIVIC CENTER

Worthy of Seattle!

November 6, 1956 Election

The state was asked to make an appropriation comparable to the amount of Seattle's civic center bond measure. Profit from the fair, if any, was to flow into the state general fund.

World's Fair Commission member Ray Olsen bird-dogged the fair's appropriation request during the 1957 legislative session. Olsen's bill funded the state's contribution by raising corporation fees, which were still billed at the rate established in 1889 when Washington became a state. The bill gave the World's Fair Commission the powers it required to acquire, develop, and build on the world's fair site, including the right to condemn property by eminent domain. The bill passed. A separate measure, also sponsored by Olsen, enlarged the World's Fair Commission to 15 members. One of these would be Al Rochester, the fair's first booster. Rochester later became the commission's salaried director.

ENTER EWEN DINGWALL Work began at once. In late April 1957, Harold Shefelman (acting for the Civic Center Advisory Commission) and Eddie Carlson (acting for the World's Fair Commission) hired Ewen C. "Ding" Dingwall, executive director of the Washington State Research Council, as project director for the development of the civic center and world's fair. (Dingwall's title would eventually be vice president and general manager of Century 21 Exposition, Inc.) He was the joint project's first paid employee, charged with overseeing the interests of both the city and the state. His office was a tiny former closet tucked away in the Civic Auditorium.

Dingwall's daughters, Emily Easton and Donnie Jewell, spoke decades later about the qualities their father brought to the job: "He was such an ethical man. It was just his core. And he was going to just, by golly, make this an honest endeavor, and one that would not lose money."

Dingwall, who was 44, brought to the job both the ability to lead and the ability to wait. Steadfastly building the project from one employee to thousands, from no buildings to dozens, from a good idea into an international accomplishment, all Dingwall's management skills were pressed into play. "There were so many people and organizations involved, each mindful of separate interests and rights — and with time pressing and everyone anxious for quick decisions, one of the toughest things was to allow each person and agency time to reach the decisions they had a right to make," Ding later recalled. "I did my share of firing from the hip, but deciding when not to come to a decision was for a long time one of my most useful functions."

Shefelman, Dingwall, and Carlson began almost daily 7 a.m. breakfast meetings in the Olympic Hotel's Seattle Room behind the Olympic Grill restaurant.

SERVING NOTICE Dingwall hired Clayton Young to be the project's coordinating architect. Trained at the University of Illinois, Young had practiced in Seattle since 1952. He was in his early 30s. It was a crucial hire: From the time the site was chosen, Young oversaw every aspect of the project's development and later coordinated postfair planning. Young had two qualities that soon came to epitomize many key fair employees: He was smart and he was young.

In April and May 1957, hundreds of individuals within the chosen area received summonses informing them that their property was being condemned. Kate Betteridge, Claude and Cecelia McPherson, heirs of Nina F. Sargent, George and Lillie Coomes, Unity Church of Truth, Annie Donnelly — the list was long.

Some of the property was bank-owned. Much property had absent landlords — children or grandchildren of early owners using their inherited houses as rental properties.

BY DESIGN The joint executive committee (representing world's fair and civic center interests) formed a volunteer Design Standards Advisory Board to help conceptualize the fair and civic center grounds. Members were chosen from a list of candidates developed by the Washington chapter of the American Institute of Architects (AIA), and included two members from outside the state: San Francisco landscape architect Lawrence Halprin and Minoru Yamasaki, an architect born and raised in Seattle whose architectural practice was in Detroit. Both men were internationally respected for their work. Seattle architects Perry Johanson, John Detlie, Robert Deitz, Paul Thiry, and Seattle's Planning Commission Director John Spaeth completed the advisory board. The board met for the first time in late August 1957.

left The Fire Alarm Communications Center on the triangle of land formed by Thomas Street, 4th Avenue N, and Broad Street was demolished to make way for construction of the Space Needle.

right More than 200 structures were demolished to clear way for the fairgrounds, including these homes dating from the turn of the twentieth century.

As early as September 1957, the Design Standards Advisory Board was considering incorporating a monorail, initially as a means of connecting the fairgrounds with the waterfront.

Clayton Young also formed a committee of local landscape architects. Community input was crucial during this early planning phase, and many Seattleites soon found themselves serving on whichever planning committee best suited their expertise. Meetings for the various committees took place at the Olympic Hotel and at the Washington Athletic Club, all at 7 a.m. Press was nearly always present, and Carlson later stressed that "the newspapers' involvement in all this was critical" to build public interest and support.

EARLY HIRES Already the project was hiring a few people who later would contribute in significant ways to the fair's success.

In September 1957, Barry Upson, 25 and a recent graduate of the University of Washington School of Architecture, joined the civic center project. Although his job was to last 60 days and initially related to the civic center only, he stayed, becoming Ewen Dingwall's assistant, the manager of the fair's New York office, and eventually director of domestic exhibits.

Upson later reflected that he was mentored by many of the high-powered business leaders he rubbed shoulders with during the course of his work at the fair. One of these mentors was Ding. Upson later reflected, "I think he was wonderful. I think he single-handedly kept the fair going. He was the reason the fair worked."

Shortly thereafter, former newspaper reporter Anne Swensson became the fair's first nonsecretarial female employee. As press coordinator, Swensson wrote press releases, handled press conferences, wrote articles about the fair for national and international publication, coordinated photography requests, and assisted with the fair's community volunteer activities such as those involving the Girl Scouts and Seattle Junior League.

A NEW MOON One of the most important moments in the history of the Seattle World's Fair occurred on October 4, 1957, when the Soviet Union launched *Sputnik*, the world's first satellite. *Sputnik*'s launch sent shock waves around the world.

People were stunned. The space race had begun, and America was already behind. This loss of pride heightened Cold War jitters, as did the stark realization that if the USSR could launch a satellite into orbit, technology to launch nuclear-armed missiles over great distances might soon follow. The Soviets had scored both a major scientific achievement and a propaganda victory.

Hundreds of Seattle residents became amateur astronomers, scouring the skies with binoculars and telescopes, hoping to grab a glimpse of tiny *Sputnik*, soaring 580 miles above. Entire families traveled up into the mountains after dark, hoping for a clearer view away from city lights. Amateur radio operators monitored the airwaves, listening for the faint "beep-beep-beep" being broadcast from above.

SEIZING THE OPPORTUNITY In the days following the *Sputnik* launch, Washington Senator Henry M. "Scoop" Jackson stated, "For the first time, our country is losing a scientific and engineering race which we were determined to win." Others in government thought likewise, and beginning in 1958 huge amounts of money began to pour into science, engineering, and mathematics education. The launch of *Sputnik* galvanized a steely drive to outdo the Soviets as soon as possible and at any cost. This nationwide shift in focus was not lost on the planners of the Seattle World's Fair.

Sputnik turned the fair's focus toward science and the urgent need for all nations to make peaceful use of space. The fair would in its time shower Seattle with a bounty of performing and visual arts, with the opportunity

opposite above Some of the World's Fair department heads: (back row, from left) Russell Mowrey (controller, 1959-1961), Clayton Young (site development), Donald Foster (exhibits), Frederic Schumacher (operations), Jay Rockey (public relations), Donald Fry (underwriting), George Whitney (concessions); (front row, from left) Harold Shaw (performing arts), Ewen Dingwall (vice president and general manager), Joseph Gandy (president), Harry Henke III (administration).

below Edward Carlson was the fair's guiding light.

to practice diplomatic cooperation among many nations, with sparkle and spangle and carnival festivities. But it was the launch of *Sputnik* that brought federal dollars to the table. It was federal participation that led to the fair's designation as an international exposition — and that brought in the world.

The day *Sputnik* was launched, Jim Faber, a *Seattle Post-Intelligencer* reporter recently hired as the fair's public relations director, was in Washington, D.C., working with Senator Magnuson's office to trace the history of federal appropriations for other U.S. expositions. Magnuson immediately saw the opportunity to shift the world's fair's focus to science.

BILLS TO PAY Five days after *Sputnik's* launch, on October 9, 1957, the state legislature approved the incorporation of the World's Fair Corporation of Washington, Inc., a nonprofit company that could raise funds from the private sector. Carlson, still chairing the World's Fair Commission, also took on the role of president for the new corporation. Governor Rosellini served as honorary chairman. Honorary vice chairmen included U.S. Senators Magnuson and Jackson; Representatives Don Magnuson, Thomas M. Pelly, Jack Westland, Russell V. Mack, Hal Holmes, Walt Horan, and Thor Tollefson; and Seattle Mayor Gordon Clinton. Upon their election to the State House of Representatives in 1958 and 1960, respectively, Catherine May and Julia Butler Hanson were added to this group.

Bills were flooding Ewen Dingwall's office. Money, or lack of it, was to become a problem throughout the development of the fair, despite disciplined budgeting. Eddie Carlson later credited Seattle real estate magnate Henry Broderick with dipping into his own pocket and quietly passing the hat among other civic leaders to tide the fair over its initial shortfall. A bright young businessman in 1909, Broderick had been the A-Y-P's youngest trustee. His appointment as a Century 21 trustee at age 77 was another arc between the old fair and the new.

On December 3, 1957, World's Fair Corporation board members Henry Broderick, Lawrence Arnold (chairman of Seattle-First National Bank board of directors), Maxwell Carlson (president of the National Bank of Commerce), Frank Dupar Jr. (treasurer of Palmer Supply Company), Ben Ehrlichman (investment banker), D. K. MacDonald (insurance broker), Emil Sick (brewery owner), and William S. Street (president of Frederick & Nelson department store) sent a letter appealing for funds to 30 other wealthy members of the board. Within the next few weeks, the plea brought in $25,000. Without generous response, it is doubtful that even Carlson's enthusiasm, Shefelman's drive, and Dingwall's leadership could have kept the fair alive.

In mid-January 1958, Mayor Clinton met with President Eisenhower and alerted him to the developing plans for the world's fair. Jim Faber and Warren Magnuson, meanwhile, were busy working to bring science and the Seattle World's Fair together. Faber bounced between New York and Washington, D.C., meeting with key scientists, including Dr. Dael Wolfle, executive officer of the American Association for the Advancement of Science and a Bremerton native whose father had worked at the A-Y-P. Wolfle connected Faber with high-caliber scientific leaders.

SCIENCE FAIR Then, just as world's fair officials began to rally scientists, America's *Explorer 1* took to the skies on January 31, 1958, beaming back data about the Van Allen radiation belts encircling the earth. Less than two months later, *Vanguard 1* became the second U.S. satellite launched into orbit, where though silent since 1964 it remains to this day as the oldest human-made object in space.

On March 15, 1958, Faber, Magnuson, Carlson, Dingwall, and 15 distinguished scientists met for dinner at the Shoreham Hotel in Washington, D.C. All agreed that the fair presented a crucial chance to showcase science.

President Dwight Eisenhower, Governor Albert Rosellini, and Mayor Gordon Clinton set the Century 21 Exposition countdown machine in motion on November 10, 1958.

Magnuson's staff drafted and won passage of legislation to finance the study of federal participation in the fair, including the appointment of a U.S. commissioner, the creation of a 16-person federal commission, and an initial appropriation of $125,000. The entire Washington congressional delegation joined to support the legislation. On August 28, President Eisenhower signed it into law.

Warren Magnuson was the fair's best friend in Congress, shepherding and protecting legislation in support of the grand project. The federal government would ultimately spend $12.5 million on U.S. participation in the fair, and the resultant United States Science Pavilion (the postfair Pacific Science Center) would draw rave reviews and attract millions of fairgoers.

A science-themed world's fair was by its nature forward-looking and should be named accordingly. Reaching ahead by decades, fair planners renamed their venture the Century 21 Exposition. The World's Fair Corporation officially adopted in the new name on July 22, 1958.

ARCHITECTURAL INTEGRITY On August 13, 1958, the Civic Center Advisory Commission and World's Fair Commission unanimously approved Paul Thiry, age 53, as primary architect for the joint project. A 1928 University of Washington graduate, Thiry had designed the Frye Art Museum and Museum of History & Industry in Seattle and the Washington State Library in Olympia. He worked closely with coordinating architect Clayton Young, whose continued focus was to ensure that prefair decisions would dovetail with successful postfair uses planned for the buildings that would be permanent. Considered the father of architectural modernism in the Pacific Northwest, Thiry would design many of Century 21's buildings, imbuing the fairgrounds with his clean design sensibility.

"This event should not be considered as merely a repetition of anything previously seen on the face of the earth. The 1961 exposition will be successful in direct proportion to the ability of the people of Washington to accept the challenge before them — to make it unique and dramatic — a foretaste of the world that is to come, rather than a record of the world as it has been. If this event is approached in that manner and all the people of the state cooperate in bringing it about, there will remain on the site, long after the fair itself has closed, a cultural center of continuing usefulness that may mark the beginning of a new era in man's understanding of and control over the universe that surrounds him."

WORLD'S FAIR COMMISSION MINUTES, JULY 7, 1958

opposite above left Paul Thiry's site plan had to incorporate existing structures including Memorial Stadium (center) and the Armory (below), within a relatively small footprint.

above right Albert Schweppe fought for the complete demolition of Civic Auditorium, but lost his case.

below Ford Motor Company Pavilion, Broad Street perspective.

MARKING TERRITORY Not all the civic seas were smooth, however. Legal and public relations wrangles with Seattle attorney Alfred Schweppe slowed momentum, as did the need to calm tempests with the Nile Shriners, the Seattle Archdiocese, and the Seattle Public Schools.

The site contained some buildings that could not be torn down because of their ownership or provenance, or because they might be useful. These included the huge National Guard Armory, High School Memorial Stadium, Civic Auditorium, Ice Arena, and VFW Hall. A small apartment house and an insurance agency, both recently constructed, were eventually repurposed for world's fair staff office space.

The newly built Nile Shrine Temple and the Catholic Sacred Heart Parish sat within the fair site, and that caused problems. When Archbishop Thomas A. Connolly of the Seattle Archdiocese got wind of the plan to acquire the parish land through condemnation, he summoned Carlson to his residence and reminded him that a number of high-ranking government officials were both practicing Catholics and (thus far) supporters of the fair.

Similarly, Harold Shefelman was summoned to a meeting of all the Nile Shriners' past potentates. Carlson went along to offer moral support and later remembered the group as "a pretty stony-faced bunch." The battle to escape the fair's eminent domain take, Carlson recalled, "united these two groups [the Shriners and the Catholic Church] for the first time in history. The fairgrounds footprint was modified to exclude the parish buildings, and the Shriners kept their property, but agreed to lease their brand new building to the exposition company during the fair."

USING WHAT'S THERE Initial plans called for the demolition of Memorial Stadium. The school district beat that down, but the Warren Avenue School lay in the very middle of the site and would have to go.

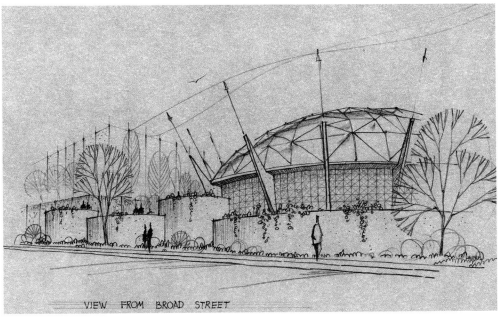

VIEW FROM BROAD STREET

THE PROTESTER: ALFRED SCHWEPPE

Alfred J. Schweppe was the fair's foremost critic, objecting on legal grounds to the use of bond-issue funding to remodel the Civic Auditorium for fair and civic center use. An attorney and opera lover who based his hatred of the Civic Auditorium on its poor acoustics, Schweppe had been a great supporter of the bond issue because it was to result in a brand new opera house — balm to the ears of all.

Schweppe waged war against the fair in both Seattle newspapers and filed three lawsuits, the last of which reached the State Supreme Court, where Schweppe's petition for rehearing was refused. In a September 1959, special-election voters reaffirmed the plan to use bond-issue monies to convert the Civic Auditorium rather than force new construction.

The National Guard Armory required modifications, especially so that its entrances could accommodate crowds. Almost all of the 27 existing restroom facilities were designed for men, so many needed to be converted for women. The uneven wooden armory floor, previously used to accommodate National Guard drill practice, required resurfacing. Attempts were also made to improve the hulking building's dodgy acoustics.

The Ice Arena received improvements, including converting some of its restrooms into dressing rooms for use by visiting performers, adding an insulation cover over the ice surface to increase spectator seating for stage shows, improving the heating and ventilation systems, and adding a portable stage platform.

The Civic Auditorium was altered most. The Design Standards Advisory Board recommended that a new concert hall and opera house be constructed within the shell of the old Civic Auditorium. This saved millions of dollars.

MAKING WAY Demolition began in pelting rain on November 12, 1958, with a two-story eight-room wood-frame house at 619 Nob Hill Avenue — future location of the Mercer Street parking garage. A-Y-P and Century 21 trustee Henry Broderick, ensconced in the cab of a 15-ton crane, let loose the wrecking clamshell's initial swing into the house's upper floor. Under an awning, a band struck up a sprightly tune. As Broderick clambered down and let professionals take over, Charles Burkman, who had lived in the house from 1897 to 1948, stood by tearfully. "That was my old bedroom," Burkman told the *Seattle Post-Intelligencer*. "It was the warmest room in the house. The chimney ran through it. There was no band music when we moved into it. I've had enough."

SAVING THE TREES

Some of the trees planted to landscape the fairgrounds were rescued from the right-of-way being cleared for construction of the Seattle Freeway (now Interstate 5). Some 80 large trees were removed from these lots. From 7428 6th Avenue NE came a 15-foot weeping cherry; 6518 Oswego Place and 5312 6th Avenue NE both yielded up their monkey puzzle trees. At 2709 Harvard Avenue N, a white birch was rescued. And so it went.

The trees were moved in early March 1959. They were stored on the former Warren Avenue School playground, the eventual site of the fair's International Fountain. Some trees that had graced structures demolished to make way for the exposition also were saved.

More than 200 houses, duplexes, multiplexes, and commercial structures were demolished. The city vacated the streets running through the fairgrounds site. Century 21 executives sought extensive press coverage of demolition as the first step of focusing the public's attention on the civic center and fairgrounds site.

Once planning was underway, citizens deluged fair officials with letters full of helpful suggestions. A number of people thought that, given the fair's science theme, the buildings should be heated and cooled with atomic energy.

BREAKING SPACE On May 27, 1959, Governor Rosellini unveiled a model of Paul Thiry's Coliseum. Although designed as a huge fair pavilion that could house multiple displays, Thiry had planned the three-acre building to be easily converted into a sports arena. At Eddie Carlson's urging, Mayor Clinton, Century 21 Exposition, Inc. (so-renamed in November 1958), Governor Rosellini, and state Department of Commerce Director Dewayne Kreager agreed that Seattle would buy the Coliseum from the state after the fair.

Century 21 Exposition officially kicked off with a wink to Washington's first world's fair. The A-Y-P had opened June 1, 1909, when President William Howard Taft pressed a telegraph key encrusted with gold nuggets

above Models of the fairgrounds were used to publicize the upcoming exposition.

below World's Fair Commission Executive Director Alfred Rochester (head of table) opens bids on Coliseum construction contract.

from the claim of George Carmack, whose lucky strike had begun the Klondike Gold Rush. Taft's signal also had started a highly publicized cross-country auto race from New York City to Seattle. Upon its triumphant entry onto the A-Y-P fairgrounds on the University of Washington campus, Henry Ford's newly invented Model T was declared the winner, although another car, a Shawmut, was later found to have deserved the prize.

On the morning of June 23, 1959, exactly 50 years after the A-Y-P contest concluded, three cars that had reenacted the Atlantic-to-Pacific race (a Model T, a 1959 Ford, and an experimental Levicar that was supposed to operate by magnetic levitation) reached the City-County Building in downtown Seattle. Seattle Mayor Clinton, Governor Rosellini, and a score of dignitaries joined them, and they proceeded to groundbreaking ceremonies for the Coliseum.

The *Seattle Post-Intelligencer* billed the celebration as a "Space Breaking" (rather than a groundbreaking), and it was: As the Ford zoomed across the finish line, Governor Rosellini pushed a switch that blasted off a small rocket carrying dirt from the Coliseum site.

ENTER JOE GANDY Eddie Carlson realized that he could no longer serve as both the World's Fair Commission chairman and Century 21 Exposition president and do his (paying) job at the Olympic Hotel. Bill Street, president of the Frederick & Nelson department store, suggested that Seattle attorney and Ford dealer Joseph E. Gandy take the helm at Century 21. Voted in on July 4, 1959, Gandy finished up his Seafair duties (he was 1959's King Neptune) and then started at the fair on September 8, 1959, a month shy of his 45th birthday.

SPACE NEEDLE: INSPIRATION

Eddie Carlson, so central to the fair's success, even conceived the Space Needle, its most spectacular and enduring icon. During a trip to Stuttgart, Germany, in the spring of 1959, Carlson and his wife, Nell, had dinner at the top of that city's television tower, then just three years old. Carlson, thinking of how monumental structures like that tower, the Empire State Building, and the Eiffel Tower often came to signify their cities, envisioned a civic symbol for Seattle and, most immediately, for the fair. By his own admission, by the time he returned home Eddie was "obsessed with the idea."

A friendly, well-connected, tireless civic booster, Joe Gandy was ideal. "My father was a *salesman*," his daughter Marilyn Gandy Scherrer later said. "He would walk into a room anywhere, and he had a presence about him, and you *knew* when he walked into the room — you just knew it. He really had quite an ability to communicate, and to get people's confidence." With Gandy's services came those of his gracious wife Laurene, to the fair's enormous benefit.

MONEY MATTERS Century 21 coffers, however, were rattling empty. State-appropriated money could only be spent on site development, not promotion. Palmer Supply Company President Frank Dupar Jr. spearheaded a drive to raise funds from local businesses, which helped, but there was a great need for a monetary infusion to meet payroll and planning demands.

Bill Street, a steadfast believer in the exposition who would help many times in many ways, suggested that Alaska Steamship President David E. "Ned" Skinner II head up fund-raising for the several million that was required if Century 21 was to survive.

Skinner was mindful of task's enormity but felt he simply could not turn it down. "This is not the sort of thing a man is asked to do every day, nor to repeat next year," Skinner later told Murray Morgan. "This was like being asked to make possible the Alaska-Yukon-Pacific Exposition. How would you have felt, looking back, if you had said 'no' to that?"

Skinner devised a plan with a coalition of local banks that then loaned Century 21 $3 million, with the credit of approved businesses serving as collateral. Only larger firms were invited to participate. They were asked to do so generously. The plan worked. Without Street's inspiration and Skinner's skillful fund-raising, there is little doubt that Century 21 would have dissolved into another civic dream gone bad.

By mid-September 1959, full federal participation in the fair had been approved and the funds appropriated. On November 10, 1959, the State Department sent invitations to the 84 nations with whom the United States had diplomatic relations, urging them to participate. Fair leaders were ecstatic. Century 21 seemed very near — so near, in fact, that to allow enough time to attract the highest caliber exhibitors from foreign nations and from domestic industry, fair planners agreed to open the exposition in spring 1962, rather than in 1961 as previously planned. On November 11, 1959, the fair dates were solidified: Century 21 would run from April 21, 1962, to October 21, 1962.

GETTING AROUND Fair planning branched out: In March 1960, Administrative Assistant Edward Stimpson, who had previously worked for the federal Department of the Interior and for the mayor's office in Seattle, opened a Century 21 office in Washington, D.C. Stimpson worked tirelessly to secure official participation from invited countries. A Paris office, directed by William and Genevieve Phillips, Seattleites with extensive European connections, opened soon after. The Phillipses traveled in Europe, signing up nations and, once official participation was assured, trying to secure commercial concessions. The Flying Squadron was deployed — a team of high-level state business leaders who helped sell the fair to their industry colleagues. By June 1960 the fair had contacted 46 nations.

Back in Seattle, after more than a year of brainstorming and negotiations, plans for a space-age monorail were beginning to solidify. A U.S. postage stamp commemorating the fair was in the works. A commemorative coin, to be issued by the U.S. mint, was being cogitated. On May 12, 1960, Coliseum construction began.

Ding, meanwhile, spent much of April and May 1960 traveling behind the Iron Curtain, soliciting exhibits for the fair. Despite Cold War tensions — on May 1, American U-2 spy plane pilot Francis Gary Powers was

above This pop-out trailer took Century 21 advance publicity to Olympia (pictured) and beyond.

below William P. Woods, chairman of the National Conference on the Peaceful Use of Space, President John Kennedy, and Senator Warren Magnuson examine United States Science Pavilion brochure.

facing page The fairground model claimed the cover of Seattle's 1961 telephone directory.

SOVIET PARTICIPATION

In accordance with Century 21's goals of fostering understanding between nations and peoples in fields of science and culture, fair officials sought the USSR's participation. Premier Nikita Khrushchev was invited to visit Seattle during his visit to the United States, Ewen Dingwall traveled to Russia, fair officials feted a Russian fisheries delegation touring the Pacific Northwest, and Joe Gandy and Senator Warren Magnuson wrote to Moscow pressing for participation. In the end, neither diplomacy nor politesse won the day. The USSR declined to participate.

left Poster showing fair site.

right Informational brochure.

brought down and captured near Sverdlovsk in the Soviet Union — Dingwall was received graciously. "There was not a single negative, anti-American incident anywhere I went," he told *The Seattle Times.* His stops included Moscow, Warsaw, Prague, Belgrade, Sofia, Athens, and Paris.

ENTER JAY ROCKEY Dingwall, Thiry, Young, Gandy, and everyone else on the fair's small staff labored tirelessly, and Ned Skinner's fund-raising — still only incipient — glimmered like a hopeful mirage. But for the fair, these were desperate times. Except for a few key boosters, local press coverage was insubstantial and national press nonexistent. Worst of all, many Seattleites remained indifferent.

Jim Faber had resigned his public relations post effective November 15, 1959. He was briefly succeeded by Seattle advertising and public relations executive Hugh Smith, who publicized Ned Skinner's underwriting campaign. In May 1960, Jay Rockey became the fair's information director and, soon after, director of public relations. Born and raised in Olympia, Rockey had managed public relations for Alcoa in New York City. Rockey

CENTURY
2
EXPOSITION

A UNITED STATES WORLD EXPOSITION
SEATTLE, WASHINGTON, 1962

ATTENTION TRAVEL INDUSTRY

Announcing New Inter-Stellar Tour Package

Leave your jet-suit at Seattle-Tacoma...Rocket direct to Mars!

- Overnight on Mars
- Hover-train over Venus' steaming Lake Celestial
- Rotodyne airtrain to Moon
- Radiant-optican view of Andromeda 1,500,000 light years away

Seriously, this tour package of the future may be all right for your long-range planning, but the most exciting travel opportunity of this decade leads to Century 21 Exposition in Seattle in 1962. And as America's Space Age World's Fair generates increased international acclaim, you have an unprecedented opportunity for profit. Travel-minded people the world over are eager to know more about Century 21. We invite you to become fully informed about the fabulous World of Tomorrow; and look forward to cooperating with you in making 1962 a year for really important travel profits.

Jay Rockey
CENTURY 21 EXPOSITION, Inc.

left Fair publicity exploited the space travel angle for all it was worth.

right Seattle World's Fair publicity mastermind Jay Rockey at the Teletype machine.

accepted the Century 21 job as an act of faith. The success of fair was far from certain, and no one on staff was sleeping easily when he came on board. "About that time, I'd say there was a desperation. I know I felt that way," Rockey later recalled. "Nothing could compare with the depths of depression from the early days — back a year or more before the fair."

A *Seattle Post-Intelligencer* business column during this period reinforces Rockey's recollections: "There are a number of people around town who — because they have not been exposed sufficiently — don't realize the tremendous business potential of Century 21. This is going to be one of the world's most memorable fairs, but the chief problem right now is to get Washington's own public attention focused on the central problem: local public support from the business community."

Rockey immediately made a splash, inviting the New York press to a dapper gathering at the Waldorf Astoria Hotel to hear Carlson, Dingwall, Gandy, and Magnuson talk up the fair.

A few months later, Joe Gandy announced that J. Elroy McCaw, owner of WINS radio in New York City, KTVW in Seattle, KTVR in Denver, and KELA in Centralia, had been named a vice president of Century 21 Exposition, Inc., His broadcasting interests would be an asset to promotional efforts.

SMALL BUT TALL Weary of having their efforts to gain official world's fair status from the Bureau of International Expositions rebuffed, in late July Century 21 officials made the bold move of announcing that, BIE approval or no, they planned to brand the exposition a world's fair. The fair, described as a "jewel box" because its 74 acres made it considerably smaller than most other expositions, now went by the name "Century 21 Exposition — America's Space Age World's Fair."

WHAT IS THE BIE?

Beginning with the Great Exposition of the Industry of All Nations at London's Crystal Palace in 1851, many countries viewed an official invitation to participate in a world's fair as both an honor and a headache. To send an exhibit, a country needed first to procure funding. As the nineteenth century rolled into the twentieth and the number of international expositions ballooned, many countries felt pressured to accept, but lacked the means to do so.

Inconsistent rules and regulations from fair to fair were another inconvenience. On November 22, 1928, delegates of 31 nations signed the first treaty governing the organization of international expositions. The Bureau of International Expositions ensures proper application of this treaty. Since the start of the twenty-first century, BIE-sanctioned Universal Expositions lasting six-months can only occur in years ending in 5 and 0, although International and Specialized Expositions can take place in other years, if they are less than three months in duration. The most recent BIE-sanctioned exposition was held in 2010 in Shanghai.

In early September 1960, Seattleites read for the first time that the fair planned to construct a tower crowned with a revolving restaurant. It was Eddie Carlson's inspiration, to be built near the armory if financing could be arranged. The following month the public learned the tower would be called the Space Needle.

ON EXHIBITS In order to keep pace with the crucial task of leasing exhibit space, Century 21's staff grew. Bill Street helped again, loaning Frederick & Nelson retail merchandising buyer Donald Foster, who soon became the fair's exhibits director. "He said to me, I've got a little project that's coming up at the fair and we need a loaned executive for a maximum of a month," Foster later recalled. "And I said, that sounds interesting. ... I never left."

Georgia M. Gellert, a savvy, stylish Seattle civic leader with extensive public relations experience, signed on as Foster's assistant. Gellert's duties included pitching the fair to potential exhibitors, coordinating the efforts of staff who were selling space from remote offices and on the road, and eventually overseeing the Interiors, Fashion, and Commerce Pavilions — a major job that including wooing funding from *Vogue Magazine*.

Foster and Gellert scored a major coup when Pacific Telephone & Telegraph Company announced that, with American Telephone & Telegraph Company (AT&T) and Western Electric, it would build a major exhibit. "It is appropriate that the Bell System, long noted for its research, would enter an exposition which has as its central theme scientific development of the future," Pacific Telephone & Telegraph President Walter Straley told *The Seattle Times*. AT&T's Bell Laboratories was working on what would become the word's first satellite capable of both sending and receiving signals (*Telstar 1*) and was actively involved in promoting science education in America's schools.

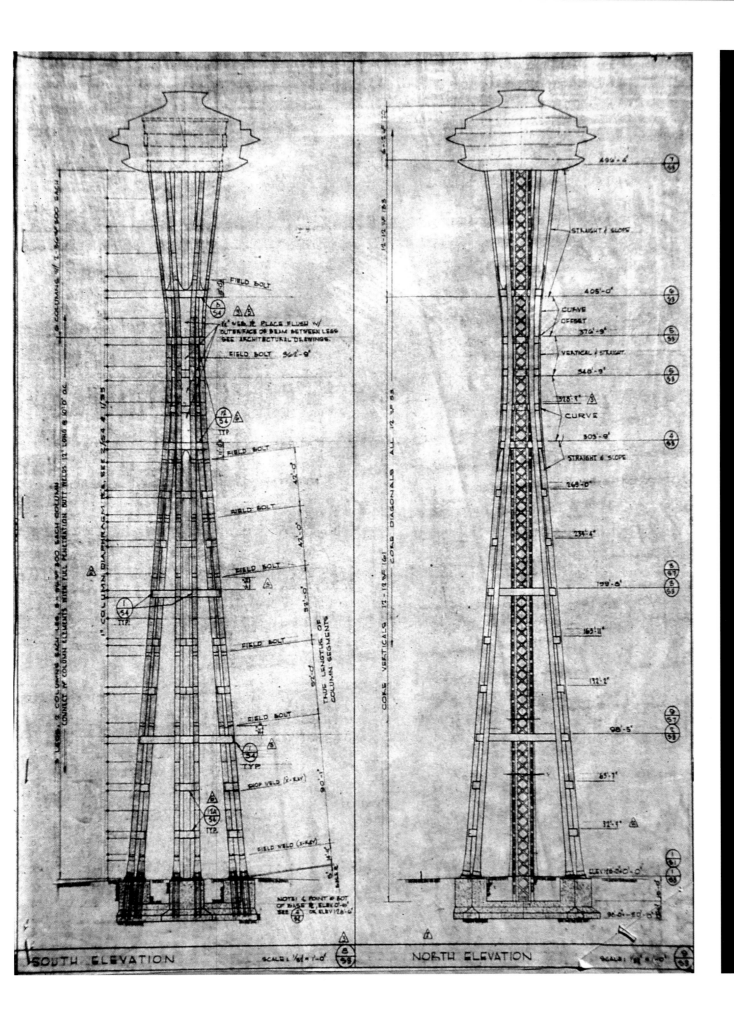

SOUTH ELEVATION

NORTH ELEVATION

SPACE NEEDLE: FUNDING THE DREAM

Eddie Carlson told real estate developer Jim Douglas his idea for a thematic tower for Century 21, and together they approached Seattle architect John Graham Jr., who agreed to work on the design. Carlson asked King County for funding but was denied. Seattle businessman and arts patron Bagley Wright joined forces with Alaska Steamship President Ned Skinner and Weyerhaeuser Corporation president Norton Clapp to assemble funding. With John Graham and Howard S. Wright (president of Howard S. Wright & Co. Construction), the men formed Pentagram Corporation, a private company, and built the Space Needle.

FIGHTING FOR BIE APPROVAL

Unless the BIE designated Century 21 a world's fair, the bureau's member nations could not participate in any official capacity. Beginning in 1958, fair planners repeatedly approached the BIE, unsuccessfully. When Joseph Gandy tried, delegates of the bureau's 23 member nations complained that the rainy weather during a Seattle fair would make viewing the Washington Monument impossible. Gandy immediately procured a large U.S. map with the state of Washington and Seattle boldly indicated, and he clarified pronunciation — not "See-tul," but "See-at-uhl."

Gandy learned exactly what the BIE required of its members and, although the United States was not one, brought Century 21 policy in line with requirements, including limiting the fair to a six-month run and providing covered exhibit space for all officially participating nations. Learning that the BIE had been burned by labor stoppages at the 1939–1940 New York World's Fair, Gandy sought help from King County Labor Council president Harry Carr, a longtime Century 21 supporter and a volunteer vice president of the fair. On April 26, 1960, Carr wrote to Gandy, assuring him that local labor unions had agreed to help the fair by promising no stoppages and to allow exhibitors to bring their own technicians onto the site for work that exceeded local expertise. Clyde Fenn made the same promise for the Seattle Building & Construction Trades Council. Gandy took these no-strike pledges to the BIE.

This Seattle information card gave easterners a visual reference for Century 21 Exposition's geographic location.

LOOKING UP The Boeing Airplane Company came on board soon after, announcing plans to sponsor a planetarium called the Spacearium jointly with the U.S. Department of Commerce. The Spacearium would be located in the United States Science Pavilion. Boeing had been a tough sell, but as Seattle's leading employer its participation was deemed essential. "Senators Jackson and Magnuson put their necks on the line big time for the participation of 'expected participants' such as Boeing," Barry Upson later recalled.

In October, Century 21 signed papers with Von Roll Iron Works of Switzerland for a Sky Ride, an aerial tramway. Von Roll was the world's largest producer of Sky Rides, including those at the Brussels World's Fair and at Disneyland. Seattle's Sky Ride, designed to carry 800 people an hour in each direction, would have 60 two-person cars.

Fairgoers also would be able to experience the space-age thrill of arriving at the fair by monorail. On October 14, 1960, Joe Gandy told the press that, after long negotiations, the plan for the Swedish firm Alweg Rapid Transit Systems to build the futuristic transport between Westlake Mall downtown and the fairgrounds was virtually complete.

GOING GLOBAL On November 8, 1960, Gandy's perseverance and steady salesmanship was at last rewarded: The Bureau of International Expositions gave Century 21 official status. Gandy considered the BIE's endorsement "a hunting license," and he immediately hit the road to bag the big game: international participation. His path was eased by an official letter of introduction written by Warren Magnuson on letterhead stamped U.S. Senate Committee on Interstate and Foreign Commerce. "Any courtesies or assistance which may be extended to Mr. Gandy will be greatly appreciated," the letter read.

In addition to the Washington, D.C., and Paris outposts, Century 21 set up satellite offices in Athens (under Athanase Makris), Bankok (Udom Yenrudi), Tokyo (Antonio de Grassi), and Manila (Marjorie Ravenholt). These local staffers did the groundwork, and then fair executives swooped in to dazzle prospects with the sales pitch.

Louis Larsen, a Seattle native who had worked for the American Automobile Association, joined the world's fair staff in November 1960. Within days, he later recalled, he was in New York with Joe Gandy, selling exhibit space. The job "was never-ending. I mean, one day I had breakfast in Brunswick, I had lunch in Moline, and dinner in West Alice, Wisconsin." Larsen's sales calls spanned the gamut "from Studebaker to Hallmark Cards to John Deere."

When major possibilities showed interest, the fair's best tactic was to get them to Seattle and show them Century 21's progress firsthand. Northwest business leaders, Governor Rosellini, the state's congressional delegation in Washington, D.C., officers of the fair, and staff all worked together to bring in exhibitors.

FOR THE ARTS In early January 1961, art lovers were delighted to learn that plans for a modest art exhibit at the fair had, under the direction of Seattle investment banker Norman Davis, morphed into a multi-gallery extravaganza. Davis had chosen curators who were experts in their respective fields and had charged them with developing first-class exhibits.

In February, patrons of the performing arts had the same thrill when Dingwall announced New Yorker Harold Shaw's hiring as performing arts director, the fair's last major staffing vacancy. Shaw was a colleague of world-famous theatrical impresario Sol Hurok. "This will not be a program designed to cater to the sporadic visitor," Shaw told *The Seattle Times*. "It will be a civic center at Century 21. That will be our underlying philosophy."

left Bureau of International Expositions informational sign.

right Ethnically costumed beauty queens admire the Coliseum model.

left Groundbreaking ceremonies for the United States Science Pavilion.

center Concept drawing for the Science Pavilion's soaring arches.;

right In this concept drawing, the Monorail hangs from its track rather than gliding upon it.

opposite above Booster brochures encouraged everyone to help promote the fair.

below Groundbreaking ceremonies for the Monorail at Westlake Mall in downtown Seattle.

MOVING QUICKLY The city council voted in early February 1961 to sell the site of the Fire Alarm Communications Center on the triangle of land between Thomas Street, 4th Avenue N, and Broad Street to sponsors of the planned Space Needle. A site survey showed this to be a good place to construct the giant tower. That the Alweg Monorail line terminated nearby was another bonus.

On February 22, 1961, fair officials ceremonially toppled an old wood-frame house, one of several dozen structures on the two square blocks bordered by Denny Way, Nob Hill Avenue, John Street, and 2nd Avenue N. This was the site where Minoru Yamasaki's glistening white United States Science Pavilion would rise, and groundbreaking ceremonies were held the same day.

Groundbreaking ceremonies for the Playhouse and Fine Arts Pavilion were held on February 28, 1961, and on the same day the Seattle City Council, in agreement with the Civic Center Advisory Commission, named the campus: Seattle Center.

In March 1961, Ned Skinner opened a second phase of the underwriting campaign. Skinner's efforts ultimately brought in $5 million to cover Century 21 operating expenses. "Everyone we asked gave willingly," Seattle Mayor Gordon Clinton later recalled. Clinton credited Skinner but also the "great cooperation" of Seattle citizens (who by now understood the fair's importance). Laurene Gandy's sentiments echoed Clinton's: "Anything is possible if the citizens will agree to it and everyone will work on it."

FULL CIRCLE Later that month, Tokyo architects Hideki Shimizu and Kazuvuki Matsushita were proclaimed the winners in the international competition to design the fairgrounds' centerpiece fountain. Shimizu and Matsushita's design was circular, with a central area resembling a sunflower's seed head. Each of the hundred "seeds" would be a tiny nozzle shooting highly pressurized water.

On March 17, 1961, Eddie Carlson (who had recently had been promoted to the presidency of Western Hotels) stepped down as chairman of Century 21 Exposition, Inc. Bill Street, so often the fair's astute advisor, had recently announced his own gradual retirement over the next year from his Frederick & Nelson post, and he took Eddie's place. Carlson continued serving as chairman of the state World's Fair Commission, the job he'd taken on at Governor Langlie's urging six years previously.

On March 28, 1961, Boeing and Cinerama announced their joint project for the U.S. government: the Cinerama lens, which created an audience viewing area of 360 degrees horizontally and 160 degrees vertically. This lens would be employed for the first time at Century 21.

MONORAIL AND NEEDLE April 2, 1961, was "Monorail Day," with groundbreaking ceremonies at Westlake Mall. The 500 spectators all got free tickets to ride the Monorail upon its completion. "The world of tomorrow is on our doorstep today," Warren Magnuson told the crowd.

A few weeks later, Seattle got another portent of "tomorrow" when the first of the giant steel wide-flanged beams that would form the base of the Space Needle arrived by rail from United States

SELLING SPACE

Exhibit staffers approached firms as diverse as the American Bible Association, the Association of Railroads, Polaroid, and Procter & Gamble to solicit potential exhibitors for Century 21. Field offices served as foxholes for Century 21 staff, who arranged sales calls, dinners, slide-shows; sent out promotional materials; and unceasingly explained the fair and its myriad potential benefits for participants. When a fish was considered big enough, Joe Gandy was deployed to land it. Once Boeing was on board, President William Allen was also enlisted to persuade attractive corporate targets into joining the Century 21 bandwagon, often ending his letters to their executives with a velvet-gloved "I want you to know that The Boeing Company will be most happy if you decide to participate."

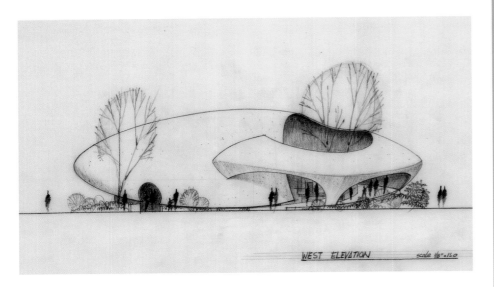

WEST ELEVATION   scale ⅛"=1'.0"

LANDSCAPING THE FAIRGROUNDS

The state appropriated $10,000 for landscaping and the city $25,000. In addition to the trees saved from the freeway right-of-way, hundreds of shrubs were purchased from area nurseries. By early 1960, groundsman Otto Holmdahl was busily arranging to secure 40,000 tulip bulbs, 20,000 gladiolus bulbs, and 25,000 annuals to be grown in six-inch pots. During the fair, many trees were in temporary pots. Landscaping subcommittee chairman James M. Ryan approached garden clubs around the state seeking donated shrubbery or financial contributions. Eventually, foreign governments also contributed plants to honor their respective countries and grace the grounds.

Above: Concept drawing for Nalley's Pavilion; Below: Early concept drawing for Space Needle.

WORLD'S FAIR, 1962

SEATTLE, APRIL 21-OCT. 21

Steel's South Chicago rolling mills and were unloaded at the Pacific Car & Foundry (now PACCAR) Renton factory. The beams, among the largest of their type ever produced, were prepared for installation at Pacific Car and then transported to the fairgrounds.

Meanwhile, the Soviet Union advanced its lead in the space race. On April 12, 1961, Soviet cosmonaut Yuri Gagarin became the first human in outer space and the first to orbit the earth.

Opening day was just one year away. Fair staffers tossed aside all pretense of working Monday to Friday, nine to five — weekends and evenings were now devoted to the million details that had to be completed in order to launch the fair. "We grabbed a chunk of sky and held on — and we're still holding on," Joe Gandy told *The Seattle Times*. Century 21 Exposition was altering Seattle, changing it, already, and the next year would be critical for both the world's fair and the city.

above Triumphal poster advertising the fair.

below Window decal used to advertise the fair.

Chapter 2

Counting Down
April 21, 1961–April 20, 1962

The site develops, staff grows, civic leaders work last-minute rescues, Monorail construction spurs Seattle's interest, and the Space Needle rises, captivating the world.

A pril 21, 1961. Century 21 would open in exactly one year, and the clock was counting down. That morning, about 100,000 letters written by Seattle school children urging friends and relatives to visit the fair were loaded onto a mail truck at exposition headquarters. The recipients had undoubtedly already heard of the Seattle World's Fair. Newspapers from New York to San Francisco to Paris to Tokyo had printed its story.

opposite Fireworks light up the half-built Coliseum.

The Seattle Convention and Tourist Bureau had 77 conventions scheduled to take place during Century 21, ranging from the International Conference on National Parks to the American Lawn Bowling Association. To help feed the coming crowds, scores of food concessions were planning menus of seafood, pancakes, coffee, and a variety of ethnic foods. One concession planned to sell burger sundaes — meat patties with a big scoop of ice cream.

At the fairgrounds, the Coliseum construction was the most visible. The four main struts of the roof were in place, ready for the 5.5 miles of cable needed to support the roof panels. To showcase this work, 21 young women in bathing suits, all 21 years old, were photographed standing in front of the building with cards that spelled out "Century 21 World's Fair."

A fireworks display at the fairgrounds that evening marked the exposition's one-year pre-anniversary. Rockets and aerial bombs exploded at 600 feet, the planned height of the Space Needle.

left Howard Wright.

right More than 250 tons of rebar was used in the Space Needle's foundation.

WELL SUPPORTED Work on the Space Needle had begun, but it was all underground. To build up, crews first had to dig down to create a 35-foot-deep, 120-foot-wide hole for the foundation. On May 22, after a dedication ceremony, a parade of cement trucks executed what was billed as the largest continuous concrete pour in the West.

At the ceremony various objects that might be "candidates for extinction" by the year 2000 were displayed. Those included a telephone, a typewriter, a pack of cigarettes, false teeth, a mousetrap, a Seattle city map, a ukulele, a diet formula, and a federal income tax form.

Ned Skinner, one of the Space Needle's principal investors, spoke of the two years of planning that went into the tower's creation and predicted that it would become "symbolic of Century 21 and the Great Northwest."

At the end of the event, Space Needle co-owner Bagley Wright's wife, Virginia, pulled a cord to symbolize the start of the 8,000-ton concrete pour, which had actually begun hours earlier. More than 2,800 cubic yards of concrete went into the hole. This would counterbalance the Space Needle's eventual 3,700 tons of steel.

Plenty of cement was also needed elsewhere. On the following day, workmen poured the first concrete pylon for the Century 21 Monorail on 5th Avenue, between Virginia and Lenora streets. The Monorail's track beams were being precast in Tacoma, but the 80 Y-shaped supporting piers were cast on-site into forms that were lying on their sides. First, steel reinforcing rods went in. As the concrete was poured into one form, steel was laid into the next. Once ready, each of the 54-ton pylons was winched up into place.

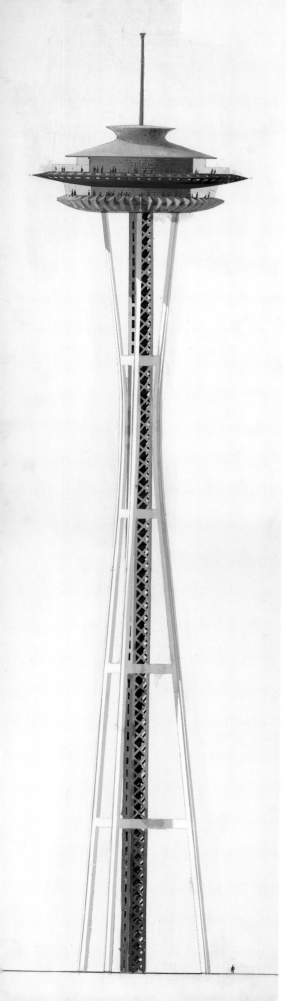

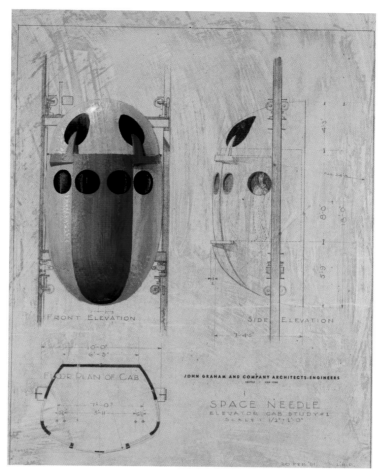

left John Graham's design drawing for the Space Needle.

above right An early design for the Space Needle elevator.

below Cutaway drawing of the Space Needle restaurant and observation deck.

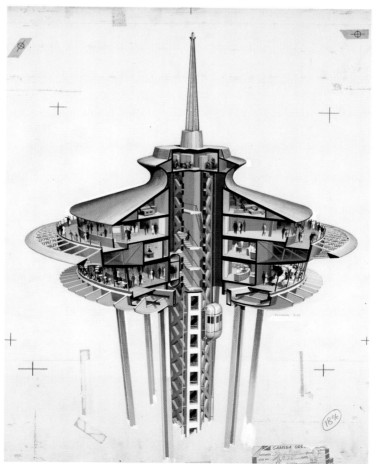

PROMOTIONAL BRANDING   Back at the main offices, planners hammered out contracts and particulars regarding concessions, exhibits, and displays. When asked decades later about the concept they used to sell the fair to exhibitors, Donald Foster and Barry Upson answered virtually in unison: "Jewel Box. Jewel Box fair. Limited in acreage, but focusing on the highest quality. We never stopped saying it."

Publicity department staffers steadily campaigned to rebrand the fair with a more nationally memorable moniker. Publicity director Bill McFarland pushed to use the name "Seattle World's Fair" instead of "Century 21 Exposition," and Jay Rockey agreed. Rockey recalled, "I really got on the Seattle World's Fair kick — that it was going to be like this: It was a world's fair, and in smaller type, Century 21. I think Century 21 was and is a great name, and we promoted the hell out of it, but a world's fair was what we were having, and if we didn't insist on that, forget about it." The new name soon gained a snappy descriptor, Rockey added: "America's Space Age World's Fair was the line that we decided to use, and flog, and I think it resonated well. It sounded like, all America's behind it!"

PAVILIONS AND PLAY   On June 1, the Seattle City Council approved plans for a large parking garage directly north of the fairgrounds on Mercer Street. Besides providing space for vehicles driven by fairgoers, the garage would pull in more than $250,000 in parking revenue.

Good news also came that day from the federal government: Dr. Athelstan Frederick Spilhaus was installed as commissioner of the U.S. science exhibit for Century 21. Spilhaus, a geophysicist, meteorologist, and inventor, was the nation's ambassador to UNESCO (United Nations Educational, Scientific, and Cultural Organization) in 1954, and he had been dean of the Institute of Technology at the University of Minnesota since 1949.

Foreign nations continued to come on board, and around the fairgrounds the pavilions that would house their exhibits began to rise. Donald Foster recalled, "One of the things that made the Seattle fair so successful was its Bureau of International Exhibitions designation as a Category 2 fair — which meant that the foreign governments didn't have to build their own pavilions."

THAT DISNEY TOUCH

George K. Whitney was named director of the Concessions and Amusements Division in September 1960, charged with developing on-site merchandise and concessions, including Show Street, the Gayway, and food services; and licensing manufacturers and retailers to use the Century 21 trademark on merchandise. Whitney had grown up working at Whitney's-On-The-Beach, his family's San Francisco amusement park, and had been hired by Walt Disney to help organize Disneyland, where he spent two years as director of rides and amusements. Century 21's Operations and Services Division Director Frederick Schumacher had also been closely involved with Disneyland planning.

On June 14, fair officials signed a $2 million contract with J. W. "Patty" Conklin and Harry J. Batt for the Gayway, Century 21's midway to be filled with rides and amusements, many of which came from France, Italy, and West Germany and would be new to American fairgoers. Director of Amusements and Concessions George K. Whitney had used his lifelong ties to the amusement industry to secure Conklin and Batt, North America's leading amusement park experts. The pair kept most of the ride descriptions secret from the press at first, but did let slip some information about the Wild Mouse, a roller coaster with two-person cars that would scatter, run, and turn — just like wild mice.

GOING STRONG Preparations for Century 21 were going strong on all fronts. In July, Public Relations Director Jay Rockey told *The Seattle Times* that his office was receiving more than 1,000 out-of-state press clippings about Century 21 each month. Nearly all of the national magazines and Sunday newspaper supplements assigned reporters to visit Century 21, and many of their stories were being saved for publication in the late fall or winter. Tony Petricelli, a *LIFE* magazine artist, was already in town working on illustrations.

On August 8, government officials from India and the Philippines announced exhibit plans for their countries. A week later, Joe Gandy returned from a 90-day tour of Central America, South America, and Europe and announced that the fair was over the hump on foreign participation. More than 35 nations had either firmly committed, or were likely to attend, and Gandy was not giving up on countries that had declined.

TRIALS AND TRIBULATIONS Construction was marred by a few serious accidents. On July 25, Alfred J. Hyde Jr., an ironworker for Isaacson Iron Works, was killed when a crane boom snapped and a cable knocked him from an 80-foot tower at the Civic Auditorium. This was the third fatal accident at the fairgrounds. On May

left A worker crosses the World of Tomorrow visitor pathway while the floating cubes and roof panels are being installed.

right A Monorail pylon is lifted into place.

opposite Conceptual artwork for the Gayway.

The rapid rise of the Space Needle provided an unmistakable visual gauge of fair progress.

10, Elmer Leith had been killed during an excavation when a sidewalk slab fell on him, and on July 12, Harry Walton had died of heat prostration.

The most significant construction woes involved the Coliseum. Miles of cables had been stretched across the building's main beams, but when it came time to attach the aluminum roof panels, 80 of them — almost 10 percent of the total — didn't fit. Urgent modifications delayed the roof installation by several weeks.

PLANTING SEEDS By now much of the fairgrounds landscaping was done, although finishing touches would be added until the last minute. On September 12, a tree-planting ceremony was held next to the Forest Industries building: Stephan Simmons planted a dawn redwood seedling. Simmons was a descendent of Pacific Northwest pioneer Michael T. Simmons, who in 1847 founded the first sawmill north of the Columbia River.

Donald Foster announced on September 17 that all but one of the open spaces for commerce and industry exhibits had been leased and that five exhibitors were vying for the last spot. Ewen Dingwall, who had boldly predicted in January 1960 that exhibit space would sell out, was being proven right.

Despite growing excitement about the fair's progress, fiscal strings were tight and would remain so. Everyone helped keep within the budget, Jay Rockey recalled. "The people who were in charge of the various departments were really dedicated, and effective, and they all seemed to respect the fact that we didn't have much money."

With this sound fiscal management came wise staff development. Special Events Administrative Assistant C. David Hughbanks later recalled how the fair's leaders — Eddie Carlson, Joe Gandy, Ewen Dingwall, Bill Street — mentored staff and recognized good work: "They took a personal interest in people who worked at the fair. If you did something that was exceptional, there was a little note that came to your office, somehow, some way, and a little card."

BENCHMARKS On September 18, with all the Monorail pylons now in place, the first two concrete track beams from Tacoma reached downtown Seattle. A special permit was granted to V. Van Dyke Trucking to haul the 76-foot, 96,000-pound beams over the Seattle-Tacoma Highway (now State Route 99). As more beams arrived over the coming weeks, workers used cranes to attach them to the large concrete piers.

But the Space Needle proved to be the true gauge of progress. From various spots around the city, people could see it grow. KOMO TV helped, placing a still camera on the roof of its studio, which faced the fairgrounds. As KOMO reporter Art McDonald later recalled, the photos of the Needle rising were spliced together and displayed during station identification announcements.

By the end of September, the structure had already risen to 400 feet, two-thirds of the way up. At this point, *The Seattle Times* began running a weekly column written by Paul Collop, the Pacific Car & Foundry Company construction superintendent for the steel on the Needle.

next

5O

SEATTLE CENTER 2012

In 1962, Seattle put itself on the map by hosting the Space Age-driven World's Fair and creating a dynamic physical legacy: Seattle Center.

As we approach the 50th anniversary of the fair, there is cause for celebration and contemplation, as our generation faces an entirely new set of priorities, challenges and opportunities.

The Next Fifty is a six-month event which will, once again, place the Pacific Northwest in the global limelight, serving as an interactive platform to illuminate the world's challenges as we explore and define our possibilities. From April 21 to October 21, 2012, millions of visitors will descend upon Seattle, with Seattle Center playing host to luminaries, exhibitions, speaker series and entertainment— to debate and define the future.

Join us today to support the 50th anniversary of the Seattle World's Fair, The Next Fifty. Your collaboration will invigorate our region and catalyze participation across the globe.

Be part of it.

TheNextFifty.org

Welcome to The Next Fifty. SEATTLE CENTER WILL COME EVEN MORE ALIVE DURING THE NEXT FIFTY, AS MILLIONS OF PEOPLE VISIT THE 74-ACRE CAMPUS TO ATTEND OVER 300 EVENTS AND ENGAGE VIRTUALLY TO CREATE OUR COLLECTIVE FUTURE THROUGH IMAGINATION, INNOVATION AND INVOLVEMENT. MARK YOUR CALENDAR, STAY CONNECTED, AND KEEP YOUR EYES OPEN TO LEARN MORE - THE NEXT FIFTY IS COMING IN 2012.

The Next Fifty will focus on our region's expertise and innovation in addressing eight focus areas:

- **ARTS CULTURE AND DESIGN** [APRIL 21 TO OCTOBER 21, 2012] THROUGHOUT THE NEXT FIFTY, DYNAMIC ARTS, CULTURE AND DESIGN PROGRAMMING WILL HELP PEOPLE BOLDLY IMAGINE THE FUTURE, CONNECT IDEAS AND PEOPLE, AND PROVIDE GLOBAL INSIGHTS.

- **SUSTAINABLE FUTURES** [APRIL 21 TO MAY 2012] THE CELEBRATION WILL SPOTLIGHT CREATIVE CONSERVATION, NEW ENERGY SOURCES AND BIG, BOLD IDEAS THAT WILL HELP US MEET THE CRITICAL CHALLENGES FACING OUR ENVIRONMENT.

- **SCIENCE AND TECHNOLOGY** [JUNE 2012] THE PACIFIC NORTHWEST'S GLOBAL LEADERSHIP IN SCIENCE AND TECHNOLOGY IS WELL-KNOWN, AND THE INNOVATIONS THAT WILL PROPEL THE FUTURE WILL BE ON DISPLAY FOR ALL TO EXPERIENCE.

- **GLOBAL HEALTH** [JULY 2012] THERE HAVE BEEN MORE DISCOVERIES IN THE LAST FIVE YEARS THAN IN ALL OF HISTORY, SETTING A PHENOMENAL PACE OF PROGRESS WE WILL SHARE, INSPIRING ALL WHO ATTEND.

- **LEARNING** [AUGUST 2012] AMERICA HAS REACHED A PIVOTAL POINT WHERE WE NEED TO EXPAND PERSPECTIVES AROUND LEARNING, EDUCATION, CULTURE AND ENVIRONMENT SO THAT PEOPLE OF ALL AGES AND FROM ALL BACKGROUNDS CAN REALIZE THEIR INTRINSIC MOTIVATION TO LEARN AND GROW.

- **COMMERCE AND THE INNOVATION ECONOMY** [SEPTEMBER 2012] SEATTLE HAS EMBRACED THE KNOWLEDGE-BASED ECONOMY TO COMPLEMENT ENTREPRENEURSHIP AND ICONIC LEADERS IN COFFEE, SOFTWARE AND AIRPLANES, ALL BUILDING THE NEW ECONOMY.

- **CIVIC ACTION** [OCTOBER 1-21, 2012] AS SOCIAL NETWORKING TRANSFORMS COMMUNICATIONS, AS GRASSROOTS INITIATIVES ARE INCREASINGLY ABLE TO MAKE CHANGE, WHAT DOES SOCIAL RESPONSIBILITY LOOK LIKE?

- **HISTORY** [APRIL 21 TO OCTOBER 21, 2012] THE 1962 WORLD'S FAIR WAS ABOUT THE FUTURE, AND SO TOO WILL BE ITS 50TH ANNIVERSARY CELEBRATION. WHAT LESSONS CAN WE LEARN FROM OUR PAST? HOW IS THE FUTURE REMEMBERED?

next
50
SEATTLE CENTER 2012

Be part of it. FROM APRIL 21 TO OCTOBER 21, 2012, PEOPLE THROUGHOUT THE COMMUNITY WILL COME TOGETHER TO ENVISION THE FUTURE OF A REGION THAT STIMULATES CREATIVE AND PRACTICAL SOLUTIONS TO THE WORLD'S GREATEST CHALLENGES. GET INVOLVED TODAY AND MAKE AN IMPACT ON TOMORROW.

Your investment matters. YOU CAN HELP MAKE THE NEXT FIFTY A HISTORICAL AND IMPACTFUL GLOBAL EVENT. WITH YOUR INVESTMENT, WE CAN ENSURE FREE AND AFFORDABLE QUALITY PROGRAMS, KNOWLEDGEABLE SPEAKERS, ENGAGING EXHIBITS AND STIMULATING CONVERSATIONS. PLEASE MAKE YOUR GIFT TODAY TO SEATTLE CENTER FOUNDATION IN SUPPORT OF THE NEXT FIFTY.

Find us on the web:
THENEXTFIFTY.ORG
FACEBOOK.COM/SEATTLECENTER
TWITTER.COM/SEATTLECENTER

305 HARRISON STREET   SEATTLE, WA 98109 | 206.684.7345 | SEATTLECENTER.ORG

Collop's columns provided intricate detail on every aspect of the Needle's construction, from girder sizes, to welding techniques, to how derricks worked, to how weather affected getting the job done. For someone who worked so high in the air, his descriptions were very down to earth.

AEROSPACE AND AUTOMOBILES Century 21 secured a definitive spot in the space age on October 1, when the National Aeronautics and Space Administration (NASA) announced that it planned to be a major exhibitor. Joe Gandy had worked out an agreement with NASA Administrator James Webb providing the government agency with 19,600 square feet of exhibit space, making NASA the second-largest exhibitor, after the U.S. government itself.

Senators Warren Magnuson and Henry Jackson played major roles in securing NASA's participation, but it was a New York senator who gave Washington an unexpected bit of publicity the next day. During a Senate debate about federal appropriations for the 1964–1965 New York World's Fair, Republican Senator Kenneth B. Keating referred to Century 21 as a "little country fair." Seattle was outraged. Keating backtracked, telling local reporters that he was "only kidding," and that he planned to attend.

That evening the city lit up for the American Automobile Association's convention. After sundown, every major downtown building was illuminated until 11 p.m. Conventioneers were urged to visit the fairgrounds to see all the progress. This may have caused traffic jams, but more than 1,000 delighted drivers returned to their home states, anxious to spread the word about the fair.

FOOD AND FUN By mid-October, the Needle's height was closing in on 500 feet. Eddie Carlson announced that the restaurant that topped it would be named the Eye of the Needle.

Ted Huggins, public relations director for the 1939 Golden Gate International Exposition in San Francisco, visited Seattle in October. In an

opposite Fearless construction workers check the joists on the Space Needle's halo.

THE OFFICIAL LOGO: "MAN IN SPACE"

Century 21's logo reflected the fair's goal of stimulating both greater understanding of science's role in the future and in world harmony. Designed by Seattle artist Robert Mathieson, the logo was composed of an arrowed-orb figure (the biological symbol for male and the astrological symbol for the planet Mars), impregnated with an icon representing the globe, and the words "Century 21 Exposition." All merchandisers who used the Century 21 trademark on their products had to obtain a royalty license and share their revenue with the fair corporation. Licensing netted Century 21 millions of dollars.

left Gracie Hansen told *The Seattle Times*, "The apple tree in Paradise will be our symbol," referring to her *Night in Paradise* show. Here she feeds a bite of the forbidden fruit to one of her dancers who has just emerged through a paper apple.

right The Eye of the Needle restaurant's rotating turntable gets a test run at Western Gear Corporation's Everett plant.

interview with Stan Patty of *The Seattle Times* he gave the fair some tart advice. "Don't rely on pretty things for attendance," Huggins said. "People want entertainment — fun — especially at night. The people who are interested in culture don't make up the gate." He noted that variety led to repeat attendance, and that "showmanship is the thing!"

Joe Gandy responded that there was going to be plenty of spectacular entertainment, and within a few days George Whitney announced the first descriptions of the fair's "Show Street." Described as "Naughty but Nice," the entertainment zone would feature song-and-dance revues, girls shows, and jazz. Nudity would be allowed, but under very strict conditions.

ENTER GRACIE HANSEN On October 25, fair officials announced that the contract to operate Show Street's major nightclub had been awarded to Gracie Hansen. She seemed an unlikely choice. Hansen's sole show business chops were producing a yearly PTA revue in the rough-and-tumble logging town of Morton, near Mount Rainier. But what the 39-year-old dynamo lacked in experience she made up for in chutzpah, perseverance, charm, and wit.

Hansen had pitched her idea for a Las Vegas/Paris-type showgirl revue a year earlier but fair officials hadn't taken her seriously. Gracie persisted. She moved to Seattle, got a job as an assistant manager at United

Savings and Loan, and began looking for investors. Robert Chinn, her boss at the bank and a prominent member of Seattle's Chinese community, rounded up 18 of his friends, each of whom chipped in $5,000. When Gracie returned to fair offices with $90,000 in her bankbook, fair planners sat up.

One week after receiving the contract to operate the nightclub (later named Paradise International), Hansen surprised everyone again when she announced that Barry Ashton — one of America's top showmen — would be producing her shows. From this point on, the press and the public wondered what this self-proclaimed "country girl from Morton" would do next.

PIECES OF PROGRESS At the end of October, the first girder to support the revolving part of the Space Needle restaurant went into place. Other fair construction was proceeding quickly. In the interest of safety and construction schedules, Ewen Dingwall closed the fairgrounds to the public until opening day.

Work was still running behind on the Coliseum — at this point renamed the Washington State Coliseum — and although much of the interior World of Tomorrow exhibit had yet to be installed, fair officials got a preview of it during the first week of November. Three officials from Donald Deskey Associates, Inc., the New York design firm in charge of the exhibit, flew to Seattle and held briefings, providing details on this complex project.

One challenge would be the installation of more than 3,200 four-foot-square aluminum cubes that would appear to float above the Coliseum floor. Visitors would ride a spherical glass elevator — the Bubbleator — into this cloud, viewing *The Threshold and the Threat*, a 21-minute multimedia spectacle with sights and sounds coming from all sides. More than 500 miles of wiring was needed for 140 loudspeakers and several hundred film projectors.

Fair staff came away impressed but worried, given that all these effects had to sync up over and over throughout every day of the fair and given the exhibit's rising costs. Still, this mix of technology and theatrics would be something fairgoers had never before seen.

On November 7, the giant doughnut-shaped track and turntable for the Eye of the Needle restaurant were given a test run in the Everett parking lot of Western Gear Corporation, its manufacturer. A makeshift platform with table and chairs was placed on the 94.5-foot-diameter ring, and a waitress/model served coffee to the architect, designer, and other dignitaries. With its one-horsepower motor, the turntable made one complete rotation in an hour, just as planned.

ARCHITECTURAL MODELS

Before the world came to the fair, Century 21 (in model form) went out to show the world its promised wonders. Fritz Ameluxen, from architect Paul Thiry's office, built the site model. It was completed in August 1960 and weighed 750 pounds. The model was trucked to Olympia and displayed in the state reception room at the Capitol. Other models included several of the Space Needle, the Coliseum, and a revised site model. In late 1961, the updated large site model was shipped to New York City, where it was featured on *The Perry Como Show*, and then to Washington, D.C., where it was displayed for several weeks at Hecht Department Store.

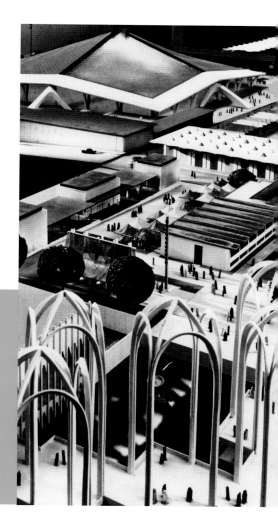

Model showing southwest corner of the fairgrounds.

below Looking down the Space Needle's shaft during construction.

BRIEFLY STATED More new buildings took shape. To lure participation by the new state of Alaska, fair officials offered free space. Governor William A. Egan gladly accepted, and National Bank of Commerce of Washington volunteered to erect Alaska's pavilion. On November 14, groundbreaking ceremonies were held for the General Electric exhibit, which would showcase an all-electric "home of the future." The next day, plans were approved for the Plaza of the States, where 50 flagpoles would each fly the flag of a different state. The Plaza of the States was Governor Rosellini's pet project — he foresaw the need to honor with proper pomp visiting dignitaries from other states.

Fair promoters were happy on November 15 when the state added an extra $100,000 to the public relations budget, and the next day they got some free publicity when John F. Kennedy visited the fairgrounds, albeit briefly. The president was in town to deliver a major foreign policy speech at the University of Washington Centennial Convocation and to attend a celebration of Senator Warren Magnuson's 25th year in Congress. After a warm welcome in downtown Seattle, the president's motorcade whisked him to the fairgrounds, drove through rapidly without stopping, and then returned downtown to the Olympic Hotel.

COMING ATTRACTIONS Show Street was generating lots of publicity. Besides Gracie Hansen's splash, another big show was in the works: *Backstage U.S.A*, directed by LeRoy Prinz, choreographer for such films as *South Pacific* and *The Ten Commandments*. Another stage show being planned was *Girls of the Galaxy*, produced by Tacoma's George M. Spray and Associates. Described as sort of a "candid-camera show," this stage review would feature 20 models posing in titillating space-age costumes. Fairgoers could snap photos of the galactic pinups with their own or rented cameras.

Puppeteers Sid and Marty Krofft hoped to have the theater for their adults-only puppet show, *Les Poupées de Paris*, ready in time for opening day. This performance — inspired by revues at the French *Folies Bergère* — would feature more than 70 marionettes in lavish costumes. Some female puppets performed strip teases during the show, and some appeared topless.

One thing that didn't remain topless was the Space Needle. By mid-November the subfloor and restaurant floor of the disk were in place, and the rail and revolving turntable were being installed. Steelworkers also got their first look at the massive gas torch that would sit atop the structure, a sign that much of the heavy lifting would soon be ending.

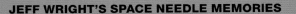

JEFF WRIGHT'S SPACE NEEDLE MEMORIES

Jeff Wright, whose father Howard S. Wright's company built the Needle, was 4 years old and probably the youngest person to ascend during its construction: "On Saturday mornings, we would tour construction sites. We got to the Space Needle one week — the restaurant and deck had been put on, but the walls weren't on. We jammed into the construction elevator, which had wire cage for walls. I was about three feet high, so I grabbed onto my dad's knees, and just — hung on for dear life. All the construction guys thought it would be cool if I got to go to the front, and sort of see the view. And I was scared to death, so I was sort of pushing back. We finally got up there, looking down 500 plus feet. I lay down on my stomach, and crawled out and my dad held onto my ankles!"

above left Workers prepare rebar and concrete for the International Fountain's base.

below left Ewen Dingwall holds up a CBS logo during a television promotion.

above right President John Kennedy and World's Fair Commission Executive Director Alfred Rochester.

BIG PRESS Paul Collop's main concern was the weather. Winter was approaching, and even small gusts of wind slowed work. Collop was also miffed that a recent *Saturday Evening Post* article had failed to credit him for designing the complex derrick used during construction, instead naming a worker for the Howard S. Wright Construction Company.

But Jay Rockey and his superpowered publicity department were thrilled with the article, one of the first published in a national magazine with large circulation. At that week's Century 21 trustee meeting, a leather-bound copy was presented to Seattle Mayor Gordon Clinton. The article coincided with a new ad campaign, with full-page promotions slated for *LIFE, Look, Time, Newsweek, Ladies Home Journal, Reader's Digest,* and many other magazines.

As always, Warren Magnuson contributed to this success. "Maggie had been the state manager for the broadcast industry here, in Olympia. They were able to convince the FCC to let promotional announcements about the fair be public service announcements, which broadcasters were required to air at the time. Here we were, sending out 30-second public service announcements about the fair, sending them out on air, and they were all free!" Bill McFarland gleefully recalled.

MONKEY BUSINESS The space race remained in the forefront of the public imagination. NASA launched a chimpanzee named Enos into orbit on November 29, in order to qualify all the systems necessary to launch John Glenn into space the following spring. Enos instantly became "the space chimp," inspiring Century 21's advance ticket sales director Louis Larsen and the press department to dream up an amusing publicity stunt.

Working with Seattle's Woodland Park Zoo, Larsen helped an orangutan named Sandra write a letter inviting Enos to hop into his space capsule the next summer and join her at the fair. News cameras flashed as Sandra placed Century 21 tickets into the package, eating a few in the process. "If Enos, described as a stable, pillar-of-the-community type fellow, succumbs to Sandra's monkeyshine suggestion, they will make a cute couple," deadpanned *The Seattle Times.*

Enos wasn't the only one receiving tickets. "Century 21 Tickets Urged as Yule Gifts," ran a headline in *The Seattle Times*. Seattle Mayor Clinton encouraged Seattleites to make it a world's fair Christmas because having tickets in hand ensured that friends and relatives would plan trips to the fair.

DOMES AND DOLE On December 2, what appeared to be a giant turtle made its way down 4th Avenue in Seattle. It was the Century 21 fountain's multinozzle dome atop a flatbed trailer. It took two hours for the 32-foot-diameter steel structure to make its way from Union Tank Works in south Seattle to the fair site.

On December 5, the last open-ground space for a pavilion was claimed when the Ford Motor Company announced that it would build a 9,500-square-foot geodesic dome next to the United States Science Pavilion. Joe Gandy, himself a Ford dealer, was ecstatic. He had marketed the fair to Ford for more than two years, persisting even after the company initially declined to participate.

More good news was announced two days later — on Pearl Harbor Day — when Hawaiian business interests optioned 10,000 feet of space for the Polynesian Playhouse and a restaurant concession. Hawaii, the nation's newest state, had not appropriated funds for official participation, but Hawaiian businesses — like Dole Food — believed the fair would be a great place to showcase island products, and they funded construction.

LARCENY AND LOYALTY The Century 21 ticket office had a scare on December 8 when a gun-toting robber fled with $130.70 and a cash tray. Louis Larsen later said that the traumatized ticket seller quit her job the next day.

Troubles continued to plague the World of Tomorrow exhibit slated for the Coliseum. Concerned over rising costs, the World's Fair Commission decided to switch contractors on December 13, opting for RCA Corporation to replace Donald Deskey Associates to finish work. Deskey had recommended RCA and offered to return $38,000 of its $317,000 fee.

After thanking everyone in his penultimate column for *The Seattle Times*, Paul Collop revealed the best story of all. On New Year's Eve, readers learned about Ethel Lyons, the ironworkers' number one fan. Lyons, a 76-year-old widow, had visited the Needle's construction site every day — rain or shine — since work began in April, often bringing pies, cakes, and other treats for the workers. After safety concerns barred the public from visiting the site, the workers bought a special hardhat for their friend, and she continued to watch from a safe distance. When the work was complete, they all gathered to have their picture taken with Lyons, whom they called the Space Needle Lady. The men who hadn't already autographed her helmet covered it in signatures. She promised to wear her "beautiful chapeau" the next spring in the Easter parade.

Throughout the prefair period, Operations and Services Director Frederick Schumacher and his assistant, Max Burland, maintained a smooth, professional, and cordial relationship with organized labor, and union members were grateful. "The fact that Seattle's World's Fair was planned and executed without labor stoppage, and this project is second only to Grand Coulee Dam in size and complexity, is deserving tribute to the efforts of Fred and Max," read a letter to Joe Gandy signed by labor leaders. Gandy, always quick to credit organized labor's no-strike agreement as a big part of the fair's success, also earned the appreciation of union members.

The World of Tomorrow exhibit
takes shape.

Union labor on the fairgrounds was by no means limited to construction workers. By opening day, 800 hourly employees falling under the jurisdiction of the Teamsters, Sales Clerks, and Operating Employees unions were on the payroll.

EVERYTHING'S ROSY With the world's fair only four months away, 1962 began with a barrage of publicity. Washington Governor Al Rosellini was the grand marshal of that year's Tournament of Roses Parade, and television viewers from coast to coast heard plenty about the upcoming exposition. Further, the Washington float, which featured the Space Needle nestled among American Beauty roses, won the parade's Class A trophy.

While in Southern California, Rosellini happened to chat with some executives from Metro-Goldwyn-Mayer Studios and suggested that the Seattle World's Fair might make a great backdrop for an Elvis Presley movie. They didn't need much convincing, and they started planning almost immediately.

PROBLEMS AND SOLUTIONS Back in Seattle, many contractors added extra shifts to finish jobs at the fair. Work on the Coliseum building was 95 percent complete, but the World of Tomorrow was only a third done — the exhibit's logistics seemed endless. The first of 3,000 cubes to be installed above the floor arrived on January 10. World of Tomorrow staff issued memos ad infinitum on the complex construction of ramps, steel cubes, and light fixtures to illuminate walkways and displays and create the desired futuristic effect; on taping of exposed edges to protect visitors from injury; and on and on. Solutions to problems spawned more problems. The fiberboard used to construct some interior walls, for example, was treated with fire retardant, making them more vulnerable to humidity and to breaking down under the anticipated heavy use.

During the months leading up to the fair, timing was crucial. The State of Nevada, for instance, was assigned a space in Domestic Commerce and Industry Building #55. The state proudly included a 100-foot-long model of Hoover Dam in its display but had to time installation around construction of Encyclopedia Britannica's exhibit nearby. If Hoover Dam was not in place before Britannica's exhibit was completed, it would be impossible to squeeze it into place. And would the floor of the exhibit building withstand the 8,000-pound truck that would convey Hoover Dam into its spot? Domestic Exhibits Director Barry Upson fielded these — and thousands of other — logistical questions.

The Seventh Day Adventists lobbied for extra space adjacent to their assigned place on the Boulevards of the World, but fair officials could not grant it. This forced the group to drop plans to build a diorama of the Garden of Eden, including the Adventists' "End of the World" sequence. They made do with a large revolving globe marked with the locations of their missions, and what a memo describes as "an exciting two or three minute motion picture film which will graphically depict assurances that the atomic age and atomic warfare, which seem imminent, does not mean the end of man's life."

The Monorail track was complete and awaiting its two trains, but the terminals were only 65 percent finished. The United States Science Pavilion was on schedule, but there was much work to be done on the Opera House, the Fine Arts Pavilion, and the Playhouse. Furthest behind was the city parking garage, which was only 25 percent complete — a major concern since it was estimated that 80 percent of the predicted 7.5 million to 10 million visitors would drive to the fair.

The best news was that advance ticket sales had topped 500,000. Thanks to a major push during the holidays, a lot of people found those Century 21 tickets in their Christmas stockings.

HIRING QUALIFICATIONS At the start of 1962, 161 people worked at Century 21, but that number grew dramatically during the next few months. The independent Space Needle Corporation had already started receiving applications from young women wishing to operate the elevators or sell tickets. In order to be an elevator operator, a woman had to be taller than 5 feet 6 inches and, according to Space Needle Manager Hoge Sullivan, had to have "the kind of personality that typified the Seattle girls."

left Construction of the Mercer Street parking garage fell behind schedule, but it was completed in time for the fair.

right On February 26, 1962, the fair's recently completed East Gate collapsed. Fair officials decided not to rebuild it, and opted instead to install 18 ornamental posts similar to those at the south gate.

By the end of January, 40 women had been hired from a pool of 300 applicants to work as demonstrators in the United States Science Pavilion. Among them were five Seafair princesses and a former Miss Alaska. The job description called for women who were young, attractive, and intelligent, and those hired were given a quick course in biology to provide them with enough background to answer questions from visitors.

Not to be outdone, the American Library Association announced that its Library of the Future exhibit in the Coliseum would have the most intelligent and attractive librarians it could find. "Gracie Hansen will think we're running competition to her girlie show," project director Gordon Martin told *The Seattle Times*.

PROTECT AND SERVE Security was a big concern. Twelve firefighters were to staff the fire-protection office, and Century 21 leased a pumper truck for emergencies. Eight police officers were already assigned for 24-hour coverage, and it was estimated that at least 60 police personnel and 90 civilian guards would be needed for the duration of the fair.

The Gayway came under police scrutiny because certain games might not be legal under the city's gambling ordinances. Seattle Police Chief Frank Ramon reluctantly allowed some mechanized bingo-type games, as long as the prizes were not cash and cost less than $15. Other games were disallowed, such as a grab-bag game in which the merchandise was not displayed, and one involving a live pig that would be sent squealing down a greased board when the player hit a target.

PROTOCOL AND PERSISTENCE The list of dignitaries planning to visit the fair was growing fast. To guard against political faux pas during their visits, Joe Gandy and Ewen Dingwall sought assistance from the U.S. Department of State, which assigned Captain Saeed A. Khan as the fair's protocol officer. Khan, a former Bengal Lancer who held joint citizenship with his native Pakistan and the United States, was charged with maintaining close contact with the Department of State and dealing with the embassies of participating nations. Seattle native Patricia Baillargeon, who had valuable protocol expertise from her years as Eleanor Roosevelt's assistant at the United Nations, and Seattleite Roger Martinsen were appointed as Khan's assistants.

ACCORDING TO PROTOCOL

Protocol for VIP visitors at the cabinet level and above was meticulously charted in advance. Scripting these high-profile visits ensured success. The visitor's time was delineated to the minute, and "Miscellaneous Information for Use During the Official Visit" decrees were distributed to host organizations. These specified name and title, correct address in correspondence and in person for formal and informal occasions, text for place cards, the order and height at which flags of foreign nations should be displayed, verbiage for toasts, languages spoken by members of the VIP party, and how much postage it would take to get an airmail letter to the VIP's country.

Program schedules detailed who would meet the dignitary (always including the Seattle World's Fair protocol officer and welcoming officials from the mayor's and governor's office). VIPs received a police escort. Official biographical sketches of the VIPs, prepared by the protocol office, were also provided to fair hosts and to the press. The VIPs, in turn, received biographical information on their Washington hosts. Remarkably — but by design — the six-month Seattle World's Fair had no protocol snafus.

In late January, the European Common Market — also known as the European Economic Community — decided to drop out of the fair. Joe Gandy immediately hopped a plane to Brussels, hoping to reverse the decision. EEC officials were so impressed with his persistence that they reconsidered.

THAT'S LIFE On February 9, Century 21 made the cover of *LIFE* magazine. The seven-page article, "How to Pull Off a Fair," praised the preparations and drove home to an international audience the exposition's scale and verve. The cover image was particularly striking. On a rare sunny day in January, *LIFE* photographer Ralph Crane captured the Space Needle against a backdrop of Elliott Bay, the Olympic Mountains, and clear blue skies. Construction workers clambered busily across the nearly finished Needle hundreds of feet in the air, a breathtaking sight that mesmerized *LIFE* readers.

Years later, Jay Rockey remembered this *LIFE* cover story as a turning point in the fair's success, something that truly captured national attention and finally allowed fair planners to catch their breath. "I'll tell you, that was about the first time I could kick off my shoes and relax — ever." The long-standing concern that the fair might fail despite all the effort put into it was finally over.

NATIONS OF THE WORLD Work continued apace. With strong organizational efforts on the part of local supporters, the United Nations announced that it would host an exhibit. On February 9, construction began on the $3 million Japanese Village, a commercial concession. The moving sidewalks at the now-completed Monorail terminals were tested for the first time, and in the Coliseum all the roof panels and cubes were finally in place.

As of February 19, 1962, the U.S. secretary of state had issued invitations to participate in the Seattle World's Fair to every nation with whom the United States had diplomatic relations.

BRIGHT SHINING FACES Jobs were being filled. More than 20,000 people applied for 1,200 positions with Century 21 Exposition, Inc., and by mid-February more than 200 had been hired. The United States Science Pavilion, the Coliseum, and the Space Needle were all hiring, and Needle management soon announced that it had chosen 31 young women out of 170 applicants.

Some of the bright young people who staffed the fairgrounds came from well beyond the boundaries of the state, and many of these — perhaps unknowingly — had their way paved by friends or relatives in high places. Lynda Kefauver, a junior at University of North Carolina, Chapel Hill, was hired by letter for a ticket-seller position. Accompanying her job offer in Ewen Dingwall's files was a letter from her father, U.S. Senator Estes Kefauver, expressing his hope that she be hired but asking that his request remain unknown to his daughter. "In other words," Kefauver penned across the bottom of his letter, "if Lynda knew I was behind this she would give me a hard time."

Eighteen was the minimum employment age, but rules were sometimes bent, as exemplified by this request from Edward Stimpson, director of the D.C. office: "Please ship employment blanks to Mr. Chauvin Wilkinson, Jr. ... He is a 17 year old who will graduate from high school this year. However, this is one that we will have to handle with special attention. Senator Ellender personally phoned Senator Magnuson on it. Senator Ellender is a very powerful force on the Appropriations Committee which voted 10 million dollars for us."

Some local young people also had an in. *The Seattle Times* President Frank A. Blethen's teenaged daughter, Diane, was encouraged to apply. Bob and Steve Camp, assistant vice president and Expo Lodging Director Willis Camp's sons, both got world's fair jobs, as did Gene and Jane Carlson (Eddie's kids) and Marilyn

opposite left Ed Sullivan was scheduled to broadcast from the fair the day after opening day, but pulled out when fair officials balked at his demand that no other network television be allowed to broadcast from the fair during its first three weeks. Undaunted, fair President Joseph Gandy appeared on Sullivan's show to promote the exposition.

right The fair received a tremendous boost when the nearly completed Space Needle made the cover of *LIFE* magazine.

Gandy (Joe's daughter). Ding's daughter Donnie worked on the grounds, and several young Dingwall relations from El Cajon, California — and their friends — applied.

Those on the fair payroll got their own glimpse of the future during meal breaks. Centuria, an automated cafeteria for employees, opened in the basement of the Armory, serving up classy entrees like salmon in wine sauce, Shrimp Louis, and tenderloin steak via a vending machine. But the big hit of the restaurant was a little machine that magically changed dollar bills into coins.

PAVING THE WAY The names of former city streets running through the fairgrounds got a world's fair make-over. Harrison Street was now United Nations Way, Republican Street turned into Freedom Way, and Thomas Street became American Way.

Despite all the progress, there were still hurdles to clear and problems to solve. Rumors spread that there would not be enough housing for the fair, causing Expo Lodging, Inc. — which had been reorganized as an official division of the fair under the direction of Willis Camp — to spend more money on advertising, assuring potential visitors that plenty of rooms were available. Governor Rosellini also stepped in when the NAACP raised concerns over fair housing. The governor firmly stated that there would be no racial bans at fair accommodations or facilities.

On February 14, the first of three high-speed elevators glided to the top of the Space Needle. The elevator's waist-high windows had yet to be installed, making it a chilly ride. For workers putting finishing touches on the Needle's disc, it was a far cry from the open-air skid on a hoist that had lifted them during construction. The old elevator, which many called the yo-yo, had made 13,500 trips.

A few days later, the nozzle test for the International Fountain attracted crowds of fair employees, who gathered to see plumes of water shoot 100 feet into the air. When workmen raised pressure to its maximum, a slight wind drenched onlookers. This problem was later solved by installing an anemometer to regulate the outflow based on wind speed.

On February 19, the first Monorail train arrived and was lifted onto its concrete beam. It boasted blue stripes on its exterior and red and beige seats. The second car — red on the outside, blue on the inside — was on its way from West Germany.

INTO ORBIT On February 20, 1962, the latest news about Seattle's world's fair got knocked off the front page when Colonel John Glenn became the first American to orbit the earth.

The impact of Glenn's achievement cannot be overstated. The Russians had already sent Yuri Gagarin and Gherman S. Titov into orbit, leaving the United States behind in the space race, since U.S. astronauts Alan Shepard and Gus Grissom had merely been lifted into suborbit. If America wished to stay competitive, a multiorbit flight was necessary to assert to the world that the United States was truly a technological power.

Glenn's mission had been postponed 10 times in two months prior to the launch, as national anticipation swelled. On the morning of February 20, hundreds of thousands of people turned on their radios and televisions and held their breaths during the final countdown. The engines roared, but the rocket at first appeared to sit motionless in a ball of fire. Then it moved skyward. Across the nation, people cheered. Some prayed, and many wept tears of joy.

Glenn orbited the earth three times and returned a national hero. President Kennedy presented him with the NASA Distinguished Service Medal, and Glenn was honored with a ticker-tape parade in New York City. Planning for a welcome parade in Seattle began almost

WILLIS CAMP AND EXPO LODGING

Expo Lodging, Inc., was a clearinghouse for advance reservations and ensured that visitors weren't gouged on lodging prices. Originally an independent organization, Expo Lodging was heavily utilized, and administration was a logistical nightmare. On February 1, 1962, Expo Lodging — by then receiving up to 2,000 mailed reservations daily — became a division of the fair.

Willis Camp, a Frederick & Nelson executive who had long been a Century 21 volunteer, was appointed assistant vice president of the fair in charge of Expo Lodging and Special Events. Camp later became special assistant to Joseph Gandy. When Camp stepped in, Expo Lodging had a backlog of 14,000 unprocessed reservation requests. Within six weeks, Camp and his team had eliminated the backlog. Some 200,000 reservations were made during the course of the fair.

immediately, in the hope that Glenn would attend NASA's space conference in May. Boosters also hoped to display Glenn's spacecraft, *Friendship 7*, at the fair.

GOOD NEWS AND MORE GOOD NEWS Everyone was talking about spaceships, but a more traditional ship made the news on February 23, when Port Commissioner Gordon Newell announced that the British liner *Dominion Monarch* was coming to Seattle during Century 21 for use as a floating hotel. This came when attempts to acquire the French liner *Liberté* fell through after months of planning. Although her glory days were behind her, the *Dominion Monarch* had 932 first-class accommodations and could sleep close to 1,500 people during the fair.

On February 25, Ned Skinner, vice president in charge of underwriting, announced some very good news: Underwriting for the fair had surpassed $5 million, a half million more than was deemed necessary to pay all the bills before opening day. That hundreds of businesses and individuals had pledged loans ranging from hundreds of dollars to hundreds of thousands was evidence of community faith in the fair's success.

ON THE MOVE The Monorail made a trial run on the night of March 3, quietly gliding along its single rail. Down at ground level, signs designed to point automobile drivers to the fairgrounds were being placed along key traffic routes. Traffic flow was a major concern, especially because the city was at the time being cleaved by the construction of the Seattle Freeway (later Interstate 5) and the State Route 520 floating bridge.

The Coliseum cubes were paneled with aluminum handled by carpenters wearing white gloves. The Opera House passed its acoustic tests. A fleet of electric cabs arrived and were taken on test runs around the fairgrounds. The first-aid room treated its first patient when Aldys Pierce, a 3-year-old boy, skinned his knee while filming a Seattle World's Fair commercial.

TICKETS AND TOTEM POLES March 15 was the final day to purchase advance ticket books, and long lines formed outside fair outlets from Seattle to San Francisco. Under the leadership of Director Louis Larsen and

CLUB 21

Club 21 was a private club for official participants, commercial exhibitors, and local VIPs. It opened on March 10, 1962, occupying the upper level of the Nile Temple, with the lower level divided into lounge areas for members of fraternal organizations. Club 21 membership applications assumed that applicants were male: the query "Married?" was followed by "wife's maiden name?" The applications were vetted by a membership committee. Membership cost $250 ($175 for exhibitors) and included two unlimited fairgrounds turnstile passes and full club privileges: dining, a supper club with entertainment, private meeting rooms, switchboard and secretarial services, and shower and grooming facilities.

Club 21 had a full Class H club liquor license to sell liquor, beer and wine by the glass, and beer and wine by the open bottle. It had 476 members — of whom Anne Swensson, the public relations office's magazine coordinator, appears to have been the only nonspouse female — plus the option of extending special one-day membership passes to adult fairgoers.

Honorary Vice President for Ticket Sales Michael Dederer, total advance ticket sales equaled $3,948,396. This was an amazing feat, giving the exposition financial ballast and allowing the fair to retire its underwriting debt months earlier than had been anticipated.

Full-priced tickets were still for sale, of course, available coast to coast through tours sold in the Sears, Roebuck catalog.

On March 20, Eddie Carlson and William Street received awards from the Municipal League for their work on Century 21. Also that day, Lummi tribal elder Joseph Hillaire left on a 30-day, 25-state trip to promote the fair. Along the way, he would carve a 35-foot totem pole that would be finished on the fairgrounds.

On the weekend of March 24, the Monorail and the Space Needle opened for preview rides. Crowds lined up at the downtown Monorail terminal before dawn, and Bob Rochelau, an Alaska motel operator, and Fred Svetich, a traveling salesman, were the first to board. Arriving at the fairgrounds, the two men rushed to the Needle, bought their tickets, and were the first ones to make it to the top. "We did it!" they both yelled, waving their world's fair pennants.

Only one elevator was operating that day, but close to 9,000 people visited the observation deck. The view of Seattle and Puget Sound left many speechless, although quite a few used the Needle's pay phones to dial up friends and say, "Hey! Guess where I'm calling from!"

FINAL WEEKS At the end of March, show producer Barry Ashton accused Gracie Hansen of misrepresenting the Paradise International revue as a "girlie show" and said Hansen had no say whatsoever in the show's production. He firmly stated that she would not be on stage during his production, and he would only allow her to appear before and after the curtain rose and fell. Hansen acquiesced, acknowledging Ashton's role as director and producer.

above left Lummi tribe member Joseph Hillaire travelled the country with Ojibwa tribe member Don McQuade to promote the fair.

above right World's Fair promotional card.

opposite Club 21 promotional card.

The fair was less than a month away, but new attractions were still being added. On April 1, negotiations were completed with water-ski impresario Tommy Bartlett for a free water-skiing show to be held inside Memorial Stadium four times a day. Work began hastily to build a 26-foot-wide concrete "aquadrome" that would circle the outer track of the stadium and would hold 100,000 gallons of water.

Workers scrambled to finish a new theater on Show Street for *Les Poupées de Paris*. The risqué puppet show was supposed to be the lead attraction onboard the hotel ship *Liberté*, but when that deal fell through the revue was left homeless. Plans were quickly drawn up for Le Petit Theatre in the last open spot of the fair's adult entertainment area.

On April 3, Donald Foster announced that all exhibit spaces had been filled well beyond the fair's original plans. More than 100 domestic exhibitors and displays representing 59 nations would occupy more than a million square feet.

Training began for some 3,500 fair employees, including staff members of exhibitors and concessionaires. Women were instructed to wear hosiery at all times and not to overdo their makeup. For men, beards and long sideburns were disallowed. The key message for everyone was to smile, always smile.

IN THE SPOTLIGHT   On the night of April 4, hundreds of photographers positioned themselves throughout the city to capture shots of a unique promotional stunt engineered by Sylvania Electronic Products. Cameras were set with a long exposure, while a helicopter carrying a bank of four Sun Guns bathed the Space Needle with intensely bright light. Flash lamps also fired on the observation deck and restaurant level, making for stunning imagery.

As the fair was about to open, widespread reports of evictions and rent-gouging brought Seattle landlords under intense scrutiny. On April 5, the City of Seattle revoked 18 hotel conversion licenses for apartment houses that had kicked out tenants to make room for tourists. Expo Lodging offered to step in and help provide solutions to this growing problem.

At the fairgrounds, work was wrapping up on the Science Pavilion, and architects Minoru Yamasaki and Perry Johanson told *The Seattle Times* that the completed structure greatly exceeded their expectations. During the design phase they had started with one arch — and then added four more. "We pushed the six buildings of the pavilion around on a model a thousand times," Yamasaki said. He hoped that after the fair the building would be used for educational purposes rather than being converted into a federal office building.

FINAL DETAILS On April 12, the Eye of the Needle served its first meal, in a test run for the kitchen and wait staff. Lunch was enjoyed by 200 fair employees, 100 at a time. To help orient the wait staff, the turntable was divided into color-keyed sections, so that the waitstaff could easily find their customers between trips to the stationary kitchen.

"The development of the Fair and the permanent Seattle Center as a partnership between City, State, Federal Government agencies and the civic leadership of this area represents the greatest single public effort in the past fifty years or since the great Alaska-Yukon-Pacific Exposition of 1909. We hope that the leadership of this area fifty years hence will be setting up similar challenges which will serve to advance the welfare, the economic and the cultural health of Seattle and the Pacific Northwest. Our warmest and best wishes to you all."

GANDY AND DINGWALL'S APRIL 4, 1962, TIME CAPSULE LETTER TO CITIZENS OF SEATTLE, 2012

After months of rehearsals in Los Angeles, Gracie Hansen's showgirls were supposed to fly north on April 13, but the 29 performers refused to board their chartered plane on the unlucky day of Friday the 13th. They arrived on Saturday to get their first look at the stage on which they'd be performing.

J. Ward Phillips, 21, had been working for the past six months setting up the Guest Relations Department. His staff was all young women from all over the country — bright, well educated, many with foreign-language skills, many hired for political reasons or as favors to influential families. They were busily figuring out the best ways to get VIP visitors around, finding ways for them to skip lines and move through the fairgrounds unimpeded. This would ultimately be accomplished by using fire exits and by asking patrons waiting in long lines to please be patient and allow the dignitary to cut in.

With a week to go, the fairgrounds were a chaotic mass of activity. Wooden packing crates lay everywhere as exhibitors unloaded their displays. Painters, carpenters, asphalt pavers, and landscapers rushed to place finishing touches. "It was like the elves came in, and all these trees got planted, lawn was rolled out, flowers were blooming," remembered Press Building Manager Sharon Lund. Jackhammers pounded, buzz saws screamed, cement mixers rattled, and generators hummed. Just before the fair opened, Assistant Special Events Director Ken Prichard, concerned about lawsuits if wheelchair users tumbled off curbs, saw that the former city streets running through the grounds were filled with asphalt and given ramps. Amid the din and the hubbub,

"This day was made possible by the unselfish, dedicated effort of our Mayor, City Council, other city officials and several hundred of our finest citizens, supported by a vote of confidence from our city electorate at two elections. ... We have endeavored to plan not for ourselves alone, but for our children and their children. We hope the generations which will enjoy Seattle Center for decades to come will believe that we have planned wisely and that we have advised our Mayor and City Council in the best interests of our community."

HAROLD SHEFELMAN TO CITIZENS OF SEATTLE, 2012

Washington State Day was celebrated on April 15, as Governor Rosellini, members of the legislature, and world's fair commissioners gathered to dedicate the Plaza of the States and the Washington State Coliseum.

SNEAK PEEKS During the next few days, reporters and other visitors got sneak previews of some of the exhibits. Entertainer Danny Kaye toured the grounds on April 17 and was most impressed by the Opera House. John Wayne visited the following day with his wife and daughter and exclaimed, "Your fair is going to be magnificent!"

On April 19, certain Century 21 personnel became the first to use Bell Systems' Bellboy devices — the world's first electronic pagers. Key department heads, maintenance personnel, and medical workers received the pocket-sized radio receivers, which would buzz whenever the person's telephone was called. The subscriber could then call a number to receive the message.

Touring the fairgrounds on April 19 were 8-year-old Debbie Smith and 9-year-old Jef Pederson, who had been chosen from thousands of Seattle schoolchildren to get a preview of the fair. They enjoyed rides on the Gayway, toured many of the pavilions, and had a lunch of hamburgers and milkshakes from the Automat. Afterward, they soared to the top of the Needle.

TOAST TO THE FUTURE World's fair officials and a Who's Who list of dignitaries gathered at the Olympic Hotel's Spanish Ballroom that Thursday evening to give the Century 21 Exposition a gala start. Months earlier, this civic appreciation dinner had been planned for Friday, April 20, the eve of opening day. Some people objected, since it was Good Friday, a sober moment in the Christian calendar. Fair officials bent to the pressure, changing the celebration to April 19 — which was Passover, a key date for observant Jews, but apparently no one raised that point.

U.S. Secretary of Commerce Luther Hodges attended the kickoff, as did Swedish Ambassador Gunnar Jaring. Other VIPs included Governor Albert Rosellini, Seattle Mayor Gordon Clinton, and Senators Warren Magnuson and Henry Jackson. Jackson arrived with his bride of four months, the former Helen Eugenia Hardin. It was her first visit to Seattle.

Toasts were offered, backs patted, champagne glasses raised. Guests dined on Puget Sound salmon and Dungeness crab, fillet of beef Wellington, and a special desert called the Century 21 Bombé — two scoops of ice cream mousse covered with flaming Grand Marnier.

below Twist Party display ad.

opposite left The Space Needle towers over actor Danny Kaye.

center Jay North — television's Dennis the Menace — enjoyed a preview of the fair before the crowds arrived.

right Film star John Wayne tours the grounds with his wife, Pilar, and their daughter Aissa.

TWIST PARTY

While Mom and Dad were getting ready to visit the fair, many local teens celebrated the grand opening of Century 21 with two days' worth of World's Fair Opening Twist Party concerts at the Orpheum Theatre. These six sold-out shows on April 20 and 21 marked Seattle's first-ever major rock 'n' roll extravaganza to be handled by a local firm.

In 1962, the Twist dance craze was at its peak. Twist fans had hoped for a venue at the world's fair to accommodate their favorite dance music, but it never came to pass. The shows at the Orpheum were the next best thing and provided Century 21 with some stiff opening-day competition from the likes of Chubby Checker, Joey Dee and the Starlighters, Gary "U.S." Bonds, and Dee Dee Sharp. With all summer long to visit the fair, many teens chose to do the twist instead.

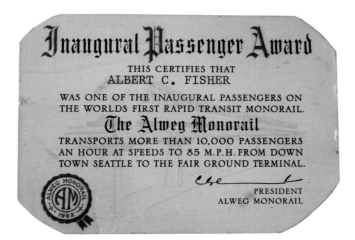

After dinner, the attendees officially christened the Monorail and then were transported to the fairgrounds, where they watched world premiers of the films *Inter-Satellite Communications* at the Bell Systems exhibit and *Journey to the Stars* in the Boeing Spacearium at the United States Science Pavilion. The Space Needle was christened with a bottle of champagne at midnight with Eddie Carlson, Joe Gandy, and Bill Street center stage. Motion Picture Association of America President (and Spokane native) Eric Johnston proposed a toast: "May we all rejoice as this beautiful city becomes the capital of the world."

READY, SET, GO On the last morning before opening day, more than 1,000 newspaper reporters gathered in the Playhouse, where they were given maps, press books, and a general briefing on the fair. Afterward they broke into small groups for a whirlwind grounds tour, followed by a massive luncheon in the Coliseum.

Final cleanup of the grounds began. Custodians swept, washers polished windows, gardeners groomed flowers, and large numbers of construction and transport vehicles were removed. Preparations continued long into the night and early the next day. Ewen Dingwall, numerous fair staff members, and Stan Patty from *The Seattle Times* worked through the night and saw dawn break over the expectant fairgrounds. The countdown clock neared zero. Century 21 was ready to blast off.

WORLD'S Seattle FAIR

SCHEDULE
★★★★★★★★★★★★★
OF EVENTS

Chapter 3

Welcome to the Future
April 21–30, 1962

The fair opens, we explore the grounds, the Opera House impresses, states are honored, and winds blow.

At 7:46 a.m. on April 21, 1962, the world's fair countdown clock stopped counting. Set in motion by former President Dwight D. Eisenhower on November 10, 1958, during a visit to Seattle, the machine had been diligently counting down the days, hours, minutes, and seconds to the start of Century 21 for the past three and a half years. With about four hours to go, the entire display went blank, save for two zeroes in the "days" column.

Century 21 General Manager Ewen Dingwall joked empathetically that the machine "obviously had a nervous breakdown." Dingwall and Donald Foster spent the rest of the morning darting around the fairgrounds, inspecting exhibits. Dingwall's electronic pager went off every few minutes, signaling him that someone had questions they needed answered.

Joe Gandy toured the grounds with a few invited guests, including U.S. Secretary of Commerce Luther Hodges. Staffers dealt with last-minute problems. At the Gayway, a display of teddy bears crashed down when a television truck accidentally backed into it. The Ferris wheel arrived late and wouldn't operate until later that evening. A few foreign exhibits had not yet arrived, and, at the Spanish Village Fiesta, almost half of the staff was absent due to a dispute with the Department of Immigration and Naturalization Services. Worst of all, the World of Tomorrow exhibit was closed to the public because of mechanical difficulties.

opposite John Raitt prepares to sing at the opening ceremonies.

NBC news anchor Chet Huntley visited the World's Fair later during the summer.

EARLY ARRIVALS Meanwhile, sparse crowds of first-day visitors lined up outside the gates. Al Carter, a Chicago musician, stopped at each gate and collected affidavits from the ticket takers, verifying that he was the first in line. In 1933, Carter had hoped to be the first one in at Chicago's Century of Progress, but another fairgoer beat him to the punch.

All the gates opened at 11 a.m., except the West Gate, where the locks had recently been changed. Frank Blair, cohost of NBC's *Today Show* interviewed fairgoers as they streamed through the south gate.

Many people made their way to the Memorial Stadium for opening ceremonies, slated to begin at 11:30. Others milled around the grounds, hoping to be the first to go into the exhibit buildings, which would open at noon.

MUSICAL OVERTURES Inside the stadium, the Vancouver, Washington, and Seattle All City High School bands played on the infield as dignitaries took their seats on stage at the west end of the field. Master of ceremonies Frank Blair of NBC introduced each of the distinguished guests to the audience, who filled the grandstands barely halfway. The Reverend Dr. Elmer H. Christie, of Seattle's Episcopal Church of the Epiphany, delivered the invocation.

Next came Harry Pelletier, president of the Musicians' Union and a drummer at the 1909 Alaska-Yukon-Pacific Exposition. Pelletier handed the Century 21 baton to Jackie Souders, director of the Official World's Fair Band. A group of Marines raised the American flag as opera singer Mary Costa sang the national anthem.

The band played "Bow Down to Washington" and "Century 21 March." Commerce Secretary Hodges, Governor Albert Rosellini, Seattle Mayor Gordon Clinton, and Joe Gandy each spoke briefly, as did other dignitaries. Between speeches, Broadway star John Raitt saluted the fair with such songs as "Hi Ho, Come to the Fair," "Seattle, U.S.A," and a rendition of "Meet Me in St. Louis" revamped to "Meet Me in Seattle." Raitt's wife, Marjorie, accompanied him on the piano, while their 12-year-old daughter, Bonnie, held the music.

Film star Danny Kaye read the Credo of Century 21. Kaye was a last-minute addition to the list of speakers, having asked to participate during a tour the day before. After the credo, the Washington National Guard fired a 21-gun salute, and the band began playing "The Century 21 Waltz."

OPENING DAY TELEVISION COVERAGE

When broadcast television was introduced at the 1939 World's Fair in Flushing Meadow, Queens, New York, it was seen by only a few hundred viewers. Coverage of the Seattle World's Fair was seen by millions. On opening day, seven stations — four in Seattle, and one each in Spokane, Portland, San Francisco, and Los Angeles — aired two full hours from the fair, beginning at 11 a.m., using 15 live cameras spread throughout the fairgrounds, including candid shots from a portable "creepy peepy" camera.

KING TV, Seattle's NBC affiliate, helped coordinate the broadcast. During the fair's first week, NBC's *Today Show* devoted almost two hours of each morning's broadcast to Century 21, with taped on-site reports from hosts John Chancellor, Frank Blair, and Louise King. The CBS network also broadcast an hour-long documentary about the fair, narrated by Walter Cronkite, who rode the Monorail and interviewed various fair officials.

At the exact moment that these photos were taken (6 min. 9 sec. before noon on April 21, 1962), Albert Fisher (right) was talking on the telephone to President John F. Kennedy at the summer White House in Florida. This photo montage documents the two of them talking together at that time.

THE ACT OF OPENING: PRESIDENT KENNEDY PRESSES THE BUTTON WHICH OPENED THE FAIR ON APRIL 21.

WAITING FOR THE PRESIDENT Unnoticed by many, 19-year-old Albert Fisher sat near the edge of the stage, clutching a telephone receiver to his ear. Fisher was hired just before the fair opened as liaison with television and media personalities and with other VIPs. On this day he was coordinating with the White House, as President Kennedy prepared to open the fair from his vacation home in Florida.

Songs and speeches blasted out of the speakers. Fisher huddled over the phone talking to various White House personnel. With only a few minutes to go, one of them struck up a polite conversation, asking how the weather was in Seattle, what kind of crowds were there, how the fair looked, and so on. Fisher responded excitedly, telling him how great it all was and how he wished Kennedy was in Seattle to enjoy it.

The last song was ending, and it was time to give Kennedy his cue. Fisher asked if the president was standing by. To Fisher's surprise, the person with whom he'd been idly chatting with for the last four minutes responded, "This is the president." Fisher patched the phone line into the audio system, and the stadium went quiet as Kennedy began his welcome speech.

OPENING THE FAIR "I am honored to open Seattle's world fair today," exclaimed President Kennedy. "What we show was achieved with great effort in the fields of science, technology and industry. These accomplishments are a bridge to carry us competently toward the twenty-first century. Many nations have sent exhibits and will send their people. We welcome them. This exemplifies the spirit of peace and cooperation with which we approach the decades ahead."

On Kennedy's desk, next to his phone, sat a telegraph key encrusted with gold nuggets — the same key President William Howard Taft had used to open Seattle's Alaska-Yukon-Exposition in 1909. But whereas the A-Y-P signal was sent directly from the East Coast, Century 21's starting signal would come from much farther away.

After explaining the telegraph key's significance, Kennedy ended his speech: "By closing this key may we not only open a great world's fair, but may we open an era of peace and understanding among all mankind." As he pressed the key downward, he added, "Let the fair begin."

left President Kennedy chats with Al Fisher while awaiting his cue.

right Opera star Mary Costa — best known as the voice of Princess Aurora in Walt Disney's 1959 film *Sleeping Beauty* — sings the national anthem.

The telegraph closed a circuit, sending an impulse to the Andover Earth Station in Maryland, which directed it toward the star Cassiopeia. At the same time, the station captured a signal that had left the star 10,000 years earlier at a speed of 186,000 miles per second. Once it was captured, the AT&T relayed that impulse to Seattle.

And so the fair began.

BOOM, CLANG, HURRAH Inside the stadium, a bank of 105-millimeter howitzers blasted a 21-gun salute. A replica of a cannon from the historic Swedish warship *Vasa* was fired. Skyrockets shot into the air, emitting hundreds of flags that fluttered to the ground. Joe Gandy pointed to the stadium's countdown timer above the stage. This one was actually working, and it now read 00:00.

The Space Needle Carillon's 538 bells clanged over 44 loudspeakers. Balloons emblazoned "See You in Seattle" were released into the air. Water-skiers gaily circled a course set up within the stadium, while aerialists rode a motorcycle across a cable running between the stadium and the Space Needle. A U.S. Air Force squadron of 10 jet fighters roared overhead, and the sun began to peek out after what had been a cloudy morning.

FIRST LOOK As the cheers and applause subsided, people streamed out of the stadium, anxious to see the rest of the fair. There was so much — what to see first? The United States Science Pavilion? One of the foreign pavilions? The rides on the Gayway? Many folks headed straight for the Space Needle and got in line for a ride aboard one of the two public elevators.

The dignitaries and VIPs were also escorted to the Needle, but they rode directly to the top aboard the service elevator. For the duration of the fair, this third elevator provided ready access to the top for many of

the fair's special guests. On this day, the speakers were all invited for a celebration lunch with the fair's top officials.

Only one thing seemed to be missing: people. Joe Gandy, Ewen Dingwall, Al Rochester, and other top brass hurried up to the Needle's observation deck, eager to assess the crowds below. Looking out over the expansive grounds, their hearts sank. Years later, Ewen Dingwall recalled the confidence-shaking moment: "It is not too much to say that it was shocking to us that there wasn't a huge crowd. There had been tremendous publicity, and we didn't know whether we were staring at a failure or what we were doing. [It turned out that] we were just looking at a situation where a lot of people didn't want to get messed up with Opening Day mobs, and stayed home."

Still, there was much to celebrate. Fair officials gathered in the restaurant with their families and distinguished guests, giddy with relief that the fair had finally begun. Even Commerce Secretary Hodges got in on the fun, offering to tell all the jokes as long as Danny Kaye provided the straight lines.

PRESS PREVIEW
Pass through gates and grounds, opening of Century 21 Exposition, April 20, 21, 22, 1962 only void thereafter
President, Seattle World's Fair

SHOCKING NEWS Fairgoers filled the restaurant. Some of them tried to catch a peek at the big shots, but most simply marveled at the panorama. Many diners lingered over lunch just to enjoy the full one-hour rotation and the 360-degree view. The room was filled with conversation and good cheer.

Then suddenly, the laughter at the dignitaries' table stopped. They had just been told horrific news: One of the air force jet fighters that had flown over the festivities had crashed into a home north of Seattle.

The details trickled in. After the F-102 jets had performed their second flyby over the stadium, the pilots circled to the east for a third. One of the planes, piloted by Captain Joseph W. Wildt, flamed out at 1,500 feet. After two attempts to restart the engine, Wildt knew he had to bail out. He set the controls

so that the plane would ditch into Lake Washington. But his ejection altered the plane's course, sending it three miles farther than he intended, straight into a neighborhood just south of the Snohomish County line.

The first house the jet slammed into was empty, its owners on vacation with their four children. The plane, now on fire and carrying the remains of that house, piled into another home across the street and exploded. Inside were Mr. and Mrs. Raymond Smith. They were killed instantly. Five nearby homes also were damaged.

Back in the restaurant, a pall settled over the crowd. Most people on the fairgrounds knew nothing of the accident. Word spread slowly, but fairgoers didn't learn the full extent of the disaster until they read about it in the newspapers.

ONGOING EVENTS Much happier opening day events included the unveiling of Paul Horiuchi's mural, a gift from the Century 21 Exposition to Seattle Center. Nearby in the Food Circus, Ethel Rosellini, wife of the governor, made the ceremonial first slice of "Paul Bunyan's 25,000-pound birthday cake," a gargantuan confection that towered 20 feet tall.

Compared with the jet crash, the day's other mishaps were minor. At the stadium, one of the water skiers slipped and smacked his head on the pool's concrete floor. An electrical problem halted the Sky Ride for an hour. A Monorail train stalled as it was leaving the downtown station and had to be rolled back into place.

A few pockets were picked, and five women had wallets pinched out of their purses. At the Lost Children Center on the first floor of the Food Circus, nurses discovered that "lost" parents and grandparents outnumbered wayward children. Although the nurses did reunite 50 sad little boys and girls with their families most lost kids ended up running around the fair having fun.

PAUL HORIUCHI'S MURAL

In 1961, the Century 21 corporation commissioned renowned Northwest artist Paul Horiuchi (1906–1999) to design and create a large outdoor mural to be located near the Space Needle and Science Pavilion. After making preliminary drawings, Horiuchi traveled to Venice to search for tiles. Although Century 21 paid for his transportation, Seattle gallery owner Zoe Dusanne helped out by arranging for Horiuchi to stay at the villa of arts patron Peggy Guggenheim.

Upon his return, Horiuchi spent months creating the mural under a large canopy. The public didn't see the completed artwork until the fair's opening day. The 60-foot-long, 17-foot-high mural was mounted on a parabolic surface, eliminating the "billboard effect" and giving it a more three dimensional quality. Unlike many of Horiuchi's other works, the mural was brightly colored for better exposure in the light of day.

Above: When Paul Horiuchi's dazzling mural was unveiled it was described as the largest artwork in the Pacific Northwest; Below: Paul and Bernadette Horiuchi in front of the Seattle Mural.

OPENING NIGHT As the sun set on the first day of Century 21, the grounds became a brightly colored jewel box. The Gayway, especially, looked magical by night. At the Playhouse, the Ceylon (now Sri Lanka) National Dancers performed the first in an eight-night run of performances. The music was supplied mainly by drums, and two fire dances were among the highlights of the show.

But the main event of the evening was opening night at Seattle's new Opera House. The show had sold out months before. Limousines arrived carrying Seattle's most prominent citizens, all dressed in their finest evening clothes and gowns.

This was the first time most people had seen the building's interior since it was the Civic Auditorium. What had been a barnlike space used for dog shows and sporting events was now a grand theater. The transformation was astonishing.

Harold Shefelman, who represented the Civic Center Advisory Commission, gave a short welcoming speech thanking Seattle's citizens for making the Opera House possible. He gave special thanks to Seattle Symphony Orchestra conductor Milton Katims and Ruth McCreery, the orchestra's manager, for their tireless efforts in championing this cause.

left Paul Bunyan's birthday cake in the food court was decorated with two tons of colored frosting and topped by replica of Mount Rainier in sugar. Taste-size souvenir packages were available for mailing.

right Feathered hats were a popular souvenir at the fair.

THE CURTAIN RISES Katims took the stage at 8:55 and received a standing ovation. He led the symphony in "The Star Spangled Banner," followed by Beethoven's *Leonore Overture No. 1*. Longtime aficionados of the symphony marveled at how well the new performance hall brought out the music's clarity and nuance.

Guest pianist Van Cliburn tore into his rendition of Rachmaninoff's *Concerto No. 1*. Since winning the prestigious International Tchaikovsky Competition in Moscow in 1958 — the first American ever to have done so — the lanky young Texan had given numerous performances within the USSR, a living demonstration that music could thaw Cold War barriers. By the time intermission rolled around, the audience had risen from their seats for numerous ovations.

The audience rose again when guest conductor Igor Stravinsky walked to the podium. The 79-year-old maestro, considered by many to be one of the greatest influences in twentieth-century music, was the star of the evening. Stravinsky led the orchestra in a variety of works, most notably a performance of his own *Firebird Suite*, which elicited the loudest cheers and applause from the audience.

Many Century 21 staff members were in the audience, including young Albert Fisher, who was still reeling from his extended chat with President Kennedy. Fisher had extra tickets that he shared with John and Marjorie Raitt, who asked if he'd like to be 12-year-old Bonnie's "date" for the concert.

The Opera House's opening night was a smashing success, a fitting end to the day's delights.

SETTLING IN With opening day hubbub now behind them, fair workers greeted visitors on Easter Sunday with new smiles on their faces. A few kinks were still being worked out. The moving walkway at the downtown Monorail terminal had to be slowed down after reports that some people were being thrown off balance. The World of Tomorrow exhibit was finally up and running, but then the Bubbleator broke down for a few hours, just after Robert Briscoe, the lord mayor of Dublin, completed his ride.

The biggest complaint of the day came from thirsty visitors — mostly those from out of state — who were surprised to learn that liquor was not being served on Sundays, due to Washington's "blue laws." Fair officials had fought unsuccessfully to find a work-around for this 1909 statute prohibiting the sale of liquor on the Sabbath. Although some other states also had blue laws, many fairgoers were disappointed.

The fairgrounds were dotted with white-capped sailors from the first units of the U.S. Navy's Fair Fleet. Over the next few weeks, 13 ships — four of which had already docked — would visit Seattle.

ROYALTY That day, fairgoers caught glimpses of royalty as Mohammad Reza Shah Pahlavi, shah of Iran, toured the grounds with his wife, the Empress Farah. One young boy wriggled through the crowd and handed the shah a present: a world's fair souvenir spoon. The shah, obviously touched, took the boy's name and address. Days later in the mail, the boy received a silver plate and dish, inlaid with gold and hand-tooled in Iran.

The shah and empress spent five hours at the fair, concentrating mostly on the United States Science Pavilion, where they were given a personal tour by Dr. Athelstan Spilhaus. The shah enjoyed testing various devices over and over and was especially intrigued by the Spacearium's journey through outer space.

After a luncheon of Dungeness crab legs and filet mignon in the Eye of the Needle, the royal couple rode the Monorail back into downtown. They then headed out to Seattle-Tacoma International Airport, where — like many other fairgoers making a grand West Coast tour — they boarded a plane headed for Los Angeles and Disneyland.

A GUEST FROM NEW YORK Meanwhile, a proud Joe Gandy toured the fair with special guest Robert Moses, New York's "Master Builder," who was heading up planning for that city's world's fair in 1964. Unlike Seattle, New York did not gain official world's fair status from the Bureau of International Expositions. Although this decision still stung, Moses had not come to Seattle to criticize but to learn. He was especially impressed with the United States Science Pavilion, noting begrudgingly that Seattle's fair officials secured government participation and funding for this exhibit at the right "psychological moment." At the end of his tour, Moses magnanimously told Gandy that the fair was "all that you have claimed for it and more."

FIRST OF THE STATES On April 23, Wisconsin became the first of many states to be honored with its own Special Day. At the Plaza of the States, Governor Rosellini and Wisconsin Governor Gaylord Nelson raised Wisconsin's flag to an honored position next to the American flag, while Boy Scouts raised the other state flags.

Attending the ceremony were 13,000 men from Wisconsin's 32nd Infantry Division of the National Guard, on leave for the day from Fort Lewis, where they were stationed. Gandy joked that Nelson was the only governor who could produce his own army.

Total attendance during the first two days was 98,143, well below what fair officials had expected. But hopes were high that with opening day and Easter behind them, more people would start visiting the fair. The grounds seemed full. At the Space Needle, people stood in line for two and a half hours, just for lunch — and for the view. The United States Science Pavilion and Food Circus also welcomed capacity crowds.

SPUDS AND STAMPS Idaho Day was celebrated on April 24, with more than 1,000 Idahoans in attendance, including Governor Robert Smylie and his family. Bands from around the state played at the flag-raising ceremony, which featured a troupe of Basque dancers from Boise.

The official Space Needle post office on Boulevards of the World was dedicated on April 25, and a new 4-cent stamp commemorating the world's fair went on sale. The first letter mailed from this post office was written by President Kennedy and hand-carried to Seattle by Postmaster General J. Edward Day. The recipient was kept secret.

WATCHFUL EYES Controversy struck Show Street when the Seattle Censor Board ordered the *Girls of the Galaxy* show closed. Heading the list of objections was that a young woman promenaded behind a large window facing Show Street, beckoning fairgoers to enter. This incited catcalling and lewd commentary from some of the coarser male passersby, which the board hoped to curtail.

The board also objected to what it deemed excessive shimmying and shaking by bare-breasted space-girl performers — in the version of the show the board had approved, the showgirls stood motionless. *Galaxy* producer Arthur Townsend vowed to remodel the building, retool the show, and reopen it.

Show Street wasn't the only section of the fair under scrutiny. On the Gayway, one concessionaire came under fire for offering live poodles as prizes. Seattle law prohibited giving away live animals in contests, and he was ordered to stop.

On April 26, curators at the Fine Arts Pavilion were embarrassed to learn that two abstract paintings had been hanging sideways since the fair began. No one had noticed, until an anonymous art lover contacted the *Seattle Post-Intelligencer*. Closer inspection revealed that French artist Roger Bissiere's signature was indeed running up the sides of both paintings.

BLUSTERY WEATHER The Hawaii Pavilion finally opened, right after the cruise liner *Matsonia* steamed into Seattle from Honolulu, via San Francisco. Honolulu Mayor Neal Blaisdell dedicated the building, and more than 4,000 Hawaiian orchids were thrown to the crowd. Originally, the flowers were supposed to be dropped by helicopter, but planners worried that high-altitude winds forecast for that day would carry the blossoms to Lake Union.

The winds arrived. By the next day, 70-mile-per-hour gusts blasted through the fairgrounds, causing tumult during Texas Day celebrations. The crowd leaned into the wind, and choral groups had to make do without a piano — the forklift meant to carry it in was off moving fallen trees. Tom Taylor, director of travel and information for the Texas Highway Department, noted that Texans prided themselves on doing things in a big way, and he tipped his cowboy hat to Seattle's blustery weather.

High winds put Space Needle elevators out of commission when one of the speed controls blew out. Eye of the Needle night manager Phil Ireland was the only passenger at the time; after waiting for more than an hour, he popped the escape hatch and climbed down the stairway inside the Needle's core. By the time the restaurant opened for dinner, the elevators were fixed.

April 28 was Montana Day, another windy day. Governor Tim Babcock attended, along with hundreds of Montanans wearing large yellow buttons that read, "I'm from Montana … The Big Sky Country." Coinciding with their visit, the naval cruiser *Helena* — named for the Montana state capital — docked in Elliott Bay.

April ended with a kickoff of Sweden Week, ushered in by another firing of the *Vasa* cannon. Senator Magnuson, of Swedish descent, joined Swedish diplomats in celebration of the first foreign nation to be honored by the fair. In the months ahead, many countries and states would receive similar tribute.

below Official Party Badge.

opposite above left Many visitors found the Art Since 1950 exhibit challenging.

above right Brochure for Gracie Hansen's *A Night in Paradise* show.

below Performers in Tommy Bartlett's water-ski show work hard to form a human pyramid.

Chapter 4

May 1962

Another *LIFE* magazine cover celebrates the fair, Soviet cosmonaut Gherman Titov and U.S. astronaut John Glenn drop in, the *Girls of the Galaxy* show is grounded, and the *Dominion Monarch* arrives to house fair visitors.

O n May 1, 1962, in celebration of Law Day, a small group of men, women, and children took the oath of allegiance at Century 21 and became American citizens. This marked the first citizenship ceremony held on the grounds, and it was a significant beginning to what would become a moving tradition at the postfair Seattle Center. The swearing-in ceremony was held at the Plaza of the States.

opposite The gleaming cubes of the World of Tomorrow exhibit.

The fair was receiving positive public response — except for the World of Tomorrow exhibit in the Coliseum. Part of the problem was lack of signage. Fairgoers entered the Bubbleator with no idea what was supposed to happen next. Transported into the cloud of cubes, many found the show — especially the narration — pretentious and overblown. Nevertheless, the exhibit was being talked about, and lines were always long.

On May 2, Expo Lodging announced expanded services: A new reservations office would open soon downtown, along with a booth near the Food Circus. Mail requests for reservations were arriving at a rate of 1,000 a day.

YOUNG AND OLD On May 3 and 4, National Science Fair finals were held in the basement of the Opera House. Budding young scientists from across the nation proudly displayed exhibits,

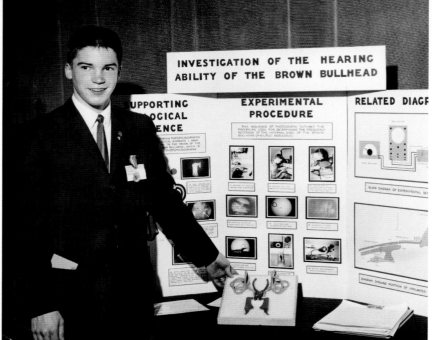

including the effect of wine on spiders, the psychophysiology of color vision, the construction of a Freon bubble chamber, and an examination of spot cycles on Jupiter and Saturn.

Century 21 honored the City of San Francisco on May 4, welcoming Mayor George Christopher and his wife, Tula, to Seattle, along with a delegation of San Francisco officials. Christopher noted that, although Century 21 was smaller in size than the 1939–1940 San Francisco World's Fair, that did not detract from its importance.

Visiting the fair that day was 101-year-old Isaac Newton Bowen, of Edmonds. The centenarian rode in on the Monorail Red Train and then headed straight for the Space Needle. "This probably is as close to heaven as I'll ever get," he told *The Seattle Times*. Bowen had attended the Alaska-Yukon-Pacific Exposition at the sprightly age of 48.

SECOND LIFE The fair's publicity staff scored yet another enormous coup on May 4, when Century 21 garnered a second *LIFE* cover. "Century 21 Opens — Out of This World Fair in Seattle," crowed headlines over Ralph Crane's illustration showing the Space Needle — its gas jet glowing — and the futuristic Monorail against a dusky blue sky. The story summed things up: "Everything's fair in Seattle — you can orbit, walk, or gawk."

Publicity just kept coming — in magazines as diverse as *Progressive Architecture*, *Vogue*, and *National Geographic* and in newspapers hailing from tiny towns and great metropolises. Reporters flocked to the Press Building like bees to a hive.

SHARON LUND FRIEL DESCRIBES PRESS BUILDING SERVICES

"We had files for anything that anyone from the working press could possibly want, and they were all prewritten, so you didn't even really have to do any reporting — you knew who, what, when, where, why, and how tall. That was the Space Needle. We had access to Western Union, and they used some of that, but most of them did their own work from wherever they were — from their hotel, or from the grounds, and then filed it later. It wasn't breaking news. We hired probably eight young men who worked as press guides, and they were available seven days a week, from morning to night. Anyone from the press who came in and needed someone to pave the way, make introductions, lead tours for the working press, these people were available. It didn't make any difference if you were from Omak, or New York City with *LIFE* magazine."

MISSION FROM MOSCOW May 5 was hectic, thanks to a visit from Russian cosmonaut Major Gherman Titov, who attracted some of the largest crowds the fair had yet seen. At times, the diminutive, 5-foot 4-inch Titov found it hard to see anything other than the Space Needle, as taller spectators gathered around him, hoping to glimpse or photograph one of the few men who'd been in outer space. Scores of news reporters compounded the crush.

Titov explored the NASA Pavilion, asking many questions through his interpreter but keeping the conversation light and personable. Afterward, he gave a short press conference before heading to the Opera House to meet his wife, Tamara, who (newspapers noted) had just had her hair styled at a downtown beauty salon. The Titovs enjoyed a performance of *The Littlest Circus* and visited Club 21 before heading out on the Monorail.

The Titovs' delight at the fair soothed Cold War tensions. Jay Rockey later remembered, "Titov and his wife came, and they really had a good time. They did things, and they laughed, and they were not rude. You sort of didn't expect that, at that time anyway."

More than 10,000 Camp Fire Girls were on hand that day to dedicate the world's fair flagpoles, funded by mint candy sales. An estimated 20,000 people — more than a quarter of the day's total attendance of 75,758 — took part in the celebration. Ewen Dingwall announced that, starting the next Saturday, the fair would open an hour earlier each day, at 9 a.m.

above Cosmonaut Gherman Titov (far left) chats with U.S. science demonstrators Merlie Ann Burton and Fiona Foyston.

below Crowds followed Titov throughout the fairgrounds.

opposite above left Gary P. Wulfsberg from Iowa won a first place award at the National Science Fair for his project, "Discovering New Compounds of Chromium and Hydroxylamine."

above right Lewis Haberly of New York won a first place award for his project, "Investigation of the Hearing Ability of the Brown Bullhead."

below Hundred-year 1962–2061 calendar.

below Jackie Cochran set more speed and distance records than any pilot, man or woman.

center Vice President Lyndon Johnson listens as Dr. Wernher von Braun speaks at the dedication of the NASA Pavilion.

opposite below right A science demonstrator speaks to a crowd of children.

above U.S. science exhibit employee emblem.

COSMONAUT CONTROVERSY Major Titov and his wife returned on Sunday. Trailed by crowds and the press, they toured the United States Science Pavilion. But then, during a coffee break with reporters, the cosmonaut sent the temperature plunging to subzero. Asked how his space flight affected his philosophy of life, Titov replied through his interpreter, "Sometimes people are saying that God is out there. I was looking around attentively all day but I didn't find anybody there. I saw neither angels nor God."

Jaws dropped. "Up until the orbital flight of Major Gagarin," Titov continued, "no God was helping make the rocket. The rocket was made certainly by our people and the flight was carried out by man. So I don't believe in God. I believe in man — in his strengths, his possibilities, and his reason."

Reporters seized Titov's frank statement. Newspapers across America, which previously had described Titov as affable and polite, now portrayed him as a godless communist. Editorials spilled barrels of ink about Soviet "antireligious propaganda."

The Titovs spent a few more hours touring the foreign exhibits, and the cosmonaut delighted some foreign representatives by telling them that he had seen their countries from the window of his spaceship. Before departing, Titov warmly pronounced Century 21 "a very good fair."

MEETING OF THE MINDS The excitement of having a Soviet space traveler at the fair was topped on Tuesday, May 8, as American space experts gathered for the Second National Conference on Peaceful Uses of Space. The conference would continue through the weekend, when Colonel John Glenn was expected to arrive.

Various NASA directors, engineers, and scientists were already in attendance, as was Jackie Cochran, the world's foremost female aviator. Cochran, who helped found the Women Airforce Service Pilots (WASP) during World War II, was the first woman to break the sound barrier and was an active supporter of America's space program.

On May 9, NASA Director James Webb and the nation's top rocket scientist, Dr. Wernher von Braun, arrived. Webb described the government's role in scientific exploration, noting that the Pacific Northwest was a key location in America's first major scientific expedition, that of Lewis and Clark. Webb went on to describe Boeing's participation in the space program, through the firm's work on the Saturn rocket, which would eventually propel men toward the moon.

THE COMEDIAN AND THE COUNT Intending to show that engineers and scientists were not just a bunch of stuffy nerds, comedian Bill Dana arrived in town in the guise of his character Jose Jimenez, an ersatz astronaut with a heavy Hispanic accent. Dana was a special guest at the conference's closing banquet at the Olympic Hotel. Although few in the crowd probably registered the thought at the time, Dana's routine underscored the fact that American astronauts were exclusively a white male fraternity.

Also visiting was another "astronaut" of sorts, from the Alaska-Yukon-Pacific Exposition. In 1909, Ed Unger had piloted a tethered balloon that took passengers 2,000 feet above the A-Y-P grounds. The 86-year-old

You are about to see...

MAN'S LIFE IN THE SPACE AGE

The theme of
SEATTLE WORLD'S FAIR
Presented by
THE STATE OF WASHINGTON
and
THE SEATTLE WORLD'S FAIR

above World of Tomorrow brochure.

opposite Colonel John Glenn stands in front of a replica of the Mercury spacecraft *Friendship 7* in the NASA exhibit.

Unger told *Seattle Post-Intelligencer* columnist Jack Jarvis that he hoped to present John Glenn with a new parachute he had invented.

Although space travel was on everyone's mind, life on the fairgrounds was down-to-earth. At the Boulevards of the World, the Philippines exhibit opened after numerous delays, attracting many visitors. The Monorail's Blue Train broke down midjourney, and passengers had to be switched over to the Red Train, which then hauled the ailing coaches back to the station for some quick repairs. The San Francisco Ballet began performances in the Opera House. And in the Arena (the renovated Ice Arena) swing fans delighted in Count Basie and His Orchestra.

FROM SPACE TO SEATTLE Just after dark, a crowd of well-wishers welcomed Colonel John Glenn at Seattle-Tacoma International Airport. After a short press conference, Glenn traveled to the Lake Forest Park home of Lieutenant Colonel Richard Rainforth, commanding officer of the Marine Corps Air Reserve at Sand Point Naval Air Station. Rainforth and Glenn had both flown in the Death Rattler Squadron during the Korean conflict.

Glenn stayed the night, sharing a bedroom with Rainforth's 14-year-old son, Kenny, who showed the visiting astronaut his model rockets and airplanes. The boy's room was plastered with newspaper clippings of his number one hero, John Glenn. *The Seattle Times* reported the visit, including a large photograph of proud Kenny and a grinning Glenn, on its front page the next day — Kenny's most fabulous clipping of all.

In the morning, Glenn went to the Olympic Hotel to meet with Governor Rosellini and Senator Magnuson. They left the building at 9:15 and were greeted by nearly 1,000 people. Some in the crowd were there to see New York Governor Nelson Rockefeller, in town for New York State Day. Others looked for U.S. Vice President Lyndon Johnson, the keynote speaker at the NASA banquet. Johnson was in his room, nursing the sore throat he'd acquired the day before while dedicating Ice Harbor Dam in Eastern Washington.

But most of the crowd wanted to see John Glenn, and most of them followed the red-haired astronaut to the Monorail station. Along with Dr. Wernher von Braun and a host of photographers, Glenn boarded the sleek elevated train and whooshed to the fairgrounds.

AN ASTRONAUT AMONG US Glenn made his way to the American Library Association exhibit in the Coliseum, signing autographs and shaking hands. He gave a short press conference at the United States Science Pavilion and then toured the exhibits. He sprawled on the carpeted floor with Senator Magnuson and the rest of the crowd to watch *House of Science*, a film by Charles and Ray Eames that introduced fairgoers to science, the scientist, and the Science Pavilion's exhibits.

He then proceeded to the dedication of the NASA Pavilion. Glenn shared the platform with Vice President Johnson, who commended the astronaut and spoke of the future of space exploration. A countdown culminated with the unveiling of the NASA logo on the pavilion's side, and Joe Gandy presented Glenn with a gold pass to the fair.

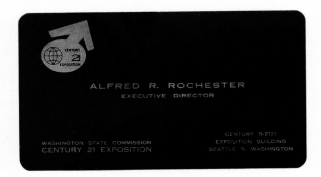

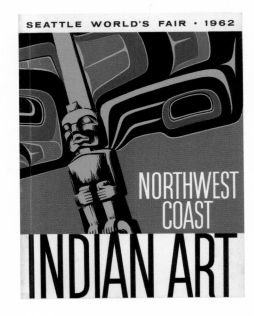

Century 21 Exposition's permanent staff operated out of three main locations: the Fair Headquarters on 1st Avenue N near the west entrance to the fairgrounds; the Blue Spruce building on Thomas Street; and the Food Circus/Armory. Each Century 21 division also had a volunteer leader selected from among the many vice presidents on the Century 21 Exposition, Inc., board of directors.

EXECUTIVE DEPARTMENT

President Joseph Gandy, Vice President and General Manager Ewen Dingwall, Assistant Vice President for Administration Harry Henke III, Assistant Vice President Willis Camp, Legal Department Director Robert Ashley, and their secretaries and assistants. Washington State Commission members with offices on the fairgrounds included Governor Albert Rosellini and Executive Director Alfred Rochester.

EXHIBITS AND CONCESSIONS DEPARTMENT

Director Donald Foster, Domestic Exhibits Manager Barry Upson, Staff Assistants Charles Hunt, Harold Douglas, and Georgia Gellert, and their secretaries. With staffers in Century 21 offices in New York, Washington, D.C., Paris, Athens, Tokyo, Manila, and Bangkok, Exhibits and Concessions marketed participation in the fair, pitching to more than 500 businesses in every major U.S. city and more abroad. Once exhibitors had signed up, the division oversaw the million details, from design and booth fabrication to daily operations to (in Gellert's case) maintaining the perfumed pools in the Fashion Pavilion.

FINE ARTS DIVISION

Director Norman Davis and his assistants and secretaries. The Fine Arts exhibits drew 1,432,352 patrons during the fair, a very pleasant surprise for planners. Norman Davis, British born but a longtime Seattle investment banker, assembled a high-caliber committee of West Coast museum directors to advise him, and he hired art professionals to oversee the main sections of the exhibit according to their expertise.

OPERATIONS AND SERVICES DIVISION

Director Fred Schumacher and, after August 1962, Maxwell Burland, Assistant Director Cliff Walker, with numerous secretaries, managers, and assistants. Operations and Services was Century 21's largest division, supervising all on-site operations: labor contract negotiations, design review, construction, utility installation, transportation services, shipping and receiving, wardrobe, medical aid, maintenance, policing concessionaires' contractual obligations, security, admissions, the fire department, personnel department, and customs and immigration.

PUBLIC RELATIONS DIVISION

Director Jay Rockey, Promotion Manager Bob Lyte, Information Manager Bill McFarland, Press Building Manager Gary Boyker (succeeded by Sharon Lund), Cyrus Noe, who served as press coordinator for all special events, and a large staff of administrative and staff assistants, secretaries, editors, and others kept this, the fair's second-largest division, humming. Rockey led a steeply uphill march to overcome early public apathy and media indifference, assembled a first-rate team brimming with newspaper expertise, and used watershed opportunities such as Monorail and Space Needle construction to wrestle national and even international media attention onto Seattle. Rockey and his team gave the Seattle World's Fair round-the-clock dedication, year after year. Their hard work garnered more than 50,000 newspaper stories, more than 1,000 magazine stories, including numerous covers, and extensive television and radio coverage, and they drew some 8,000 reporters to the fairgrounds during the course of the fair.

PERFORMING ARTS DIVISION

Director Harold Shaw, Assistant Directors Fred Vogel and Phil Tippin, Director of Publicity George McPherson, Hospitality Committee Chair Madeleine Sayres, Civic Center Manager Don Johnston, and their secretaries and assistants. New Yorker Harold Shaw had been an assistant to famed impresario Sol Hurok, and he had substantial contacts that helped him secure performers from nations participating in the fair as well as from across the United States and Canada. The Performing Arts Division provided 2,500 programs on the fairgrounds over the course of the fair.

SPECIAL EVENTS DIVISION

Director Louis Larsen, Assistant Directors Bill Borah and Ken Prichard, and a staff of secretaries, assistants, and coordinators. Before taking the helm at Special Events, Louis Larsen managed the fair's extremely successful advance-ticket-sales campaign. Special Events coordinated Special Day celebrations and all Plaza of the States ceremonies, handled all VIP visitors not handled by the Protocol Division, and included Guest Relations, the team of bright young folks who led special tours. The Special Events Division also produced the closing ceremonies.

PROTOCOL DIVISION

Protocol Officer Captain Saeed Khan and Protocol Assistants Patricia Baillargeon and Roger Martinsen. The protocol office handled foreign and high ranking U.S. VIPs of cabinet level and above, coordinating security, managing schedules, issuing invitations, and maintaining close relationships with the commissioners general of the 23 official foreign government exhibitors; liaising with the U.S. Department of State, Governor Rosellini's and Mayor Clinton's offices; and briefing all participants in every protocol event. Khan's excellent working relations with the embassies of all the nations participating in the fair, coupled with an encyclopedic knowledge of protocol and exacting standards and his staff's expertise, netted the Seattle World's Fair a spotless diplomatic record and greatly helped further international good will.

Above left: Alfred Rochester's metallic business card; Center left: Guidebook for the Northwest Coast Indian Art exhibit; Below left: Century 21 security badge; Above right: KING 5 TV television camera; Center right: Jackie Souders leads the Official World's Fair Band; Below right: Sign for Governor Nelson Rockefeller's car on New York Day.

After a luncheon in the Arena, Glenn helped present a plaque in the name of President Kennedy to Senator Magnuson "for his contribution to the advancement of the sciences." After the ceremonies, the astronaut had time for a quick ride to the top of the Space Needle before moving on to the NASA conference at the Opera House.

The highlight of the conference was a televised discussion involving Glenn and eight other panelists. Audience members directed most of their questions to Glenn, and the first were related to Soviet cosmonaut Titov's professed atheism. Glenn responded, "The God I pray to is not small enough that I expect to see him in outer space."

Other questions addressed the use of space monkeys instead of astronauts, whether the Russian flights were hoaxes, and various aspects of technology and space travel. Glenn answered in a reserved and somewhat bashful manner, but he also made sure that the other panelists were heard from.

The eight other men at the table were members of the 100,000 Foot Club — test pilots who had reached that altitude in balloons, rockets, and experimental aircraft. The panelists answered questions with aplomb, but Glenn held the spotlight. The *Seattle Post-Intelligencer* noted that the other astronauts "might as well have been eight guys named Joe." One of those anonymous Joes was Neil Armstrong, the first man — seven years later — to step onto the moon.

BACK TO EARTH May 11 was Seattle and King County Day, capping a week's worth of Washington State celebrations honoring Spokane, Pierce County, Walla Walla, and Pasco. The Seafair Pirates kicked off the day's events, running around the fairgrounds brandishing sabers and yelling, "Arrrrrr!"

Iowa Day was held on May 12, and Governor Norman Erbe joined Governor Rosellini in saluting the Hawkeye State. Erbe, visiting with his wife Jackie and their three daughters, was no stranger to Washington,

left: *Backstage U.S.A.* neon sign.

right: *Backstage U.S.A.* brochure.

having been stationed at Moses Lake during World War II. School Patrol Day was also celebrated, and 1,600 young members of school safety programs gathered in Memorial Stadium to receive praise from Governor Rosellini.

The *Girls of the Galaxy* show reopened, but Ewen Dingwall shut it down again almost immediately. He stated that it did not meet the standards of the fair.

Dingwall also looked with a sharp eye on the *Backstage U.S.A.* revue, after receiving complaints from spectators that the showgirls didn't do anything. The intended allure of the show was a "backstage" view of young women in various stages of undress, but most of the semiclad ingénues just sat knitting, reading, or writing letters. Director LeRoy Prinz vowed to liven up the act. The fair struggled to find a balance between too much sex and no sex.

AUTHORS AND MOTHERS   In the Opera House, Rod Serling, Ray Bradbury, and other writers held a panel discussion titled "Science Fiction in the Space Age" before an audience made up mainly of teenagers. Bradbury, author of *The Martian Chronicles* and numerous short stories, described space travel as "the single most important step to be made by the human race." Serling bemoaned the lack of serious science fiction on television, noting that even his show *The Twilight Zone* would soon be going off the air.

Both Bradbury and Serling brought their families, calling into service both the Guest Relations Department and the Hospitality Committee. Headed by fair employee Madeleine Sayres (wife of *Slo-Mo-Shun* hydroplane driver Stan Sayres), the Hospitality Committee entertained the fair's entertainers. Committee members ferried performers to and from the airport, showed off the town, hosted parties in their own homes, and met all special requests — from babysitting to particular brands of booze.

Another television personality visiting the fair that weekend was Edd "Kookie" Byrnes, hair-centric star of the hit show *77 Sunset Strip*. Wishing to avoid adoring fans, Byrnes wore a fake mustache and a black topcoat, and fair officials kept his arrival a secret. A few fairgoers recognized him, but it is unknown whether any of them asked to borrow his comb.

May 13 was Mothers Day, and plenty of dads and kids treated Mom to a day the fair. An impromptu appearance of the Rainier Beach Grandmothers Kitchen Band, a group of about 300 grandmothers from around Puget Sound delighted everyone. The fun-loving grannies wore hats and dresses decorated with clothespins, plastic forks, and kitchen utensils. They paraded around the grounds playing music on kazoos, buckets, pots, pans, and washboards.

On Monday, May 14, due to overwhelming demand, the Eye of the Needle began serving breakfast. Plenty of other folks preferred the Belgian Waffle House, one of the fair's biggest concession hits.

GIRLS GONE WILD Trouble was brewing in the heavens over on Show Street. *Girls of the Galaxy* producers vowed to defy closure orders, claiming that Dingwall had no legal right to shut them down. In response, Century 21 guards confiscated employee passes. The cast paid their own way into the fair, only to discover that the building's gas and electricity lines had been disconnected. They moved ahead anyway, readying themselves in the dressing room by flashlight. Just before showtime, the stage crew located an emergency electrical outlet in the ceiling, and the lights went on, along with the show.

While a sparse crowd — mostly newsmen — watched dancer Patty Herman perform *Around the World in Sexty Minutes*, the Seattle Police Department positioned fair guards outside, waiting for the show to end. After the spectators exited, two large trucks moved in to block the entrance before anyone could go in to see the second show. The guards also set up wooden barricades. Jose Duarte, the show's comedian, tried to get through the line with coffee for the cast, but he ended up in a tussle with one of the guards and was arrested for disorderly conduct. Exotic dancer Fantasia tried to wriggle her way in under one of the trucks, but the guards pushed her back.

One of the show's backers promised that the show would run again the next night. But the next evening, after closed-door discussions, Ewen Dingwall held a press conference, stating that the *Girls of the Galaxy* show was closed by mutual consent.

below The old world look of the Belgian Waffle House made it very easy to find.

opposite Many people relaxed around the International Fountain after dining at one of the nearby restaurants.

BELGIAN WAFFLES

Originally showcased at the 1958 Brussels World's Fair, Belgian waffles were introduced commercially into the United States at the Seattle World's Fair. Made with yeast-leavened batter — which made them lighter, thicker, and crispier than other waffles — and topped with whipped cream and strawberries, the confection quickly became one of the most talked-about food treats at the fair.

Century 21's Belgian Waffle House was managed by Belgian Chef Walter Cleyman, who also ran a smaller waffle booth on the Gayway. Cleyman baked waffles at the 1958 Brussels fair, where the treat was originally called the Brussels waffle by its creator, Maurice Vermersch. In 1964, Vermersch opened a waffle stand at the New York World's Fair, and, although that fair is often credited with first popularizing the confection, it is Seattle that actually holds the honor.

below Seattle Mayor Gordon Clinton
rings the Friendship Bell as Kobe
Mayor Chujiro Haraguchi looks on.

center Evalyn Van Vliet expresses
delight at being named the one-
millionth visitor.

opposite below The Bell Telephone
Systems exhibit showcased many
breakthroughs and innovations that
are now commonplace.

above Bell Systems cartoon depicting
Chip Martin, College Reporter, being
given a tour of the Bell exhibit.

FINE MUSIC There was probably not much crossover appeal, but disappointed *Girls of the Galaxy* fans could opt to see Isaac Stern perform at the Opera House. On May 15, the noted violinist stole the show as the Seattle Symphony Orchestra's guest soloist. Stern thrilled the audience with an impeccable performance of Beethoven's *D-Major Violin Concerto*. The symphony also debuted *Visions of Poets*, a choral-orchestral arrangement of Walt Whitman's poems composed by Benjamin Lees.

Denmark Days began on Wednesday, May 16, and continued until Sunday. In the Plaza of States, Danish officials joined Lieutenant Governor John Cherberg, Mayor Clinton, and Joe Gandy. The World's Fair Band played the Danish "Champagnegaloppen." Each night Opera House audiences enjoyed performances by Denmark's most famous comedian-pianist, Victor Borge.

At the Boulevards of the World, Mayor Clinton joined with Mayor Chujiro Haraguchi, of Kobe, Japan, to celebrate the Seattle-Kobe Sister City Program. The two mayors rang a one-ton Friendship Bell — later called the Kobe Bell — that was a gift to Seattle from Kobe. Mayor Clinton was one of the earliest proponents of the nationwide Sister City Program instituted by President Eisenhower in 1956.

THE FIRST MILLION On May 18, the NASA Pavilion received a very special visitor — John F. Victory, the first employee of the National Advisory Committee for Aeronautics. Victory had joined the committee when it was created by President Woodrow Wilson in 1915 to focus on aeronautical research and development. The agency was dissolved in 1958, and was succeeded by NASA, which took over its predecessor's assets and personnel. Dr. Victory retired in 1960, but still took an active interest in the space program. He was a living link between the days of biplanes and booster rockets.

At the Bell Telephone Systems Pavilion, telephone engineers made some changes that allowed visitors to dial directly to various cities and get a recorded weather report. A few clever users realized that these were open lines and made personal calls around the country. Bell removed the speaking mechanisms on these phones.

Twenty-eight-year-old Evalyn Van Vliet got a big surprise when she walked through the gate on May 19. A man told her to stop where she was. A blue carpet was rolled out in front of her and Joe Gandy came over and gave her a big kiss. She was given a portable television set, $100 in trade dollars, a Space Needle ashtray, a cruise to Victoria, B.C., an envelope full of fair tickets, and a sport outfit in a world's fair print. Van Vliet was the one-millionth visitor to Century 21.

By now fair officials were pleased with attendance numbers. As the weather improved, crowds grew, and it wasn't even summer yet. Many people were repeat visitors, some returning dozens of times. On this day, attendance topped out at 66,923. Only the crowd on the day Soviet cosmonaut Titov visited was larger.

FRESH FRAGRANCE On Monday, May 21, thousands of Canadians came to celebrate Vancouver, B.C., Day. Many of them had the day off of work for Victoria Day, their own national holiday.

And because it was exactly one month since the fair opened, the 20,000-gallon Revlon Fountains of Fragrance perfumed pool at the Fashion Pavilion got a new scent. The "Intimate"–scented pool had been drained the night before, scrubbed with detergent, and refilled. Georgia Gellert poured in the right amount of "Jolie Madame," adding a fresh new aroma to the exhibit.

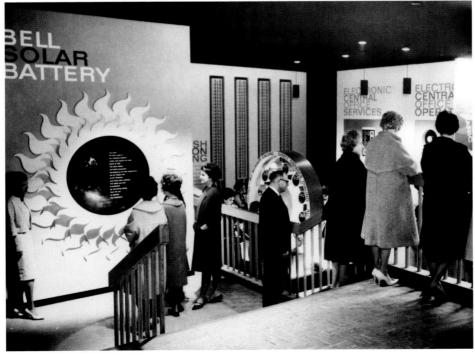

GREENWICH MEAN TIME   ORBIT NUMBER   COUNTDOWN   ELAPSED TIME   TIME TO RETROFIRE

above left *Vogue Magazine* sponsored fashion shows featuring models sporting next season's looks as they strutted and posed above Revlon-perfumed fountains.

above right The NASA tracking station was used to monitor Scott Carpenter's triple-orbital flight.

opposite Visitors to the NASA Pavilion learned about the many satellites and space capsules that circled, or soon would be circling, the planet.

Keeping the perfumed pools clean was a challenge for maintenance staff. Something — either the painted concrete lily pads across which the glamorous models strutted during daily fashion shows, or items tossed into the pool, or maybe the perfume concentrate — caused the formation of an unglamorous scum across the water's surface. The pool was vacuumed thrice weekly and repainted more than once. Although the scent attracted crowds, sometimes the smell went off, repelling them. Dingwall requested that staff attend to the situation he called "unsatisfactory and even, to some, offensive."

GOOD SHOWS   The controversial *Girls of the Galaxy* show reappeared — but this time with Ewen Dingwall's approval. The show had been completely revamped, new acts had been added, all without any nudity. Dingwall stated that it was "now a good show for the money."

Renowned clarinetist Benny Goodman and his orchestra began a week of performances in the Arena that night. The group was en route to a tour in the USSR and spent their Seattle days rehearsing and preparing for that trip.

On May 22, folk singer Theodore Bikel played a single show at the Opera House before a large audience. For three hours, Bikel interspersed more than 30 songs with jokes, informal thoughts on history, and explanations of why certain songs affected him personally. His diverse music included songs from Israel, Ireland, Spain, Hungary, and Russia. Bikel told his Hospitality Committee minders that he enjoyed Seattle and the fair so much, he didn't even want to waste time sleeping.

THE VIEW FROM SPACE   On May 24, crowds gathered in the NASA Pavilion, where six television screens displayed network broadcasts of astronaut Scott Carpenter's triple-orbit flight. Carpenter's space mission lasted five hours, the last 30 minutes frighteningly suspenseful. Carpenter overshot his reentry point and splashed down 250 miles from his target. The room was silent as fairgoers, along with television viewers around the world, waited to see if he had survived the landing.

below Riding the Bubbleator into
the World of Tomorrow was one of
the most memorable experiences of
the fair.

opposite above left Tamar Ivask was
quite surprised when she learned that
she was the one-millionth passenger
aboard the Monorail.

above right Oregon Governor Mark
Hatfield (center) stands proudly with
members of the United Indian Tribes
of Oregon.

One of the people watching was actor Jack Lemmon, in town to visit the fair with his 7-year-old son, Christopher. Glued to the television displays in the NASA building, Lemmon started chain smoking as Carpenter began his reentry. After what seemed like hours, the entire room erupted in cheers when the astronaut was found safe.

MUSICIANS AND POLITICIANS   At the Opera House that evening, Eugene Ormandy conducted the Philadelphia Orchestra performing works by Ravel, Wagner, and Rachmaninoff. The audience was especially impressed by 19-year-old pianist Susan Starr, who had recently taken second place in the International Tchaikovsky Competition. Starr had first soloed with the orchestra at the age of 6.

Secretary of State Dean Rusk arrived at the fair on May 25 to deliver a major policy speech. Speaking to a near-capacity crowd in the Opera House, he described the U.S. goal to make the frontiers of space an arena of peace, not of war and military might. He challenged the Soviets to do the same.

Afterward, Rusk spent the rest of the morning touring the fair with his wife, Virginia, and Benny Goodman. Rusk was most impressed by the World of Tomorrow exhibit and its strong plea for peace among mankind. His only complaint was that the presentation was too short — he wanted time to ponder.

RIDERS AND INSIDERS   Tamar Ivask became the Monorail's one-millionth passenger and was handed a gold pass to the Monorail along with $50 in fair admissions. As cameras flashed, she exclaimed, "I have no hair-do! I am just out of the kitchen!"

WORLD OF TOMORROW

A trip to the World of Tomorrow began with the Bubbleator operator urging visitors to "step to the rear of the sphere" before ascending into a floating structure of cubes bathed in light. "Utopia! Century 21! First floor! Step off into the future, please. We've all got to do that sometime."

According to the official guidebook, the prologue of the presentation titled *The Threshold and the Threat* compressed the next 39 years into 40 seconds, illustrated by possible futures projected onto the cubes. Suddenly, the threat of nuclear war is displayed. A family is seen desperately awaiting help in a fallout shelter, but the voice of a child banishes their plight with words of compassion. The narrator beckons visitors to enter the city of the future.

Seattle's terrain is apparent, but much has changed. Jetports, monorails, and highways interlace the region, allowing people to live far from the city center, with plenty of room to move about. The factories of tomorrow are automated and located in attractive industrial parks. Offices are filled with devices that send micromail, transmit correspondence, and even communicate with each other.

Without warning, visitors are returned to the family in the fallout shelter, for whom time is running out. The lights dim, and they are met with silence, followed by the voice of President Kennedy from his inaugural speech, calling upon everyone to use the knowledge of the present to build a brighter world of tomorrow — a world free of the threat that clouds the threshold.

At the United States Science Pavilion, Athelstan Spilhaus broke up a "racket" that two opportunistic young boys had been operating. The junior science laboratory was open to children ages 8 to 13, and adults were allowed in if accompanied by a child. The budding entrepreneurs noticed many unescorted adults who wanted access to the junior science experiments, so for 25 cents a pop the youngsters masqueraded as their children. Spilhaus asked the young entrepreneurs to leave, and a "children only" sign quickly went up.

OREGON TRAIL Oregon Day was May 26, attracting throngs of visitors from the neighboring state. One train arrived from Portland with 1,257 fair-bound Oregonians, including Governor Mark Hatfield. Hatfield noted that it was the longest passenger train assembled in Portland since World War II.

The United Indian Tribes of Oregon bestowed a special honor on Hatfield, making him their Tah-keia-me-u Oh Hut or En-che-ca — "Head Chief" in the Nez Perce and Warm Springs languages. Hatfield was given a feathered Indian bonnet and a pair of white moccasins. His wife received a beaded purse.

VISITORS FROM ABROAD British Week began on May 27 with a visit from Her Majesty's ambassador to the United States, Sir David Ormsby-Gore. The ambassador spoke at the Great Britain Pavilion, noting that Britain set the stage for international exhibitions when Queen Victoria opened the first one in London's Crystal Palace in 1851 — the same year, Ormsby-Gore pointed out, that Seattle was founded.

The fair also welcomed more visitors from behind the Iron Curtain: 11 Soviet hydroelectric engineers, who spent most of their time at the hydroelectric exhibit and the Hall of Industry. The next day a party of 16 prominent Soviets arrived. The group was made up of scientists, economists, philosophers, historians, and film workers, and their stop was part of a 20-day tour of America, sponsored by the USSR's Institute of Soviet-American Relations.

Some Monorail passengers bought this pin so that their friends back home would know they'd ridden on the futuristic transport.

On May 28, the American Cancer Society dedicated its Man against Cancer exhibit in the Washington State Coliseum. The star of the dedication was William Gargan, a former Hollywood "tough guy" who had lost his larynx to throat cancer. Gargan had learned to talk again using an esophageal voice, and the crowd stood silent as he swallowed air to help him speak about the importance of cancer research and the risks of smoking.

PULLING INTO PORT The big news on May 29 was the arrival of the retired ocean liner *Dominion Monarch*. Joe Gandy and other officials had spent months trying to secure a hotel ship for the Seattle waterfront. Steaming into Elliott Bay, the *Dominion Monarch* dwarfed other vessels. Rising 10 stories high and longer than two football fields, the 27,000-ton behemoth turned heads along the waterfront as it was welcomed by aerial bombs and

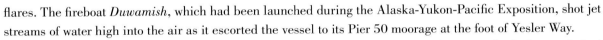

CENTURY 21 CALLING

The Bell Systems Pavilion introduced many advances in the world of modern telephone communication, including direct dialing, call waiting, conference calling, touch-tone phones, and pagers. Although speed dialing was demonstrated through the use of punch cards, most of the other innovations came to be used exactly as displayed. Fairgoers also got their first look at a solar battery, which turned light into electricity.

During the fair, Bell Systems produced *Century 21 Calling …*, a short promotional film that highlighted its exhibit as well as other aspects of the world's fair. In it, a young boy and girl arrive at Century 21 aboard the Monorail and proceed to visit the Gayway, a few foreign exhibits, and the United States Science Pavilion. Then they take a detailed tour of the Bell exhibit, where they marvel at each new innovation. They end their day atop the Space Needle, looking out over a beautiful Puget Sound sunset.

flares. The fireboat *Duwamish*, which had been launched during the Alaska-Yukon-Pacific Exposition, shot jet streams of water high into the air as it escorted the vessel to its Pier 50 moorage at the foot of Yesler Way.

At the fairgrounds, the Opera House received its first visit from Alfred Schweppe, who had wrangled with the city over the bond issue that funded conversion of the Civic Auditorium. After touring the building, which he described as "very lovely," he admitted that he was happy at how things turned out.

HOLIDAY HIGHLANDERS Wednesday, May 30, was Memorial Day, and the first holiday since the fair opened brought in 54,662 people. The more popular exhibits had lines a block long. Scottish bagpipers wandered the fairgrounds and were joined by groups of highland dancers for two concerts near the Great Britain Pavilion.

Bagpipers were a great hit with fairgoers. Special Events Director Louis Larsen recalled years later. "We had a Vancouver Day. And I'm big on bagpipe bands, because I guarantee you, if you have a big impact day, and you have a crowd, and you take a bagpipe band, and they play, you can move the crowd from here to there." Larsen also laughingly remembered that traveling with pipers could lighten bar tabs: "You take a piper in there, and you'll never spend a dime for a drink."

The month of May ended with the dedication of the International Fountain, sponsored by the American Waterworks Association, in town for its annual convention. One of the fair's most charming symbols was thus officially honored as the Memorial Day weekend unfolded and fair crowds surged. Summer was beginning, the summer of 1962, the world's fair summer. It would belong to Century 21.

above Bell Systems' Princess Phone, introduced in 1959 and produced by Western Electric, boasted an illuminated dial and a choice of colors: white, beige, pink, blue, or turquoise. Miniature versions of this phone were popular souvenirs in the Bell Systems Pavilion.

opposite The *Dominion Monarch* steams into Elliott Bay for use as a floating hotel.

Chapter 5

June 1962

HRH Prince Philip, Duke of Edinburgh, strolls the grounds, the Seattle Symphony strikes up *Aida*, the 1909 Alaska-Yukon-Pacific Exposition gets a fond nod, and attendance nears the three million mark.

The grandest event of British Week was the visit of His Royal Highness Prince Philip, Duke of Edinburgh, to the fairgrounds on June 1. Prince Philip's visit to Seattle lasted only 27 hours, and his wife, Her Royal Highness Queen Elizabeth II, did not accompany him. Still, Prince Philip's visit constituted a massive project for the Protocol Division. As usual, Saeed Kahn's staff organized details down to the least minutia, and, as usual, everything played out brilliantly. His Royal Highness was greeted by Washington's highest official, Governor Albert Rosellini, with the rest of the political and world's fair VIP entourage standing by.

The prince's visit was a huge treat for British expats, but many only glimpsed him. One member of the crowd lining 4th Avenue as the limousine slid by was reported to have cried, "'Ere 'e Comes! ... And there 'e goes."

The same day, members of the National Science Planning Board and the Science Advisory Committee for the United States Science Pavilion arrived in town. "This is what we wanted," said Dr. Dael Wolfle, executive officer of the American Association for the Advancement of Science. At the Brussels exposition, Wolfle noted, the United States Pavilion displays were too technical and most fairgoers could not fathom them. Seattle's science exhibits were far more user-friendly.

opposite The fair's south entrance gate reminded some visitors of modernistic totem poles.

BOOKS AND THE BARD Still, science had its challengers, including good old-fashioned picture books. The children's library at the American Library Association exhibit offered free programs every half hour from 10 in the morning until 10 at night, and kids adored it, turning the 21 available seats in the cozy theater into a sort of musical chairs game. The exhibit was stocked with books, storytellers plied their trade, and motion pictures and film strips were a steady draw.

Shakespeare fans were rapturous over *Romeo and Juliet*, directed by Franco Zeffirelli and played by London's Old Vic touring repertory players at the Opera House. "Zeffirelli has treated *Romeo and Juliet* as though he had never heard of it previously — and the result is a production that ranks with the best theater you've ever seen," *Seattle Post-Intelligencer* critic John Voorhees enthused.

Seattle was the last stop on the production's American tour, and the players must have been completely charmed by the welcome Madeleine Sayres and the Hospitality Committee provided. The actors arrived at their hotel to find 700 roses awaiting them. The Old Vic's offerings also included George Bernard Shaw's *Saint Joan* and Shakespeare's *Macbeth*.

QUESTIONS AND ANSWERS For outside fun, kids visiting the fair could pay 50 cents for a golden (plastic) Key to the Fair. These operated talking storybook machines throughout the fair. The NASA Pavilion book began with a countdown and simulated rocket blast and then described the contents of the pavilion. At the International Fountain, the storybook provided statistics: how high the jets shot water, how many of them operated, how often the carillon played.

NASA offered each pavilion visitor a chart titled "The Earthman's Guide to Outer Space." Filled with interesting statistical data about the planets in our solar system, the brochure cheerfully invited fairgoers to "plan your vacation now for an exciting holiday on one of these nine planets or the moon."

Fairgoers who visited the League of Women Voters booth liked trying out the Rockwell Manufacturing Company's voting machines. All things lunar prevailed here as well: "Should the nation landing on the moon first own it?"

Anyone needing that question translated could ask the Guest Relations staff. "In French, German, or Japanese, the answer to the most-asked foreign question at the Seattle World's Fair is: L'Aiguille de l'espace ...Wel traumnadel ... Matento. The questions, posed in a score of languages by visitors from more than 100 countries concern first — the Space Needle," the *Seattle Post-Intelligencer* reported. Guest Relations staff fielded questions, comments, and complaints in Chinese, Danish, French, German, Italian, Latvian, Norwegian, Spanish, Japanese, and Portuguese. Clad in easily recognizable crisp blue uniforms, the division's interpreters also assisted the fair's many foreign exhibitors.

above Romeo (John Stride, extreme left) watches the duel between Mercutio (Alec McCowen, left) and Tybalt (Thomas Kempinski, right) in the Old Vic's production of *Romeo and Juliet*.

below Seattle World's Fair Talking Storybook key.

Four Men Who Made the Fair

Fair employees worked tirelessly, and all deserve credit for the exposition's success. Four men's extraordinarily complementary efforts deserve particular mention: those of Edward Carlson (the visionary), Joseph Gandy (consummate salesman and face of the fair), Ewen Dingwall (for detail and follow-through), and Al Rochester (senior statesman and link with past glories).

EDWARD CARLSON (1911–1990)

Edward Carlson, Century 21's mastermind and main engine, rose through the ranks of the hotel industry, from pageboy to president of Western Hotels (now Westin Hotels and Resorts) and later of United Airlines. Finances forced him to leave the University of Washington without finishing his degree, but he would later state, "Even without a college degree I have found life very generous." Carlson returned life's favor, providing the Seattle community with steady leadership and exemplary public service throughout his business career.

In April 1970, the University of Washington recognized Carlson's longstanding dedication to the Northwest community by awarding him the Alumnus Summa Laude Dignatus, the highest honor the school and its alumni organization can bestow. Harvard Business School considers Carlson one of the great business leaders of the twentieth century, and *The Wall Street Journal* described his leadership style as "gentle generalship." Edward Carlson died on April 3, 1990. In 1992 the Carlson family funded the Edward E. Carlson Leadership and Public Service Center at the University of Washington. The Carlson Center encourages University of Washington students to contribute meaningfully to their community as effective citizens and future leaders.

JOSEPH GANDY (1904–1971)

As president of the Century 21 Exposition, Joseph Gandy traveled the world as an emissary for Seattle and the Pacific Northwest, winning support from the many nations whose participation in Century 21 truly made the fair a global event. "Joe liked a challenge," Laurene Gandy later recalled. "Anything that was uphill, Joe liked. He went into it so Seattle could have its civic center — the World's Fair was simply a vehicle to get the civic center. He felt this was so right for the city, and I think it has been." Of her own considerable role in Century 21, Laurene Gandy modestly admitted, "Where I was needed, I helped."

Gandy held a law degree from the University of Washington. During World War II, he served as the chief deputy regional director of the War Production Board for Washington, Idaho, Oregon, Montana, and Alaska. Gandy was secretary-treasurer of Smith-Gandy Ford, a Seattle Ford dealership he cofounded in 1946. He chaired the United Good Neighbors fund-raising drive in 1953, served as president of the Seattle Chamber of Commerce in 1956 and 1957, was crowned Seafair King Neptune X in 1959, and was a two-term president of the Seattle Symphony Orchestra Association. Gandy also founded the Central Association and served as that group's first president, founded the Seattle Junior Chamber of Commerce, served on the boards of the Youth Symphony Orchestra, the Urban League, the Washington State Highway Users, Junior Achievement, the Seattle Municipal League, the World Affairs Council, the Seattle Art Museum, and Greater Seattle, Inc. In 1969 he headed up the United Arts Council, Seattle's first consolidated drive to raise money for arts and cultural groups. Joseph Gandy died on June 13, 1971.

Above, from left: Washington Governor Albert Rosellini, a World's Fair Service Scout, Nell Carlson, and Edward Carlson on the fair's Edward E. Carlson Day, September 23, 1962; Below, from left: Joseph Gandy, *Denver Post* publisher Palmer Hoyt, Alfred Rochester, Ewen Dingwall.

EWEN DINGWALL (1913–1996)

Ewen Dingwall's influence on both the fair and Seattle Center was enormous. He oversaw and managed every aspect of the fair and served as first executive director of Century 21 Center, Inc., later resuming the helm at Seattle Center at a crucial moment in the center's development. Born in Seattle, Dingwall held a degree in journalism from the University of Washington. He worked for the Municipal League, as Mayor Bill Devin's assistant, and then for the Washington State Research Center before becoming Century 21's first hire. Ewen Dingwall died on October 25, 1996.

ALFRED ROCHESTER (1895–1989)

Al Rochester, a lifelong Seattle resident, was active in the Democratic Party and served on the Seattle City Council (1944–1956). Century 21 Exposition's original booster, Rochester served as executive director of the World's Fair Commission from 1960 to 1963 and was a constant presence on the fairgrounds. Amiable and affable, Al Rochester was an officer of the Pioneer Association of Washington State, chairman of the King County USO, and chairman of the Easter Seal campaign. He organized and chaired the local Infantile Paralysis Foundation chapter, was director of Red Cross and Heart Association campaigns, and was twice president of the Young Men's Democratic Club of Seattle and King County. Seattle Mayor Charles Royer declared September 24, 1984, Al Rochester Day "to honor this dapper and charming man who has played such an important role in the history of our city." Al Rochester died on February 4, 1989.

below Sermons from Science gave
visitors an electrifying experience.

opposite left Childcare was available
in the Christian Witness Pavilion.

above right Sermons from Science
brochure.

below right The stained glass window
in the Christian Witness Pavilion won
an award from the Stained Glass
Association of America.

Kids enjoying the shooting show at the Quick Draw Theater on the Gayway got an eyeful beginning in early June, when two curvaceous cowgirls joined the cast. Mikki Frantz and Barbara Bouchet, formerly showgirls in the adults-only *Peep Backstage* attraction on Show Street, lost their jobs when they were discovered to be underage. (Bouchet would later play Miss Moneypenny in the 1967 film *Casino Royale*.)

The pair swapped grease paint (and not much else) for six-shooters, form-fitting jeans, Western boots, and cowboy hats worn at angles more perky than functional. Frantz, 19 and the mother of a 5-month-old, expressed relief to be working fully clothed. "I felt like a monkey in a zoo. I'm really a housewife at heart," Frantz told *The Seattle Times*. "My biggest problem is spinning the weapon," she lamented. "I've broken five fingernails so far."

SINGERS AND SHRINERS Seattle Symphony conductor Milton Katims, meanwhile, was putting performers of a different sort through their paces. Working in a large warehouse on Pier 91, Katims rehearsed a cast of 333, readying them for three upcoming sold-out Opera House performances of Giuseppe Verdi's *Aida*. Soprano Gloria Davy, who was singing the title role, had made her Metropolitan Opera House debut in the part in 1958, the first African American artist to sing the role at that famous venue. Seattle native Robert Joffrey, who had recently choreographed *Aida* for the New York City Opera, was busily rehearsing dancers for Katims's extravaganza.

On June 3, Dr. Jonas Salk, whose creation of the polio vaccine had earned him near deity status among American parents, spoke to scientists, educators, and community leaders in the United States Science Theater in the Science Pavilion. Introduced just seven years before the fair, Salk's vaccine had produced an 85 to 90 percent drop in polio cases nationwide, sparing the lives of tens of thousands. "His work means more than that of any living scientist," Joseph Gandy told the *Seattle Post-Intelligencer*.

Downtown, meanwhile, Northwest Shriners, decked out in turban hats, curly-toed shoes, and billowing pasha pants paraded down 4th Avenue toward the fairgrounds. Although parades had been held at least weekly during the Alaska-Yukon-Pacific Exposition, Century 21 Exposition planners discouraged such off-grounds pageantry. Their rationale was that parades, watched for free, might siphon off potential ticket buyers. For older Seattleites, the Shriners parade was a happy reminder of Washington's first world's fair.

SCIENCE AND SALVATION

Three buildings at the fair were associated with religious groups: the Christian Science Pavilion, the Christian Witness Pavilion, and the Sermons from Science Pavilion. Each offered answers to fairgoers grappling with discrepancies between Christian religious traditions and scientific knowledge.

At the Christian Science Pavilion, fairgoers could read about many religions from around the globe and learn about what the teachings of Christian Science called the "spiritual science demonstrated by Christ in the healing of sickness and sin." The Christian Witness Pavilion was primarily devoted to child evangelism and to helping assuage fear of thermonuclear annihilation with Christian teachings about the hereafter. The Sermons from Science Pavilion held a 300-seat theater in which fairgoers could watch Dr. George Speake of the Moody Institute of Science deliver his famous lecture relating scientific knowledge to the Christian gospels using film, electronic gear, and crackling electricity.

10,000,000 SOULS WILL VISIT CENTURY 21 . . . WITNESS TO THEM THROUGH THIS AMAZING GOD-INSPIRED SCIENCE DEMONSTRATION!

Everywhere in the world today men are asking such searching questions as: Is there a God? Can I know Him? Do I really count in the scheme of things? Am I accountable for my conduct? What is the soul? Is there an afterlife? Is Christian faith compatible with the findings of modern science?

Sermons From Science answers these questions and many more. It confronts men with God and the necessity of the acceptance of Christ as their Saviour.

FOR BY HIM WERE ALL THINGS CREATED . . .
COLOSSIANS 1:16

WITNESS FOR CHRIST BY HELPING TO MAKE SERMONS FROM SCIENCE POSSIBLE

DR. GEORGE SPEAKE
IN PERSON

George Speake received a degree in mechanical engineering from the University of Pennsylvania. He served for 10 years as a Navy pilot . . . in the South Pacific during World War II. The past 14 years he has served on the staff of the Moody Institute of Science. His dynamic personality and dedicated life add much to his work in Sermons From Science. Sermons From Science shows the union between man's scientific achievements and God.

Dr. Speake's demonstration will include:
• A complete portable science laboratory • A frozen shadow • One million volts of man-made lightning • A flashlight that talks • The cry that shatters glass • Eyes that see in total darkness • Modern marvels from test tube and flask • Liquid light • Invisible energy setting steel aflame • Electron magic with a ribbon of rust • Metal rings floating in air

EYES ON DESIGN June 3 was Architects Day, and visiting architects from around the world weighed in on Century 21's buildings. Most liked the smaller size of the fairgrounds, compared with those of other expositions, and the colors, which were described as "gay" and "kaleidoscopic." Grouping buildings for a smaller site was "rather difficult," according to Royal Canadian Institute of Architects President John Davies, but "they have done rather well." Sir William Graham Holford, president of the Royal Institute of British Architecture, opined, "When the fair is over and only the permanent buildings remain, I think there will be an entirely different feeling, one of simplicity."

The architects whose buildings graced the fairgrounds were honored at a ceremony in front of the Horiuchi mural. The Seattle chapter of the American Institute of Architects presented medals to the architects and to Clayton Young, whose tireless efforts as site coordinator had been integral to the fair's successful built environment.

The AIA information booth, a temporary structure designed by Seattle architect and preservationist Victor Steinbrueck, on the International Plaza, was staffed primarily by members of the AIA Women's Guild — wives of the almost exclusively male membership. These women, sometimes joined by leading local architects like Fred Bassetti, Arnie Bystrom, Norm Johnston, and Don Meyers, were on the fairgrounds daily to field questions about fair buildings and to distribute information about Seattle's architecture.

The United Nations exhibit nearby was proving popular, especially its Speaker's Circle, a replica of an ancient council ring where fairgoers could listen to visiting international relations experts in an informal setting. Designed by Fred Bassetti and landscaped by Richard Haig, the United Nations exhibit was adorned with flags of all member nations and was staffed by more than 150 volunteers.

FOLLIES AND DOLLARS Century 21 crowds had plenty to choose from off the fairgrounds as well as on. Greater Seattle's annual Seafair festival, enjoying its 13th summer of pirates, clowns, King Neptune, hydroplane races, and parades, designated 1962 the World's Fair Edition. Seafair's popular Green Lake Aqua Follies were also a "go," and musical theater fans could look forward to professional productions of *The Music Man* and *Annie Get Your Gun*. The Aqua Follies theme for 1962 was "Salute to the World's Fairs" — from London's 1851 Crystal Palace Exposition right through Century 21. Comedian Bob Hope arrived in Seattle in early June to firm up plans to bring in his own variety review show from Hollywood.

above left From left, William Ku (assistant to Minoru Yamasaki), Perry Johanson (Architect, Naramore, Bain, Brady & Johanson), Philip Evans (U.S. science exhibit commissioner), Francis Miller (U.S. science exhibit deputy commissioner), and Minoru Yamasaki (architect), examine a model of the Science Pavilion.

above right United Nations Pavilion Speaker's Ring.

opposite Assistant Special Events Director Ken Prichard captured this aerial view of the fairgrounds from the Goodyear Blimp.

World's Fair Trade Dollar Days officially began on June 4. Miss Trade Dollar, Lonni Schaumburg, described by the *Seattle Post-Intelligencer* as "a stately blonde," christened trade dollar headquarters — a pontoon boat parked at University Plaza in downtown Seattle — with a bottle of champagne.

June 5 was Hawaii Day, and Hawaii's governor, William F. Quinn, demonstrated the hula for an enthusiastic group of reporters. North Dakota shared Hawaii's Special Day, but Governor William Guy, also present at the press conference, was forced to concede the dance contest — North Dakota had no hula equivalent.

CANNONS AND KANSAS Sweden Day was not until June 6, but Seattle's considerable Swedish population couldn't wait to begin celebrating. Joe Gandy and Miss Maritime of 1962, Donna Nonemaker, welcomed Captain Gunnar Dahlquist, master of the Swedish Johnson Line freighter *Seattle* that was berthed at Pier 28. Crew members firing the ship's cannon wore seventeenth-century costumes. Sweden Day festivities included performances by the Svea male chorus and the Nordiska Folkdancers, after which the crowd was invited to join the dancing — from folk to the twist.

Starting on June 6, Roy Rogers fans could dial CEntury 5-7980 and hear recorded greetings from the cowboy filmstar. The service built interest in the upcoming Roy Rogers show, scheduled for a two-week run in Memorial Stadium.

Fairgoers attending Plaza of the States ceremonies on Kansas Day (celebrated June 7) were supposed to have been greeted by Miss Sunflower. Unlike most beauty queens associated with the fair, no newspaper sang praises to Miss Sunflower's sleek charms — not really surprising, since she was a 500-pound yearling bison. In the end, Miss Sunflower's scheduled fair debut was canceled for fear the noise might panic her. As planned, she became a permanent resident at Woodland Park Zoo.

ACCESSIBILITY

Leo Weisfield, chairman of Washington's Employ the Handicapped Committee, raised the issue of considering the needs of people with physical disabilities in a November 28, 1960, letter to Clayton Young, the site coordinator. Weisfield pointed out that accommodations for fair visitors who were elderly, disabled, had babes in arms, or who might otherwise have trouble navigating steps and stairs should be planned for. Young forwarded Weisfield's letter to the architects and designers participating in the design process. Further attempts to make the grounds more accessible to people using wheelchairs included creating asphalt fillers at all major curb lines and placing wooden ramps with nonskid surfacing over stairs. Ida Daly, director of the Seattle Handicapped Club, visited the grounds with members of the club in early June and found the United States Science Pavilion, which was under federal rather than fair control, the most difficult part of the fairgrounds to navigate by wheelchair.

DIVAS AND DAREDEVILS *Aida* opened that night — the first opera performed in the world's fair Opera House. Gloria Davy and her fellow singers received high marks, but *Seattle Post-Intelligencer* critic John Voorhees called the costumes "lavishly overdone," adding, "In Acts I and II it became almost impossible to find the soloists since the stage was filled to overflowing with priests, soldiers, fan carriers, emblem carriers, slaves, scribes, sedan carriers, flower girls, and the general population. All of them seemed to be endlessly moving about for reasons I was never able to discern."

The hoi polloi were better pleased with Circus Berlin. The European circus troop was settled into Memorial Stadium for a run of twice-daily shows scheduled to last most of the summer. Some people saw the show for free despite the high wooden fence erected to block freeloaders' views of paid events in the stadium: Circus Berlin's aerial show was clearly visible to anyone who cared to look up. The sloped walkway between the Press Building and the Spanish Village Fiesta was an especially easy place from which to peek into the stadium, and it was usually crowded during shows.

Crowds ballooned when Circus Berlin added 18-year-old Thomas Kluger, who walked the high wire blindfolded and hooded. Kluger terrified the audience when, during one of his first performances, he nearly lost his balance midwire and fought, pole flailing, not to fall. He later admitted that he had stubbed his toe. "That was not a good performance," he abashedly told *The Seattle Times.*

WELCOME MAT Operation Smile kicked off on June 10. The program was designed to encourage Washingtonians to welcome fair visitors. Throughout the state, Century 21 distributed a booklet titled *You Are an Official Host for the Seattle World's Fair.* One aspect of the campaign called for communities to stop visitors' cars, explain the program, and offer passengers free lodging for the night along with free entertainment. About 100 communities in the state agreed to participate.

below left The Spanish Village Fiesta offered exotic flamenco dancing, delicious paella, and thirst-quenching sangria, among other pleasures.

below right World's fair souvenir badge.

opposite above World's fair trade dollar.

below Boy Scouts Gary Olint (Troop 357, Seattle) and Robert Forrest (Troop 115, Idaho) with Ruth Ekman.

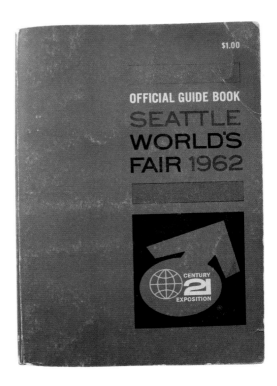

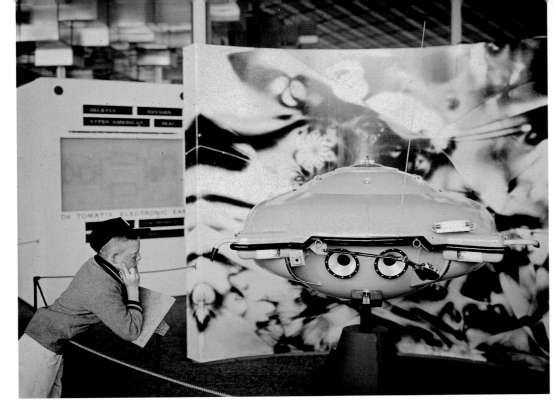

Fair officials were smiling that day: Shortly after noon, the Seattle World's Fair welcomed its two-millionth visitor. The influx of children, now enjoying their summer vacations, put attendance ahead of projections. "Countless thousands of families throughout the nation had been waiting only for the final report cards of their children," chortled the *Seattle Post-Intelligencer*, "and now that school is out, many of those families are already Seattle-bound."

The news did not reach Seattle for several weeks, but on June 10, a climbing party led by Richard E. McGowan of Edmonds planted a large Seattle World's Fair flag atop the 20,320-foot summit of Mount McKinley, the highest point on the North American continent. It was another link with 1909, when a party from the Mountaineers Club planted an Alaska-Yukon-Pacific Exposition flag and a "Votes for Women" banner at the summit of Columbia Crest on Mount Rainier.

Looking beyond the heady excitement of the fair, 16 civic leaders founded Post-Fair Unlimited, a non-profit organization dedicated to keeping worldwide attention focused on the Pacific Northwest after the exposition closed. One of its main goals, according to the *Seattle Post-Intelligencer*, was "achieving maximum long-range benefits from the World's Fair and that part of the exposition officially designated as 'Seattle Center.'" The group included many who had been working toward the civic center project's success for years, Harold Shefelman and Eddie Carlson foremost among them. Wheeler Grey, formerly president of the Seattle Chamber of Commerce, chaired the new organization.

ON THE GO Century 21's benefit radius was widening already. Airlines reported steadily increasing traffic from Europe and Asia as people from around the globe trooped to the fair. Once in the Pacific Northwest, many visitors traveled on to California, British Columbia, Alaska, and other destinations.

The Official Guide Book: Seattle World's Fair 1962 sold for $1 on the fairgrounds and was included in the advance ticket packages many tourists had purchased. It included a section on Seattle and the Northwest.

French Ambassador Hervé Alphand and his chic wife, Nicole, arrived at the fairgrounds on June 11 to officially open the French exhibit in the Washington State Coliseum. France was the fair's largest foreign participant, and the couple's visit occasioned a reception at the Washington Athletic Club and a black-tie candlelit dinner at the Sunset Club, hosted by Joseph and Laurene Gandy.

Perhaps because of the French festivities, the day drew the fair's highest attendance yet: 68,552. Traffic on the Seattle-Bremerton ferry route had increased so much that three extra trips were added each way. The beautiful but aging streamlined art deco ferry *Kalakala*, already making three trips daily, doubled her workload. Since many of the riders were walk-ons, Seattle Transit System added extra buses between the downtown ferry terminal and the fairgrounds.

The plethora of similar-looking world's fair medals, coins, trade dollars, and medallions was causing such confusion that *The Seattle Times* ran a feature explaining which was which. Fairgoers could purchase (1) George Tsutakawa's official bronze collector's medal, selling for $1.95; (2) a three-coin series of official souvenir medals, one featuring the Space Needle, one the Monorail, and one the Million Dollar Display, selling for 50 cents each; (3) the $1 trade dollar, good at all participating businesses; and (4) bags of 1,000 silver dollars sold by the Million Dollar Display concessionaires for $1,500. The silver dollars were minted before 1904 and could not be collected until after the fair because they were part of the display.

BRING THE KIDS Still taunting the censors, Harold Shaw outdid himself, announcing to the press that Gracie Hansen's Paradise International nightclub and the naughty puppet show *Les Poupées de Paris* would soon introduce father-and-son nights. Sons, he hastened to say, would have to be at least 18. (Legal drinking age was 21.) Mother-and-daughter nights were on the drawing board, Shaw said, "but first I want to see how this idea goes."

Governor Albert Rosellini declared himself shocked and wrote to fair officials asking them to take steps "to assure a more adequate regard for morality." His office, the Associated Press reported, had received more than 1,000 letters of complaint.

"It's time that young people learn not to be ashamed of their nude bodies," Harold Shaw shot back. Nudity at the fair, he added, would "be a boost to President Kennedy's physical fitness plan. Americans don't have beautiful bodies. The best way to stimulate beautiful bodies is to see them." Improved physical fitness, and particularly youth fitness, was among Kennedy's stated presidential goals.

ON THE BOARDS The Ukrainian State Dancers opened at the Opera House on June 18. It was the 110-member troop's first appearance in the United States. Audiences thrilled to the dazzling costumes and rousing folk dancing, which included the *prisiadka*, the famous kicking dance done from a squatting position. The standing ovations the troop received underscored the importance of cultural exchange, melting the Cold War chill for at least a few hours.

The same night, the Playhouse Theater of Houston, Texas, opened a two-week run of *The Fantasticks* in the Playhouse. The New York production of the musical, by Tom Jones and Harvey Schmidt, was two years into its eventual 42-year off-Broadway run at the Sullivan Street Playhouse. Fair audiences were excited at the chance to see the show, whose fresh, simple staging and memorable songs had generated much positive press.

Writer and comedian Carl Reiner, visiting the fair with his family — wife Estelle, son Rob, 15, and daughter Ana, 13 — got the chance to tour the grounds unrecognized by his fans. Reiner, who had recently won an Emmy for his scripts on the very popular *Dick Van Dyke Show*, had inadvertently left his toupee at home in Los Angeles. Since so few television viewers had seen him without it, he was able to enjoy the fair in privacy.

AMERICAN AMBASSADORS U.S. ambassador to the United Nations Adlai Stevenson visited the fairgrounds on June 19 to dedicate the United Nations Pavilion. Stevenson praised the volunteers who had worked so hard to raise funds for the pavilion and to staff it. Stevenson also delivered a major address in the Opera House, expressing the belief that the Soviet Union would eventually call off the Cold War and speaking to the complex relations between communist and noncommunist nations within the United Nations: "If communism is a problem for the U.N., so is the U.N. a problem for communism. The U.N. is a community of tolerance, and this is a terrible frustration for the totalitarian mind."

That same day Mrs. America 1962, Lila Mason, attended Michigan Day ceremonies. Hailing from Detroit, the 39-year-old mother of three was enjoying the travel that went along with her title, while her husband, Cleve, kept the home fires burning. As part of her competition for the Mrs. America title, Mason was required to bake and frost a cake, prepare a chicken dish, and pack a picnic basket, all in under 2 hours and 45 minutes.

HAPPY TRAILS Governor Rosellini designated June 21, 22, and 23 as Washington State Indian Days, urging Washingtonians to study the culture and heritage of the state's tribes. Miss Indian America of 1962, Brenda Bearchum, of Adams, Oregon, arrived at the fairgrounds by helicopter to participate. Other participants included members of the Makah, Yakama, and Colville Confederated tribes who worked at the world's fair Indian Village, members of more than a dozen other Pacific Northwest Indian tribes, George Pierre of the Seattle Indian Center, and the Seattle Boy Scouts.

above The neon sign for *Les Poupées de Paris* enticed fairgoers into the slightly naughty puppet extravaganza.

opposite above left U.S. ambassador to the United Nations Adlai Stevenson addresses the crowd on United Nations Day.

below left A quiet moment in the tranquil lobby of the Playhouse.

right Miss Indian America, Brenda Bearchum.

UNITED NATIONS
DAY
DEDICATION CEREMONY 10:45
AMBASSADOR
ADLAI STEVENSON
TODAYS SPEAKER
CLARK EICHELBERGER 2 PM
DR BROCK CHISHOLM 3 & 7 PM

Everett DuPen's Fountain of Creation featured abstract bronze sculptures depicting the history of humanity.

Where there were Indians, there had to be cowboys. Western stars Roy Rogers and Dale Evans rode in on a helicopter rather than on horseback, landing at Northgate Mall. World's fair Executive Director Al Rochester, Northgate President Jim Douglas, Seafair Queen Linda Juel, and some 3,000 excited children greeted the pair. At the fairgrounds, Roy Rogers was made "an honorary chief of the Indians of this state," according to *The Seattle Times*. Governor Rosellini "got to be an honorary sub-chief." Each received a blue-tipped bonnet, a membership in the Eagle War Bonnet Society, a painting by Carol Orr of the Moses band of the Colville Tribe, and a lifetime license to hunt and fish on the Colville Indian Reservation. Rogers and Evans were opening their Western variety show in Memorial Stadium on June 23.

June 22 was A-Y-P Exposition Day at Century 21. Festivities included a parade of vintage automobiles, a fashion show featuring 1909's finest apparel, a concert band playing 1909 tunes, and speeches recounting the glory days of Washington's first world's fair. Special guests were Al Rochester, Mabel Chilberg (sister of A-Y-P President J. E. Chilberg), Henry Broderick (the only trustee of both A-Y-P and Century 21), Frank Richardson Pierce (a guard at A-Y-P), and Eleanor Taft Hall (President William Howard Taft's granddaughter).

FUELING UP Jack Jarvis, the *Seattle Post-Intelligencer* reporter whose frequent "Our Man at the Fair" column put him on the fairgrounds almost constantly, wrote on June 22 about an ailment from which he, and probably scores of others working at the fair, suffered: world's fair stomach. "I can resist anything but temptation," Jarvis joked. "This was my breakfast the other morning: Four cups of coffee and some vitamin pills at home at 6 a.m. A Belgian waffle, a slice of pizza, two plain donuts, a Coke, and a handful of saltwater taffy at 10 a.m. Lunch consisted of three aspirin tablets washed down with hot chocolate. Dinner was a Mongolian steak sandwich, a

scone, and more coffee at about 6 p.m. followed at home at 9 p.m. by a peanut butter sandwich and a glass of milk. Six more cups of coffee lulled me to sleep at midnight. ... My clothes are getting tighter every day."

On June 23, the Space Needle's gas torch, which had been out of commission since early June, was relit. The torch's interior mechanisms had been redesigned to offset the effects of wind. It consumed enough natural gas each day to heat 200 homes.

As if trying to compete with the torch, temperatures that day rose to the mid-80s. Some of the fair's 66,000 visitors found it hard to be prepared for the heat wave. Leonard Rock Jr., a Boy Scout assisting with North Carolina's Special Day ceremony in the Plaza of the States, fainted as he was holding that state's flag, pulling the flag down with him. Young Leonard was quickly revived, and the weather took the blame for the incident.

LET ME ENTERTAIN YOU   At the conclusion of the North Carolina ceremony, Paula Bane, who had sung the national anthem at all 26 state days so far, was presented with a dozen roses and named Our Lady of Song. Only Jackie Souders's World's Fair Band was permitted to accompany Bane during the ceremonies. Ever busy, Souders also led the pit band at Gracie Hansen's Paradise International nightclub.

The warm weather continued, giving Carol Vaughn, an exotic dancer from Show Street's *Backstage U.S.A.*, the chance to beat the heat while lathering up a little publicity for the attraction. Clad in a golden swimming suit and carrying a towel and soap, Vaughn strolled from Show Street to the Canada Pavilion, where she stepped into the Fountain of Creation, designed by Everett DuPen, and frolicked in the cool spray. The crowd, many of whom Vaughn had gathered à la Pied Piper as she crossed the fairgrounds, snapped photographs. All Show Street

ECHOES OF A-Y-P

Separated by the Great Depression and two world wars, Seattle's fairs were distinguished from other expositions by two facts: the Alaska-Yukon-Pacific Exposition and Century 21 both intentionally created buildings designed for postfair use, and they both closed their books in the black. In 1909 the A-Y-P celebrated the present, including Washington's recent enrichment by Yukon gold rush wealth. In 1962 Century 21 focused vividly on the future, an imagined place toward which the city, state, and country were fervently reaching. Nostalgia was anathema, and although A-Y-P received the occasional civil nod from its bright young progeny, the earlier fair was recast as a tinny, jingly, antiquated event — a sepia-toned past pushed aside for a Kodachrome future.

attractions except Gracie Hansen's and *Les Poupées de Paris* were floundering financially — management hoped Vaughn's stunt would refresh sales figures as much as it did her own.

A few days later, *Backstage U.S.A.* became so desperate that it announced plans to add a children's event, *Circus Backstage*, that would use the existing set and would feature clowns (one of them a fully clothed female), a juggler, and a unicyclist. Five circuses were to be held daily between 10:45 a.m. and 2 p.m. One hour after the last circus, the exotic dancers would again take the stage.

LONG LINES On June 28, fairgoers' impatience with long lines became evident at the United States Science Pavilion. Regular opening time was 10:15, but Roy Rogers was filming his television show in the courtyard, causing a slight delay. Staff members explaining the delay to the crowd — the lines stretched two full blocks — were met with catcalls and boos.

At the Space Needle lines could stretch to five hours. The Eye of the Needle restaurant took no reservations, making it first come, first served. People were generally patient, although some who joined the line for breakfast found it was lunchtime by the time they claimed a table. Space Needle elevator operator Kathy McGuiness told the *Seattle Post-Intelligencer* that local residents minded waiting far more than tourists did. "It's something out-of-towners won't see again, so they are more patient." The Ford Motor Company Pavilion and the Bubbleator ride up into the Washington State theme show in the Coliseum also required extended waits.

The number of employee and volunteer workers at the fair had reached 8,000. Some 2,000 of these worked for the fair corporation and the rest for concessions and in exhibits. The United States Science Pavilion, the NASA Pavilion, and the Coliseum were separate from the fair corporation, but their staffing was handled by the fair at the exhibitors' request. This was the peak of employment on the fairgrounds during Century 21. "It was a kind of magic period," Ewen Dingwall later recalled. "We were having so much fun and had such a feeling of exhilaration about it — we had been working a long time on it. It was coming off very, very well and we really enjoyed it."

By the end of June, a total of 3,174,760 people had passed through the gates. Local, national, and international votes were in: Century 21 Exposition, the Seattle World's Fair, was a smashing success.

below This colorful paper fan was a 1962 fair souvenir, but its old-fashioned style hearkened back to the 1909 fair.

opposite above left Crowds waited hours to reach the entrance of the United States Science Pavilion.

above right Century 21 Exposition celebrates Alaska-Yukon-Pacific Exposition Day.

below This driving game sponsored by Mobil gave fairgoers a chance to test their driving skills under various simulated road conditions, then ranked their performance.

Chapter 6

July 1962

Billy Graham speaks to the faithful, Sal Durante drops the ball, and *Telstar 1* broadcasts images of Century 21 through space to an eager European public.

O n July 1, 1962, the Seattle World's Fair marked its highest Sunday attendance yet with 58,673 people enjoying a damp and cloudy day. The Space Needle welcomed its one-millionth visitor, either Mr. or Mrs. Jack Gruber, who arrived at the same time. The lucky couple received a free dinner at the Eye of the Needle. Higher in the sky, the Goodyear Blimp *Mayflower II* flew over Seattle.

At ground level, thousands of travelers from around the world arrived by buses from their temporary home in Auburn, where the Wally Byam Caravan Club had circled its wagons. The Caravan Club, doing its part to foster world peace and understanding, had set up camp at Red Square in Moscow the year before. The Auburn rally included close to 2,000 Airstreams, Avions, Spartans, and more, filled with more than 7,000 people eager to see the world's fair. During the weeklong rally, Auburn's population temporarily grew by 50 percent, much to the delight of local merchants.

opposite The moon rises behind the Space Needle.

CAUSE TO CELEBRATE Fair officials received good news on July 3, when bookkeepers announced that, based on attendance numbers, Century 21 had passed the break-even point and would make money as long the expected total of nine million visitors passed through the gates before they closed. Ewen Dingwall took the news in stride, noting that if attendance did drop off for some reason, "we would trim the budget accordingly." Part of Ding's concern was that people might stay away on holidays and weekends, fearing large crowds.

And true enough, the next day, Independence Day, only 54,971 fairgoers arrived, about half of optimistic predictions. But those who did attend enjoyed a star-spangled Fourth of July filled with flags, fun, and fireworks.

At the Plaza of the States, fairgoers enjoyed a patriotic program of speeches and music sponsored by Seattle Post No. 1 of the American Legion. The highlight of the event was the swearing in of 75 new citizens by the Immigration and Naturalization Service. The evening's fireworks show, usually held at Green Lake, was shot off over Elliott Bay so that fairgoers would have a better view.

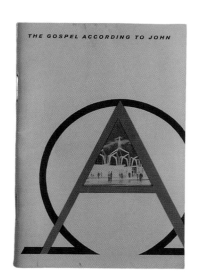

SERMON IN THE STADIUM Alaska Day celebrations on July 7 featured a visit from Governor William Egan and his wife, Neva. The Blue Angels flying team, in town for a show at Sand Point Naval Air Station and over Lake Washington, added to the excitement. But more exciting to many fairgoers was a glimpse of Christian evangelist Dr. Billy Graham as he toured the fair.

Graham spent quite a bit of time in the United States Science Pavilion, where he exclaimed, "As far as I can discover, nearly all scientists of any stature are coming more and more to believe that an intelligence underlies the universe. They may not call it God, but they know it is there." Graham also enjoyed many other exhibits but he did not visit Show Street. Earlier, at a press conference, he had proclaimed that girlie shows contributed to a moral breakdown in the United States.

The following day, Graham gave a Sunday sermon in Memorial Stadium to an overflow crowd estimated at 20,000. At 3 p.m., when he stepped up to the podium, sounds from the Gayway, the Space Needle Carillon bells, and all live music were silenced in observance of the occasion.

"When we go into outer space," he cautioned, "we take our sins and depravity with us." Graham responded to cosmonaut Gherman Titov's comment about not seeing God in space, likening it to "a little earthworm sticking his head out of the ground and saying I don't see any Khrushchev, therefore there is no Khrushchev." At the end of his sermon, Graham challenged audience members to "come forward and accept Christ." More than 1,600 people streamed onto the field to confess their sins.

ART EXHIBIT

The Fine Arts Pavilion's five main galleries housed these impressive shows over the course of the fair: Art Since 1950: American; Masterpieces of Art; Art of the Ancient East; Art Since 1950: International; Northwest Coast Indian Art; Northwest Painting and Sculpture; Adventures in Art (showcasing ceramics, mobiles, and glass); and Countries of the Pacific Rim — the finest assembly of art shown in Washington until that point. Museums from across the country and around the world loaned artworks. Seattle art collector Bagley Wright later recalled, "The contemporary art on display during the fair was shattering to people. They'd never seen that — they'd never seen Jackson Pollock. They'd never seen Rauschenberg. ... There was a lot of thinking that New York artists, so-called, were just products of hype. And so this show made a great difference."

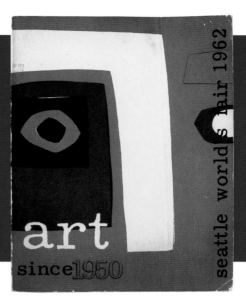

CROWNING AND CLOSING Philippines Week celebrations also began on Sunday, with ceremonies and songs in the International Mall. Philippine Senator Rogelio de la Rosa saluted the fair, and crowds were entertained by the 35-member Bayanihan Company of dancers and singers. Afterwards, Phebe Anne Porras was crowned Miss Filipino American in a contest sponsored by the Seattle-based newspaper *Filipino Forum*.

That night, fair officials held a two-hour late-night emergency meeting to respond to a storm of protest that had erupted after hundreds of prospective visitors lost their advance deposits for Traveler's Village, a trailer camp east of Lake Washington that had closed its doors in June due to financial troubles. Although the fair and Expo Lodging were not responsible, fair officials stepped in and repaid those who had lost deposits — issuing checks totaling more than $95,000 to some 1,400 families. Thus was a public relations disaster averted. Fair officials hoped to recapture some of this money later through the courts.

EYES ON THE PRIZE One of the fair's most talked-about publicity stunts took place on July 9, when Sal Durante attempted to catch a baseball for $1,000. Months earlier, the young Brooklyn fan had snagged Roger Maris's record-setting 61st home run at Yankee Stadium, and he was invited to Seattle to catch another ball — tossed from the observation deck of the Space Needle.

The promotion was almost cancelled after a University of Washington physics professor calculated that an object thrown from the Needle would reach speeds of up to 140 miles per hour before it reached the ground, arriving with enough force to crack open someone's skull. Not wanting to risk such a mishap, fair officials moved the stunt over to the Gayway, where the Yankees fan would catch a ball thrown from the top of the Ferris wheel.

Durante brought his own mitt and, before the event, he practiced catching a few balls tossed by folks who had gathered to cheer him on. The big moment arrived when Seattle Rainiers pitcher Tracy Stallard — who had served up Maris's historic home run while pitching for the Boston Red Sox — climbed aboard the Ferris wheel and rode it to the top.

Durante caught two practice throws easily, even showboating one behind his back. The next toss was worth $1,000, and the audience hushed accordingly. Stallard hurled the baseball downward, Durante held up his mitt, the ball hit the glove's sweet spot … and promptly fell out onto the ground.

Heartbroken, Durante turned from the crowd. Not only had he lost face. The recently married young man had hoped to win the money for his bride, who was about to give birth back home. Just before he left for New York — and unbeknownst to the press — fair officials handed him a check for $1,000 anyway.

LOUD AND CLEAR On July 10, the communications satellite *Telstar 1* was launched from Cape Canaveral and subsequently relayed the first transatlantic television signal in history. Constructed by AT&T's Bell

Telephone Laboratories, the satellite captured microwave signals from a ground station in Andover, Maine, which were then amplified and rebroadcast in England.

Unlike NASA's *Echo* satellite, which had been launched in 1960 and only acted as a passive reflector of radio signals, *Telstar* was the first communications satellite that could actively direct and amplify telephone calls. Hours after *Telstar*'s launch, one of the first long-distance phone calls in space-age history took place between Senator Magnuson in Washington, D.C., and Governor Rosellini and Ewen Dingwall atop the Space Needle.

Fairgoers listened in on the six-minute conversation broadcast over the public address system, as Rosellini greeted Magnuson and thanked NASA and AT&T for launching the historic satellite. Ewen Dingwall got on the line next and was clearly excited by the clarity of Magnuson's voice. Ding exclaimed, "Senator, you sound as though you're calling from the foot of the Space Needle, instead of back in Washington, D.C. This is what you call a good connection. I think it is astounding."

ON POINTE That afternoon in the Opera House, 200 budding ballerinas between the ages of 8 and 14 were more concerned at how well they would be received by Janet Reed, ballet mistress for the New York City Ballet. Reed was auditioning the young dancers for parts as sprites, pixies, and fairies for the upcoming production of *A Midsummer Night's Dream*, to be held at the fair beginning on July 24.

The girls were nervous as they demonstrated their arabesques and pirouettes, hoping to be one of the lucky 28 chosen for the show. When Reed found a child's dancing to her liking, she nodded approval, but at least once, she called a halt to the proceedings, pointed at the audience and said, "Your teachers must be dying."

Century 21's top leadership was exclusively male. Nevertheless, women were present in many capacities. Among paid staff, Georgia Gellert (exhibits) and Anne Swensson and Sharon Lund (press department) held positions of greatest authority. Lund, who was 23, remembered, "I didn't see any privilege. I didn't feel that anyone had made accommodations for me because I was a woman, or denied me because I was a woman. I didn't think of it being a sexist situation, ever. I knew I could do the job."

The daily details of every male department head were managed by highly competent secretaries, all female. Most departments had women working as assistants and coordinators, albeit at a low ratio. Among hourly employees, women were well represented. Reflecting mores of the era, the most visible of these were hired at least partly on the basis of physical attributes — height and beauty (Space Needle elevator operators); attractiveness and capacity for science (United States Science Pavilion demonstrators); clean-cut good looks (guides).

Female performers abounded, most visibly in Show Street attractions, where their physical attributes were usually on full view. Women were also represented in every aspect of the performing arts — from circus performers to water skiers to ballet and folk dancers, to actors and singers.

Several of the international pavilions, most notably India's, had female managers, and most had female staff representing their countries and cultures to the world.

If the wives of top fair brass who played important diplomatic and leadership roles bracket one end of female participation in Century 21, Gracie Hansen frames the opposite end of the spectrum. Fifty years hence, Hansen tops the list of memorable women who shaped the fair.

GRACIE HANSEN (1922–1985)

Short, brash, witty, and possessing a seemingly inexhaustible list of helpful friends from all walks of life, Gracie Hansen and her Las Vegas–style nightclub Paradise International were destined to make some of Century 21's most vivid memories. Born in Shreveport, Louisiana, and raised in Longview, Washington, Hansen's theatrical credentials prior to mounting her impressive Show Street attraction consisted mainly of voluminous knowledge of Hollywood movies and producing the annual PTA follies show in Morton, Washington, where she managed the state liquor store.

Upon learning about the Seattle World's Fair, Hansen decided she had a mission in life: to save the fair from science. In this she succeeded, hiring nationally famous nightclub producer Barry Ashton, a bevy of leggy female performers able to manage feathered headdresses and chorus-line kicks while baring their breasts, and a performing dog who stole the show. Hansen drew publicity as honey attracts flies, and she ensured that no fair visit was truly complete without her trademark welcome — "Hello, suckers!" — and drinking and dining through her show, *A Night in Paradise*.

LAURENE GANDY (1908–1993)

Laurene Gandy had an official schedule on the fairgrounds nearly every day of Century 21 — primarily guiding visiting VIP families and female VIPs through the fair. Her thorough efforts (all completely volunteer) smoothed the way for these important fairgoers, as evidenced by the many thank-you letters she received — from Eunice Kennedy Shriver at Hyannis Port to the families of ambassadors from Belgium, France, and Great Britain. She also supported her husband in his efforts and endured long and frequent absences as he traveled the globe to promote the fair. Her role in the success of the fair cannot be overestimated.

For 25 years following the fair, Laurene Gandy provided leadership for Seattle Center, serving as a steering committee member during the formation of Seattle Center Foundation and as its first president.

THE WIVES: "OUR FAIR LADIES"

Women married to Century 21 executives were also married to the fair. Their home lives turned upside down, their presence commanded at fair functions large and small, their expertise as tour guides for female dignitaries expected — those married to the fair's all-male leadership provided Seattle with service of the highest caliber, unpaid, with grace, upholding protocol. Some wives enjoyed the spotlight, others shunned it. Betty Lou Dingwall's daughters recalled their mother's shyness when meeting celebrities and sitting at head tables. Nell Carlson was a steady presence at Eddie's side. Steve Camp remembered his mother, Marty, as "the perfect partner for someone who was involved in a lot of social events, a lot of evening parties — she just loved doing it." Marilyn Gandy remembered that her mother, Laurene, "for the six months of the fair, entertained almost every breakfast, lunch, and dinner."

Left: The irrepressible Gracie Hansen;
Right: Joseph and Laurene Gandy were
as much a fixture of the fair as the
Space Needle.

RAILS AND RIDES On July 11, Sixten Holmquist, president of Alweg Rapid Transit Systems, announced that the Monorail trains would stay in service after the fair closed while the city decided whether to keep the system. The news was met with interest by visiting transit officials from Los Angeles, who were exploring the possibility of building a monorail system to ease their city's traffic woes.

While folks pondered the role of monorails as public transport, traditional railroads were enjoying a resurgence of passenger service, thanks to the Seattle World's Fair. The postwar boom in automobile sales had led to a steep decline in passenger rail use, but during the fair the three lines that served Seattle — Northern Pacific, Great Northern, and Union Pacific — all ran extra trains for the first time in years.

Over on the Gayway, a new ride was dedicated: the Space Wheel, designed by veteran amusement manufacturers Elmer and Curtis Velare. Unlike a Ferris wheel, which supported each passenger carriage with two arms, the Space Wheel held each of its cars on the end of a single spoke, hidden behind the passenger's view, providing the rider with the thrill of seemingly floating in space.

MORE MILLIONS The fair welcomed its four-millionth visitor on July 13 when 7-year-old Christine Graham walked through the East Gate with her family. The excited little girl was showered with gifts. Lew Fine, emcee of *Backstage U.S.A.*, was standing by with a box of Philippine cigars just in case number four million was a man. Thankfully, Christine didn't receive those.

New Mexico Day was celebrated on July 14 with a visit from Governor Edwin I. Mechem, who was welcomed by two noteworthy honor guards, Bert Parks and Barbara Williams, stars of *The Music Man* production at the Green Lake Aqua Theater. To the surprise of no one, Parks led the World's Fair Band in a rousing performance of the hit musical's "76 Trombones."

below The Space Wheel was a big hit with thrill seekers.

opposite Christine Graham laughs at the antics surrounding her after being named the fair's four-millionth visitor.

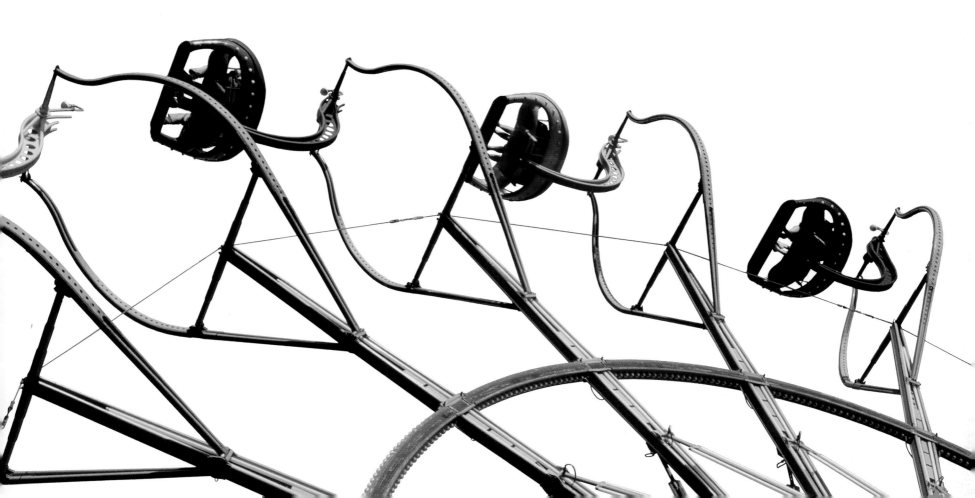

Children's Week kicked off that weekend with the Huckleberry Hound and Yogi Bear show, featuring costumed versions of the well-loved cartoon characters. On Sunday in the Arena, champagne music lovers enjoyed (*a one and a*) two shows by Lawrence Welk and the Lennon Sisters.

REST AND RESCUE Because of the long lines waiting to get into the Eye of the Needle restaurant, on July 17 Eddie Carlson's Western Hotels installed rows of chairs at ground level, relieving many weary feet. People still had to walk through the snaky maze of chains directly in front of the elevators, but those waiting to get that far could now rest first. A new electronic sign displaying waiting-time estimates was also installed.

On July 19, one of the fair's VIP guests walked down the "blue carpet" on all fours, to the delight of press photographers. That guest was Baron, a heroic black Labrador who had stayed with his mistress — 5-year-old Vicki Spiwak — for more than 50 hours after the child had become lost in the Cascade Mountains a month earlier. Baron had kept her warm, and it was his barking that led to her rescue. Baron received a Space Age World's Fair Medal from state Senator (and world's fair Commissioner) Michael Gallagher before touring the fair. The furry, well-behaved dog was the first "nonprofessional" animal to be allowed on the grounds.

JERSEY SORE If anyone was growling and snapping that day, it was a group of a hundred New Jersey visitors who had caravanned across the country to take part in their state's celebration. Upon their arrival the day before they had found their campsite — assigned to them by Expo Lodging — to be nothing more than a dusty, rutted, stump ranch along Pacific Highway South, 20 miles from the fair.

The visitors were outraged and went to the press. Fair officials took immediate action. Expo Lodging manager Willis Camp quickly found a campsite with tall trees, sewer facilities, and trailer hookups. Oddly though, 15 campers opted to remain at the stump ranch.

The day before New Jersey Day festivities, all of the previously disgruntled Garden Staters were given a world's fair welcome by Joe Gandy and Jay Rockey, including free admission to the fair and a free lunch in Club 21. To seal the deal, Native Americans performing in the Indian Village offered the New Jerseyans the pipe of peace. Another public relations blunder was averted, and everyone was happy.

HALFWAY THERE   On July 21, Antonio Garrigues y Díaz-Cañabate, Spain's new ambassador to the United States, was guest of honor at a reception held in the Spanish Village Fiesta. Garrigues was quite impressed with the village's authenticity and spent the day touring the rest of the fairgrounds.

The fair was now at its halfway mark — three months down and three to go. Ewen Dingwall excitedly told the *Seattle Post-Intelligencer* that the fair "exceeded our expectations by far!" Joe Gandy felt that attendance would remain high, even after Labor Day, when local visitors would fill the gap left by vacationers. Dingwall and Gandy both praised the fair's staffers and exhibitors, claiming "we couldn't have done it without them."

Most importantly, a combination of strong advance ticket sales and continued good attendance allowed the fair to repay its underwriters ahead of schedule — a truly astonishing feat.

above The Sermons from Science
Pavilion showcased marvels of
science as evidence of a divine plan.

below Pedal-powered rickshaws were
one of the many ways visitors toured
the fairgrounds.

opposite above left The Flight to
Mars ride on the Gayway provided
plenty of scary fun.

above right Television viewers in
Europe got to see the fair live, thanks
to the *Telstar* satellite.

below Minoru Yamasaki's design for
the United States Science Pavilion
reminded many visitors of a cathedral.

On July 22, Sunday services began in the Christian Witness Pavilion. Each Sunday until the close of the fair, a different Protestant denomination invited fairgoers to meet with their congregations and to join them in prayer.

SEATTLE BY SATELLITE On July 23, the *Telstar 1* satellite made history again when the United States and Europe exchanged planned television programs for the first time. The 20-minute *America to Europe* program included live broadcasts of a Cubs-Phillies baseball game, Colonel John Glenn speaking from Cape Canaveral, a crowded Detroit expressway, a view of Mount Rushmore, and best of all for those in Seattle — scenes of Century 21.

The fair received 90 seconds of airtime, with sights and sounds broadcast from around the grounds and commentary by KING 5's Charles Herring. In Europe, 54 cameras filmed scenes from Austria, Britain, France, Germany, Italy, Sweden, Switzerland, Yugoslavia, and the Vatican, including views of the Eiffel Tower, the Coliseum, Big Ben, and more. Televisions were set up throughout the Century 21 grounds, so that fairgoers could watch both the American and European broadcasts.

Earlier in the day, Japan Week festivities began in the Plaza of the States with a visit from Japanese Ambassador Koichiro Asaki, who spoke of the important bond between Seattle and its sister city, Kobe. The Bon Odori Dancers gave outdoor performances and the Bunraku Doll Theatre held shows at the Playhouse all week.

LEG WORK In the afternoon, the Space Needle's revolving restaurant came to a halt when 8-year-old Mary Plunkett got her shoe caught between a partition and the turntable. Firemen had to free the little girl, who was uninjured but very frightened.

On July 24, the New York City Ballet held its Northwest premiere of *A Midsummer Night's Dream*, in the Opera House. The young dancers who had passed Janet Reed's rigorous audition two weeks earlier performed admirably.

Seven Explorer Scouts from Hibbing, Minnesota, arrived at the fair after bicycling 1,615 miles cross-country. Since bikes weren't allowed on the Lake Washington floating bridge, the young men set up camp at Lake Sammamish and were then driven into Seattle, where they received a free night's stay on the *Dominion Monarch*. The teens planned to return to Hibbing by car.

MINORU YAMASAKI (1912–1986)

Minoru Yamasaki was a Seattle native and a 1934 University of Washington School of Architecture graduate. During World War II, Yamasaki, then establishing his architectural practice in New York City and thus well outside the Japanese internment zone, was able to spare his parents and brother from internment by moving them into his small apartment.

At the time of his selection as architect of the Century 21 United States Pavilion, his work was already internationally known. He had designed the United States Pavilion at the Agricultural Exposition in New Delhi; the American consulate offices in Kobe, Japan; and airports in St. Louis and Saudi Arabia, among many other projects. Postfair, his work included Seattle's IBM Building (1964), Rainier Tower (1977) and Square, and New York's World Trade Center (1976).

St. Mary's Chinese Band made an impressive showing at the fair.

POCKETS AND SKYROCKETS Walter VanCamp, managing director of Greater Seattle, Inc., announced that the world's fair trade dollars were a hit and that more than one million of the "fun coins" had been sold. He noted that, besides their use in trade, the medallions were sought after by coin collectors. One fair official exclaimed, "You can get an idea what a trade dollar will be worth by asking a coin collector what he would give for a medallion of the Alaska-Yukon-Pacific Exposition."

On July 25, Nat King Cole performed the first of four nightly shows in the Arena. The first half of his *Sights and Sounds* extravaganza featured Cole supported by the Merry Young Souls, a group of young singers and dancers. The second half was more traditional, with Cole singing his hits, including "Mona Lisa," "Ballerina," and "Paper Moon." Cole also sang, "Mr. Cole Won't Rock and Roll," a medley in which he parodied pop music.

Japan Week ended with a bang on the night of July 27, with a huge fireworks show over Elliott Bay. The display was organized by Tokyo fireworks expert Kyosuke Ogatsu, who had won a Grand Prix for his show at the Brussels World's Fair. Century 21 fairgoers could see the skyrockets from just about anywhere on the fairgrounds, but many vied for the best seats in the house — atop the Space Needle.

SEAFAIR ROYALTY The last weekend of July was one of the hottest yet that summer, with temperatures hovering around 90 degrees. Sun worshippers came out in droves, not only to enjoy the world's fair, but also Seafair, Seattle's annual citywide summer festival. On Saturday, July 28, tens of thousands of people lined 2nd Avenue to watch the gala Seafair parade, with its colorful floats and scores of marching bands.

After the parade, Seafair royalty were escorted to Century 21, where they ruled over Seafair Day activities. Holding court in the Plaza of the States, King Neptune Rex XIII (Cecil H. McKinstry), his Prime Minister (Don Kraft), and retiring Queen of the Seas (Linda Juel) oversaw a two-hour showing of musical acts and marching bands, while the Seafair Pirates and Seafair Clowns scampered among a delighted audience.

above Singer Nat King Cole, center, signs an autograph for Special Events Director Louis Larsen, right.

below To defray the $500 per day costs of guards and insurance for the Million Dollar Display, exhibitor Lawrence McBride made the coins available for sale to fairgoers as souvenirs, deliverable when the fair ended.

opposite above This Space Needle souvenir medallion featured the Needle on one side and an aerial fairground view on the other.

below *Music Man* star Bert Parks leads the World's Fair Band in a rendition of "76 Trombones."

above Ken Prichard's day-by-day activity roster in the Special Events Division was an important stop for reporters covering the fair.

below Robert Godden's coloring books of the World's Fair are valued by collectors today.

opposite left Ticket booth at the South Gate.

right The downtown Monorail station was the point of entry for many fairgoers.

The Bon Odori Dancers, who had performed during Japan Week, added a touch of the Far East to the festivities. The International Five, made up of singers from Italy, Peru, Turkey, Scotland, and Spain, sang the songs of many lands. More than a dozen marching bands filled the plaza with pomp and glory, but the biggest crowd pleaser was the St. Paul Indianhead Boy Scout Drum and Bugle Corps, which gave two encores and was invited to return to the fair on Sunday.

ROBERT GODDEN (1928–1985)

Seattle artist Robert Godden produced much of the artwork featured in fair publications. The fair's official guidebook features Godden's work and that of Ross Swift, his frequent collaborator. Century 21's two coloring books — one starred a human family visiting the fair and the other a family of mice — were also Godden's work. Godden produced many of the illustrations in print advertisements used by local firms to promote the fair, the city, and area businesses. Other artists who produced work for the fair included George Kutha, John C. Ray, Harry Bonath, Irwin Caplan, Ted Rand, and James Edward Peck.

FIVE MILLION On July 31, Colleen Mantyla of Roosevelt, Utah, became the five-millionth fairgoer when she passed through a West Gate turnstile with her husband, Donald, and three children. Fair officials, who had been watching excitedly, rolled out the Century 21 blue carpet and hung a sign reading "5,000,000" around Mantyla's neck. Reporters and photographers rushed in as Joe Gandy handed the startled — but delighted — woman a large white orchid. Bundled into two pedicabs, the Mantyla family was conveyed to the International Mall. They were then showered with gifts ranging from a carved West African mahogany wall plaque to a toy dog stuffed with 100 world's fair trade dollars.

The march toward five million had been only 698 short of the mark when the fair closed the night before. Jay Rockey described how million-mark fairgoers were selected in a letter to Canadians planning the Pacific National Exhibition in Vancouver: "We have five gates, and, quite frankly, we must simply choose one of the gates arbitrarily as the special gate. In the case of the five-millionth, we chose the West Gate, since the others had been used on numbers one, two, three, and four. ... We pre-selected a family before they got to the gate. ... They didn't know they were being chosen, but we usually can 'screen' them in the line outside pretty well."

Summer was only halfway over, and there were many millions of visitors to come.

Chapter 7

August 1962

Attorney General Robert F. Kennedy and family see the fair from Eye of
the Needle to the Gayway, John Glenn's *Friendship 7* goes on display, and
postfair plans are firming up.

A s August began, Seattle leaders were working to envision the postfair
Seattle Center, sometimes with differing agendas. United States Science
Pavilion architect Minoru Yamasaki brokered peace between members
of the business and cultural communities and the Civic Center Advisory
Commission. "If you surround the Civic Center with only cultural activities — except for
those events — you will have a dead Center. ... I think you should have a Center which
is active. A place where people want to come at night — that they go there because they
have a good time. You should have all sorts of activities," Yamasaki explained presciently.
If Seattle Center were developed to include all sorts of activities, he added, visitors would
get "culture by osmosis."

Ballet fans were beside themselves with joy as New York City Ballet's two-week
run in the Opera House continued during August. The chance to see world-class dancers
like Melissa Hayden and Jacques d'Amboise performing the classic *Swan Lake* and to
experience George Balanchine's choreography was simply stunning.

opposite The City of Berlin Pavilion
told the story of Berlin's struggle
following the recent erection of the
wall dividing the city.

Seafair Queen of the Seas Linda Juel made her final appearance at the fair on American Automobile Association Day. Juel swung a samurai sword to cut a cake and helped hand out cupcakes frosted with the AAA initials. Then, in a ceremony at the Green Lake Aqua Theater, she passed her crown to the new Seafair queen, Gail Reid. But world's fair officials were not content to bask in her glory or that of other local queens such as Miss Seattle (Linda Humble), who was also a Space Needle elevator operator, Yakima's Miss Peaches and Cream (Beverly Stine), or Miss Good Posture for Washington State (Judy Marie Wise). Instead they announced their upcoming Miss Century 21 Employee contest. The winner and her two princesses would be chosen by popular vote, with a coronation planned for August 17 in the Olympic Hotel's Spanish Ballroom. Fairgoers were permitted to cast one vote for each $1 fair ticket purchased.

ARABS AND CHERUBS United Arab Republic Week opened on August 2 with a ceremony in the International Plaza near the UAR Pavilion. "By hosting this fair, your city of Seattle, the state of Washington, and the United States of America are widening this area of international cooperation to a new important dimension," UAR ambassador to the United States Dr. Mostafa Kamel told fairgoers.

Some of the younger fair staffers, along with the public relations crew, were planning a thrilling race for August 8 and 9: Pedicabs, those popular fair conveyances powered by strong young men, would be loaded with beauty queens and raced across the fairgrounds. This event, as close as Century 21 might get to movie heartthrob Charlton Heston's Roman chariot race in the popular 1959 movie *Ben Hur*, was sure to delight fairgoers and garner press coverage. But Century 21's safety director, Ben Snook, forbade the event, reasoning that city ordinances banned "competitive racing" in city streets. Undaunted, the young staffers continued to pursue the project.

Romance bloomed for Robert "Bob" Maloy, sponsor of the fresh fruit concession in the Food Circus, and Helena Havlik, a staffer in the Niagara Therapy Manufacturing booth. The couple married in Club 21 on August 2. Havlik told the *Seattle Post-Intelligencer*, "I tried most of the eating places in the Food Circus, and when I got to the strawberry shortcake at Bob's booth, he said, 'Have one on the house,' and I did."

GENERAL MOTORS

SMILE, YOU'RE ON CANDID CAMERA Some fair occurrences not even Jay Rockey's PR machine could have imagined. Mildred and Lester Dancey of Clarksville, Tennessee, challenged themselves to drive to Seattle and on the cheap — the *really* cheap. "To the World's Fair and back or bust on $99!" proclaimed the hand-lettered sign on the back of their Volkswagen Beetle. The Danceys hopscotched between free lodging provided for them by relatives, friends, and friends of friends. Their total expenses on the trip west were $45, leaving plenty for the return trek. They planned to spend several days at the fair before heading back home.

Fairgoers, a few anyway, were caught unaware and ended up on the very popular television program, *Candid Camera*. Host Allen Funt and his photographers staked out hidden camera locations all over the grounds. In one stunt filmed in the Food Circus, the *Candid Camera* crew assembled an upside-down room — with chairs, tables, lamps, and trash baskets with paper in them fastened to the ceiling — and marked the door "Information." Funt's teenage son Peter was strapped into a chair upside down. No one who entered the room mentioned the odd setup.

The pedicab race appeared to be taking shape despite being banned. Newspapers announced that at 9:30 a.m. on August 8 and 9, 18 pedicabs, powered by robust young men, would race around the International Fountain, each laden with a beautiful young woman. In order to make the contest fair, each cab would haul enough variously sized coconuts to bring the total cargo weight (female + fruit) up to 140 pounds.

SPACE CHARIOT The Mormon Tabernacle Choir arrived triumphantly, 380 members strong, at King Street Station on the afternoon of August 5, ready to dazzle music lovers. It was the famous choral group's first visit to Seattle since performing at the Alaska-Yukon-Pacific Exposition.

John Glenn's *Friendship 7* space capsule, in which the astronaut made his historic three orbits around the earth, went on display in the NASA Pavilion on August 6. The spacecraft replaced a replica that had been on display since the fair opened. Glenn's craft was concluding a 25-city round-the-world tour and had been viewed by some eight million people.

this page NASA Pavilion displays gave a space-hungry public its first chance to learn in depth about the organization.

opposite Dripping with juicy strawberries and whipped cream, Belgian waffles were a hit at Century 21.

Fairgoers were the first ordinary Americans to see and touch the capsule on its home soil. "It gives me a sort of funny feeling — a good feeling," world's fair security guard Joe Gordon told *The Seattle Times*. "It's great to know our country could do it." After its Seattle display the capsule was scheduled to end its trip at the Smithsonian Museum in Washington, D.C.

Barbara Le Sage, 104, came from her home in Butte, Montana, to see the capsule. Born in 1858 — 45 years before the Wright brothers flew — Mrs. Le Sage had followed the news of John Glenn's historic mission with great interest. "I was up at 3:30 in the morning to watch the flight on television," she told *The Seattle Times*. "I prayed all the way until he was safe." Like many other visitors to the NASA Pavilion, Le Sage gently touched the craft's exterior.

A CROWD OF KENNEDYS Tragic news reached Seattle by radio and television late August 5, confirmed by the *Seattle Post-Intelligencer* the morning of the 6th: "Marilyn Monroe Is Found Dead at Home." Monroe, 36, enormously famous and so iconic that her image was among those featured on the illuminated cubes in the fair's Washington State Coliseum show, *The Threat and the Threshold*, had been discovered by her housekeeper, a probable suicide. Details unfolded over the following days, jostling against headline news concerning one of the fair's most prestigious visitors: U.S. Attorney General Robert Kennedy, his wife Ethel, and four of their seven children.

Robert and Ethel Kennedy arrived the following day, wearing comfortable shoes, in the company of Kennedy's sister, Eunice Shriver, and trailing children like ducklings. The grownups headed for the foreign exhibits, signing guest books in each pavilion they visited, while the kids hit the Gayway, chaperoned by Rose Hill from Guest Relations, and Dorothy Sorter from Special Events. Joseph Kennedy, aged 9, chomped gum before discarding it as he boarded the Wild Mouse — a wise

move, considering how quickly the roller coaster whipped its riders around. Joe must have carried his Chiclets to the fair with him — following Walt Disney's lead on one way to maintain tidy grounds, sale of chewing gum was forbidden at Century 21.

Fairgoers shouted out to the popular political family and snapped pictures, while Eunice Shriver, using an inexpensive point-and-shoot camera, snapped back. During a 3 p.m. speech at the Playhouse, Robert Kennedy saluted the Pacific Northwest, equating Western pioneers with those who pushed toward the New Frontier, the theme the Kennedy administration applied to its policies and programs: "The future today demands of us the resolution, the sacrifice, the courage, and the faith of the pioneers," Kennedy told the crowd. Every one of the 800 seats in the Playhouse was filled, and hundreds more people stood in the drizzle outside the theater.

AT THE RACES The pedicab races, it now appeared, were off. Ted Eastwood, who managed Century 21's division of Air Mac Industries (operators of the pedicabs) said their insurance underwriters feared damage to fairgoers, the pedicabs, the virile peddlers, the beauty queens, even the coconuts, which were scheduled to be given away during Miami Day festivities after the scheduled races. Fairgoers were instead directed to the international championship baton-twirling contest in Memorial Stadium, where 1,300 twirlers were competing.

Even without permission, Gary Boyker (at the time the fair's Press Building manager) and Special Events Assistant Coordinator J. Ward Phillips "borrowed" a couple of pedicabs and took two beauty queens — Phillips later remembered that his was Miss Junior America — for an impromptu race. They meant it in fun and for public relations, but both men were reprimanded. Phillips recalled that the hardworking young staffers, with few days off, were responsible beyond their years, but sometimes their youthful spirits carried the day.

CITIZEN NIXON Richard M. Nixon, who had served eight years as Dwight D. Eisenhower's vice president, and then narrowly lost the 1960 presidential race to John F. Kennedy, arrived at Seattle-Tacoma International Airport later that afternoon with his wife, Pat, and daughters Tricia, 16, and Julie, 14. The family spent August 9 on the fairgrounds, receiving the blue carpet treatment and a warm bipartisan welcome. Nixon, who was hoping to win the 1962 California gubernatorial election, signed autographs whenever requested.

Even unflappable Laurene Gandy admitted feeling fear when fair crowds surged in to get a better look at the Nixons. Eventually the group split up: Nixon with Joe Gandy and Willis Camp, Pat Nixon with Laurene Gandy and Willis Camp's wife, Marty, and Julie and Tricia with the Camps' teenage son, Robert. This strategy dispersed the scrum sufficiently to allow free movement.

The following morning, Nixon visited Nathan Eckstein Junior High School student Karen Anderson's home at 6521 29th Avenue NE, in Seattle's Bryant neighborhood. Karen, 11 at the time, had written to Nixon after the election and offered her condolences for his loss to Kennedy. Nixon replied, eventually becoming a pen pal with Karen, who had been in the hospital with broken ankles when she wrote and was, at the time of Nixon's visit, recovering from skin grafts. Anderson's parents, sister, church pastor, and neighborhood friends crowded in to meet the politician.

COCONUTS AND MOCCASINS The fair was breaking attendance records almost daily, and there were nearly 80,000 people on the grounds for Miami Day on August 9. Floridians found a unique way to celebrate: They hired a Seattle-King County Health Department truck to spray orange blossom scent onto the crowd in the Plaza of the States, bringing the sunny fragrance of their home state's famous fruit to Century 21. They also handed out coconuts, some 2,500 of them, and staged a fashion show — from bathing suits to evening clothes — of clothing designed and fabricated in Florida.

below Former Vice President Richard Nixon, Julie Nixon, and Pat Nixon approach the fairgrounds by Monorail.

opposite left, from left David Kennedy, Attorney General Robert Kennedy, Robert Kennedy Jr., and Ethel Kennedy tour the fairgrounds.

right Robert Kennedy tosses coins in the United States Science Pavilion as Science Pavilion Commissioner Athelstan Spilhaus (far left), aid Ed Divine, Special Events Director Louis Larsen (to Kennedy's right), and Ethel Kennedy look on.

above Seattle World's Fair pennant.

center A beauty queen holds enough coconuts to bring her up to weight for a pedicab race.

below Puyallup Daffodil Queen 1962 Sharon Silvernail (front, third from left) and her princesses; including Ouida Weaver (second from left), Pat Flynn (fourth from left), Darlene Gose (fifth from left), Robin Holmes (back row, far right), and Sharon Biehn (back row second from left); (others could not be identified).

opposite Strong young exposition employees pedaled beauty queens in a cross-fairgrounds race, defying a ban on such events.

above Julie, left, and Tricia Nixon in the Great Britain Pavilion.

opposite above left Gracie Hansen's Paradise International was only quiet in the mornings — afternoon fashion shows and the Barry Ashton's nightclub act kept things busy at all other hours.

above right Several performers in Gracie Hansen's show wandered through the fairgrounds trailing reporters during a photo op, and made a stop at a Gayway booth to admire an enormous stuffed donkey.

below Gracie Hansen's bitten-apple logo gave a wink to the Biblical story of Adam and Eve.

Somehow, *Girls of the Galaxy* was hanging on, despite meager audiences. The show was living proof that nudity alone was not exciting. Dissatisfied fairgoer Paul Kessler wrote to Ewen Dingwall, stating, "In 30 years of going to 'adult' shows, I have never seen a worse show. 1. Dirty building. 2. Poor sound. 3. Poor seating. 4. Last, but not least, the show itself 'stunk.'"

The Indian Village, also on Show Street, had money troubles too. Performers, claiming they had not been paid for three weeks and therefore could not buy food, closed the show after staging a protest in which (according to Stan Patty in *The Seattle Times*) they boiled their worn-out moccasins, making reference to earlier days when such boiled leather might have been consumed to stave off starvation. The kettle they used supposedly had been given to the grandfather of one of the performers by Washington's first territorial governor, Isaac Stevens.

UNUSUAL JOURNEYS After waiting patiently in the usual long line to ascend the Space Needle, 27 fairgoers had to summon an extra helping of the virtue. As their elevator ascended for what should have been an 86-second ride, a minor electrical fire at the base of the Needle triggered a stall at the 120-foot level. The patrons and their unflappable elevator operator, Nancy Sutherlin, were stranded for 90 minutes. Sutherlin, a former airline stewardess, helped maintain calm even after the capsule-shaped elevator dropped 20 feet before its emergency brakes took hold.

The air in the elevator soon became stale, and most of the women removed their high-heeled shoes in order to stand more comfortably. All of the passengers commended Sutherlin for calmly explaining the elevator's safety features and for her help in maintaining morale.

Gracie Hansen's morale was certainly high that day. She and a chartered busload of her Paradise International performers, along with reporters, photographers, and press agents, stormed Morton, her old hometown. Gracie's triumphant return was prompted by the 20th annual Loggers' Jubilee, for which she had been chosen homecoming queen. Wearing a dress spangled with silver sequins, sitting in an open convertible, she led the Jubilee Parade. She presided over a demonstration of logging skills, after which she was presented with a golden ax.

Alan Crowe, 16, rode his bicycle to the Seattle World's fair — peddling all the way from his home in New Brunswick, Canada. His expectations for Century 21 had grown over the course of his 3,350-mile journey, Crowe wrote in a special feature for *The Seattle Times*, and he was not disappointed: "The fair is like the pot of gold at the end of a rainbow. If I could have ridden my bike around the fair I could say with a good deal of truth that I had cycled around the world."

Meanwhile, 80-year-old John F. Stahl showed it was possible to get to the fair the old-fashioned way — no matter how far away one lived. Stahl, nicknamed Old Iron Legs, arrived on the fairgrounds just before noon on August 13 (his birthday), completing the 900-mile walk he'd started in San Francisco on May 9. "I feel good, not even a blister," Stahl told *The Seattle Times*. Al Rochester, 68, met Stahl as he passed through the gate, and the two men danced an impromptu jig. Stahl had earned his moniker in 1939–1940, when he had walked from the Panama Canal to Austin, Texas.

HEALTH AND PROSPERITY Korea Week festivities began with a heartfelt speech by Dong Hwan Kim, chargé d'affaires of the Korean Embassy in Washington, D.C., at a fairgrounds press conference. "The tragic consequences of the Korean War left us virtually nothing but misery and hunger," he told fairgoers. "Certainly, our survival and recovery would not have been possible without the unselfish

cooperation of the free world, especially that of the United States." He toasted the crowd with a ginseng beverage, drinking to their health, prosperity, and victory against communism.

Members of the Civic Center Advisory Commission started an intense session of postfair planning by going together to the Space Needle observation deck — and looking down. The group's most pressing decisions concerned which of the temporary buildings on the site would stay and which would go. They were also weighing the question of whether the City should manage Seattle Center or if they should contract with a private group.

The next day, the VIPs at the Space Needle were the Smiths — the Hamilton B. Smiths — of Rock Springs, Wyoming. The family had won local notice the year before by being the very first people to inquire at Expo Lodging. Summoned to Seattle on a free tour, they'd explored the partially completed fairgrounds and the Pacific Northwest. Now that the fair was actually happening, the Smiths — joined by the Frank Smiths, a New York family who had won a radio contest — were back to experience its glory.

Meanwhile, Gary Kunst, a 6-year-old San Francisco boy, became the fair's six-millionth customer.

About 100 local residents had already been hired as extras for Elvis Presley's upcoming film *Meet Me at the Fair* (later retitled *It Happened at the World's Fair*). Film crews were on the fairgrounds after dark, shooting the Monorail and other recognizable fair features. Presley was expected to arrive in early September, stimulating some young female fans to ponder skipping one of the first days back at school to see the King.

A random-sample visitor survey in mid-August discovered that about one-third of out of towners were staying in private homes, with friends or relatives. When those fairgoers headed back to their borrowed digs, they were exhausted — most spent more than five hours per visit exploring the fair.

Happy news surfaced on August 17: The very popular United States Science Pavilion would reopen the day after the fair closed. Its name would change to Pacific Science Center. World's Fair Commission President Edward Carlson made sure this valuable resource was not lost to the community, leading planning for the transition and incorporating the new organization as a nonprofit foundation.

TWISTING THE NIGHT AWAY   Early in the morning on August 18, Mobil Driver Game employee Patricia Ann Thearse Dzejachok, of Bellevue, was named Miss World's Fairest — also known as Miss Century 21. Her title was bestowed at an employee dance at the Olympic Hotel. The dance began at 10 p.m. on August 17, so that fair staff could attend after work. Judy Hansen and Yvonne Van Bronckhorst were Pat's princesses.

That day Roman Catholic participants in North American Liturgical Week began arriving in Seattle. Attendance of 5,000 was expected, making it the largest religious gathering during the fair. The conference was intended to provide a period of spiritual and intellectual enrichment as well as an opportunity for prayer and study. One of the most hotly debated questions during Liturgical Week was whether the Mass, or at least major portions of it, should be celebrated in English rather than in Latin — an issue at the upcoming Second Vatican Convention (Vatican II) that would open in Rome on October 11.

On a lighter note, young fairgoers were thrilled with the free outdoor Dancing Under the Stars events that had recently been instituted. Hundreds gathered on Saturday nights to twist to music from the bandstand in the International Plaza. The dances had been added to placate teens, only some of whom enjoyed the fair's more highbrow musical offerings.

As attendance increased, so did trouble. Seattle Police Department Lieutenant Dave W. Jessup, who was assigned to the fair, sent a memo to his supervisor, Captain L. J. La Pointe, expressing alarm over the dance series. "The teenage dances are slowly degenerating into a teenage orgy," Jessup wrote. "Each week there has been an increasing amount of juvenile vandalism, drinking, and disorderly conduct. ... I strongly recommend that these dances be discontinued immediately." The dances were allowed to continue, but security was increased, and the bands hired were chosen with an aim of minimizing frenzy.

below Seattle's cultural options expanded enormously during the fair, including the chance to buy tickets to London's famous Old Vic theater company.

opposite left Visitors to the Government of Mexico Pavilion admire handcrafts.

above right World's Fair Bandleader Jackie Souders oversees the Twist.

below right Miss Century 21, Patricia Ann Dzejachok.

BOOKING THE PERFORMING ARTS

Performing Arts Director Harold Shaw estimated that the number of performances combined with total seating capacity in the fair's performance venues was equivalent to changing the program in a full Broadway season every two weeks. Shaw literally traveled the globe signing world-class talent for the exposition. He told *The Seattle Times* on August 19, 1961, that the performing arts could help an American public that "urgently needs to understand other peoples. Science has made such gigantic strides in recent years that most of us are left breathless. However, the humanities and arts are far behind, and it is important to us and to the world that we close the gap."

TROUBLE BEHIND THE SCENES The Indian Village performers who had departed the fair in the wake of that concession's financial troubles regrouped and opened an Indian Village of their own at the Ilahee Ranch Restaurant in Federal Way. The group included four couples, two other men, and three children from Washington, Oregon, Montana, Alberta, and Oklahoma. They were living in two teepees formerly pitched on the fairgrounds. They felt the concession's manager had taken advantage of them. He had fled Seattle when charged with embezzlement and was still on the lam. "But this is show business," their spokesman, Chief Jim Owens, told *The Seattle Times*. "It's a rough racket."

Spanish Village Fiesta entertainers were learning that lesson too. Their concession was very popular, but expenses were high. When backers revealed that they were $200,000 in the hole, Ewen Dingwall and other fair leaders closed them down. The fair was the Spanish Village's largest creditor, so the best choice seemed to be for the fair to manage it and try to recoup what was owed. Dingwall reorganized the concession, announcing that 50 employees (all of whom had been brought to the fair from Spain and were being fed and housed) would be departing. This led to arguments among the Spanish Village workers — no one wanted to go home. In the end, the popular La Tuna musicians and the Spanish dancers stayed, and cooks, waiters, craftspeople, and other staff went back to Spain.

TYKES AND TIDDLYWINKS The Wenatchee Youth Circus opened in Memorial Stadium on August 22. Billed as "The Greatest Little Show on Earth," the circus showcased 80 performers between the ages of 3 and 18. "The boys and girls have it all organized," their director Paul Pugh (also known as Guppo the Clown) told *The Seattle Times*. "They do it all — the rigging, the supervising, the performing, everything. They're wonderful."

Rumors that Soviet ships were massing in Cuba began to appear on the front pages of newspapers. The ships — some passenger liners and some cargo ships — were apparently being unloaded at night under strict security. "This is the system employed in Cuba when Soviet ships bringing military equipment are being unloaded," a story in the *Seattle Post-Intelligencer* cautioned.

On Saturday afternoon, August 25, what might have been the first tiddlywinks contest held at any exposition took place in the Plaza of the States. Billed as a world championship, the match pitted Oxford University's tiddlywinkers against the World's Fair All-Stars, a freshly organized enterprise. Since arriving from Great Britain, the Oxford team had already matched their skills against teams in San Francisco and Los Angeles. They had a team sponsor: Guinness Stout. The Seattle team was sponsorless, but Gracie Hansen granted them Louie, her performing cocker spaniel, as a mascot. Despite the participation of world's fair Protocol Officer Saeed Khan, a Cambridge graduate who had served in Her Majesty's Bengal Lancers and — apparently — knew his tiddlywinks, Oxford carried the day.

ART SHOW AND MEXICO The Masterpieces of Art show in the Fine Arts Pavilion was ending after Labor Day. The display, drawn from America's most prestigious museums, included works by Titian, Rembrandt, Goya, Kandinsky, and Picasso. Before the month ended, the Fine Arts Pavilion welcomed its millionth visitor.

Belgian waffles were a Seattle World's Fair craving, and felt novelty hats adorned with foot-long feathers had a following, but nothing surpassed the mania for giant novelty stuffed animals that, by the end of August, had become an overwhelming feature of daily life at Century 21. The locally manufactured oversized plush toys were sold and given away as prizes on the Gayway. "The out-sized French poodles,

left Sculptor Henry Moore's *Reclining Figure III* was displayed just west of the Exhibition Hall.

right The fair's stuffed prizes sometimes exceeded the size of those who won them.

opposite above John Provost, star of the television show *Lassie*, with Lassie.

below Kiosk advertising upcoming performing arts events.

tigers, and smirking cats have become Fair symbols second only to the Space Needle," opined the *Seattle Post-Intelligencer*. "To stroll the Gayway with one under an arm is to radiate prestige as a dime-pitcher or ring-tosser par excellence." The toys were about two-thirds as tall as an average adult and weighed as much as a large toddler. Tired of trying to squeeze the stuffed fauna into their already crowded elevators, the Space Needle instituted a special toy-check room at the base of the Needle and thereafter prohibited fairgoers from ascending with their fuzzy friends.

Mexico Week began on August 27, and Mexican Ambassador Antonio Carillo Flores and his daughter, Lupita, 19, were on hand for the festivities. Ballet Folklórico de México performed in the Opera House, Mexican high fashion was modeled in the Playhouse, and the Mexico City Police Department's motorcycle drill team dazzled the crowd with precision displays. A Mexican Fiesta, complete with a stunning buffet of delicious food prepared by members of Seattle's Mexican community, followed the Ballet Folklórico's gala opening night. It was the internationally famous dance troop's first U.S. appearance.

BACK TO SCHOOL Fair attendance leveled off as summer waned, families readied children for the school year, and vacationers from out of town headed home. Jay Rockey expressed the hope that local families would come back to the fair once the crowds had thinned and would enjoy shorter wait times for the Space Needle and the United States Science Pavilion. Pavilion staff estimated that 90 percent of all fairgoers visited the building — shorter waits there were worth talking about. Repeat business had been an important part of the fair's success so far.

The World's Fair Service Scouts were due back at school, which meant an end to the helping hands they'd lent all summer at the fairgrounds. The boys — some 450 of them from Washington, Oregon, Montana, Idaho, and Alaska — had bunked at Fort Lawton, spending about six hours daily on the fairgrounds. One of their regular tasks was helping out during the state days honor ceremonies at the Plaza of the States. The scouts resigned en masse on August 30, some jumping into the DuPen fountain to cool off and celebrate.

left Ron Dewar was the fair's lucky
number 7,000,000.

right Wenatchee Youth Circus aerial
performers traverse the high wire.

CUPS AND CORPS The Brazil Pavilion seemed immune to the late-summer slump. Deputy Commissioner Ruy Pereira De Silva told the *Seattle Post Intelligencer* that the pavilion was giving out at least 3,000 free cups of Brazilian coffee every day and almost as many samples of iced maté tea. Fairgoers found the smell of freshly brewing coffee magnetic, and the Brazil Pavilion usually had a crowd. "It is the finest coffee in the world, no doubt about that," Pereira De Silva asserted.

The final day of August honored the Peace Corps, created by President Kennedy in 1961. Peace Corps Associate Director Warren W. Wiggins told fairgoers, "This is an appropriate time for Peace Corps Day because the corps is entering the eve of its biggest departure ... we will double the size of the Peace Corps in terms of volunteers serving overseas."

At 9:05 that evening, the fair welcomed its seven-millionth visitor, Rod Dewar, a teacher. He was the first Seattleite to be a "millionth" fairgoer. Free Space Needle and Show Street tickets, 10 days free fair admission, and $100 in trade dollars were showered on Dewar and his date, both of whom expressed pleasure that they'd arrived at the gate later than planned.

It was a fitting ending to the fair's full summer. Seattle paused to catch its collective breath — and then headed into Century 21's final stretch. Even with all that had been accomplished, landmark events — including the soul-stirring Canadian Tattoo and Elvis Presley's dizzying week of filming at the fair — were yet to come.

PRODUCT LICENSING

The fair licensed many products. Century 21 had official paper luncheon, dinner, and cocktail napkins, coasters, drinking straws, litter bags, drinking glass covers (designed for the hotel and motel trade) — all imprinted with the official logo and trademark phrase "America's Space Age World's Fair." Tacoma mattress maker Spring Air produced an officially licensed Century 21 mattress. Costume jewelry, fabric yard-goods, casual men's shirts, a crayon-sketch Christmas card depicting the Three Wise Men riding their camels past the Monorail and Space Needle while the Star in the East shone in the sky, a Seattle world's fair mobile emblazoned with "Let the kiddies build their own World's Fair!," along with the usual pennants, banners, flags, decals, and bumper stickers — all these items were licensed. Licensing fees brought significant revenue.

Top row from left: Space Needle pens; logo coffee cup; tag from the official Century 21 mattress; world's fair luggage;
Center row from left: Contests held during the fair, such as the American Lawn Bowling Association Tournament, often used the official logo; portable radio; postcard mobile; coloring set;
Lower row from left: Sugar packets; ashtray; woman's blouse of world's fair fabric with Space Needle pen in pocket; juice glasses.

Chapter 8

September 1962

Elvis Presley arrives to shoot a movie and teenagers swoon, the Canadian Tattoo thrills thousands, and postfair planning gathers momentum.

September brought what might have been Century 21's most unusual visitor: a large chunk of ice from the North Pole. The ice was brought to Washington, D.C., by two nuclear submarines, the USS *Skate* and the USS *Seadragon* — which had carried a Century 21 Exposition flag and a Washington State flag to the subs' historic rendezvous beneath the polar ice cap. The crews had carved off the chunk of ice after their vessels made a joint surfacing at the pole. A U.S. Navy plane carried Washington Senator Henry "Scoop" Jackson, several navy commanding officers from the submarines, and the ice from the "other Washington" to Seattle. Dry ice kept the precious chunk of polar ice frozen.

On Monday, September 3, the *Skate*'s commander, Seattleite Joe Skoog, and Charles D. Summit, the Nashville, Tennessee, resident who had commanded the *Seadragon*, were honored at the Plaza of the States. Governor Rosellini and Senators Jackson, Warren Magnuson, and Hubert Humphrey of Minnesota took part in the ceremony. At a reception afterward, dignitaries enjoyed Washington apple juice served over chips of polar ice.

opposite from left Governor Albert Rosellini, *It Happened at the World's Fair* producer Ted Richmond, Elvis Presley, Colonel Tom Parker, and the film's director, Norman Taurog. Even Elvis seems surprised to be presenting a ham to the governor.

The *Seadragon* was berthed at Pier 91. Its freezers carried backup polar ice chunks, just in case the ice for the fair should melt before its moment in the limelight. Lest the drinking of apple juice make the *Seadragon* and *Skate* appear frivolous, Senator Jackson reminded the public that the real purpose of their rendezvous had been to demonstrate that the United States "can meet the Soviet submarine threat under the ice. ... The best way to get a submarine is with another submarine."

THE SHOWS GO ON Maurice Chevalier, billed as "the boulevardier of show business — singing his world famous songs as only HE can!" — opened a week's performances in the Opera House on September 4. Unlike some performers who were too busy working to soak in the fair, Chevalier enjoyed several special tours of the Century 21's most famous features. The Hospitality Committee squired him everywhere, including around Lake Washington on a private yacht.

Tickets were selling quickly for Hal Holbrook in *Mark Twain Tonight*. Holbrook's one-man show had been an off-Broadway hit, and Seattle audiences looked forward to the show, called "uproariously funny" by *Time* magazine.

For those who'd loved *Aida* — or those who'd found it slightly overwhelming — the famed D'Oyly Carte Opera Company brought its productions of Gilbert and Sullivan's *The Mikado*, *The Gondoliers*, and *The Pirates of Penzance* to the Opera House. The London-based company had been performing works by Gilbert and Sullivan since 1875.

Performing Arts Director Harold Shaw was pleased with the work he'd done to bring impressive talent to the fair, but he nevertheless resigned in early September, leaving affairs to his assistant, Phil Tippet. Shaw expressed pride that 70 percent of fairgoers had attended a performing arts event.

left Bob Hope examines a mannequin of Nipper, the RCA Victor "His Master's Voice" pup.

right Fair Assistant Vice President Willis Camp's 16-year-old daughter, Georgine, was whisked past crowds of screaming teenaged girls to watch Elvis filming *It Happened at the World's Fair*, and had the thrill of briefly meeting the King himself.

MELONS AND MISSILES Attendance surged as 171,463 people streamed through the turnstiles over the three-day Labor Day weekend. They might have been surprised when entering the Food Circus to find the new display straight from Hope, Arkansas: a 140-pound watermelon. It was greatly appreciated by a large group of visiting underprivileged kids who gobbled it up when offered the chance.

Newspaper photographs of the enormous melon hardly served to distract the public from the news from Cuba, which grew darker daily. President Kennedy issued a formal statement that addressed Russia's ongoing shipment of missiles into that country. "The United States in conjunction with other hemisphere countries will make sure that while increased Cuban armaments will be a heavy burden to the unhappy people of Cuba, they will be nothing more," the statement ended grimly.

VISIT FROM THE KING Elvis arrived on the fairgrounds bright and early on Wednesday, September 5, to begin on-location shooting for MGM's *Meet Me at the Fair* (released as *It Happened at the World's Fair*). Presley's first scenes were on the Monorail Red Train, and he and his child costar, Vicky Tiu, with Seattle extras Linda Humble (Miss Seattle and a Space Needle elevator operator), Joan Seller (also a Space Needle elevator operator), Thelma Reddick, and Harry Dearinger, went back and forth along the short track as filming progressed. Other local extras, hired at $10 per day, milled about on the station platforms, while 25 uniformed off-duty policemen maintained order. The 100-member MGM crew swarmed busily, and dialogue director Jack Mintz ran the stars through thier lines.

Though it was the first day back at Seattle Public Schools, plenty of teenage girls were present to shriek and swoon. The King's female fans came in all ages: Joyce Bucknell, a Spokane mother of five who was president of the Our King Elvis Presley Fan Club, was so smitten that she'd named her youngest baby Elvis.

above "I Was There" pins were produced in many colors. This unusual version sports a ribbon and — for some unknown reason — a model bomb.

below Elvis, members of his entourage, and fair staffer Albert Fisher on location at the fair.

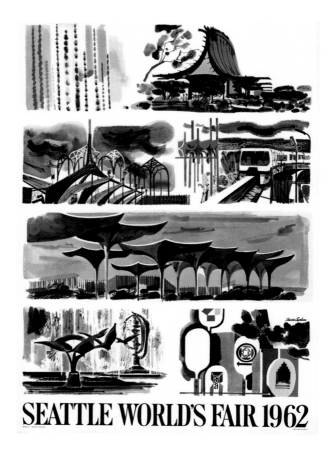

SEATTLE WORLD'S FAIR 1962

left Irwin Caplan's world's fair poster drew inspiration from scenes across the fairgrounds.

right Brazilian fashion models provide a photo opportunity.

One Seattleite who got a chance to see the King close up was 18-year-old Sue Wouters. The teen enjoyed four dates with Presley — and his bodyguards — at the New Washington Hotel, the star's home during Seattle filming. Wouters's mother, Betty, was a secretary to Al Fisher, one of the fair's film and television VIP handlers, and Sue was visiting her as Presley filmed his scenes. Elvis spotted Sue, introductions followed, and before Sue knew it, she was being chauffeured to the New Washington to watch television, listen to music, and drink Coca-Cola. Elvis kissed her, Sue told *The Seattle Times*, and was a thorough gentleman. Nevertheless, she admitted, dating Elvis Presley cost her the company of her steady boyfriend.

In spite of media hoopla and adoring fans, Century 21 staffers remember the King as humble. "He wasn't extraordinary," Public Relations Director Jay Rockey, who was present during most of Elvis's time on the grounds, remembered later. "He always called me Mr. Rockey. ... He was calm, well-spoken, nice looking, clean."

CARNIVAL AND CANADA Brazil Week wrapped up on September 7 and 8. Brazilians at the fair attended a special mass at Sacred Heart Church, marking Brazilian Independence Day, and enjoyed a gala reception in the Brazil Pavilion that night. The next afternoon, the Century 21 soccer team was awarded the Brazil Pavilion cup they'd captured in a stirring game against a Tacoma team several nights before. "Carnival 21" followed. It was a condensed version of the Mardi Gras carnival held each year in Rio de Janeiro.

The first wave of Canadians who would be participating in Canada Week and the grand Canadian Tattoo began arriving in Seattle on the evening of September 6. In the vanguard were 36 horses from the Royal Canadian Mounted Police Musical Ride, which arrived at King Street Station on a Great Northern Railway train. Many Seattle families made the trip downtown to watch the horses and their red-coated riders detrain and parade

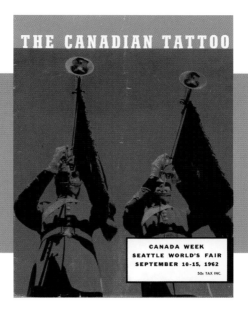

THE CANADIAN TATTOO

CANADA WEEK
SEATTLE WORLD'S FAIR
SEPTEMBER 10-15, 1962
50¢ TAX INC.

WHAT IS A "TATTOO"?

The official Canada Week souvenir program explains, "In the 17th century, in Holland, British troops were billeted in towns and villages where local inns became the social centers for the soldiers. To get them back to their billets at night it became necessary for innkeepers to turn off their beer taps and stop selling liquor. ... It was notified to all concerned by a drummer marching through the billeting area beating a 'call.' ... When the innkeepers hear[d] it, they remark[ed], 'Doe den tap toe,' which, freely translated, means: 'Turn off the taps.' ... In modern times the 'tattoo' has developed into a military display of spectacular proportions designed to entertain audiences of thousands."

to the fairgrounds. The horses were stabled in the lower level of the Opera House, which had been lined with temporary plywood stalls carpeted with hay and wood shavings.

The Royal Canadian Engineers, meanwhile, had transformed Memorial Stadium into a replica of Fort Henry, erecting a realistic-looking stone facade across the entryway to the field. The facade was built of 400 sections of plywood that fit together like a jigsaw puzzle. (The original Fort Henry was built in Kingston, Ontario, during the War of 1812.)

In addition to the 600-man Tattoo, Canada Week events included the Montreal Theatre Company's American premiere of Gratien Gelina's study of French Canadian life, *Bousille and the Just*; daily concerts by a 100-piece Canadian military band (the largest musical unit ever assembled by the Royal Canadian Air Force, done specially for its fair appearance); films produced in Canada; and the daily performances by the Royal Canadian Air Force aerobatics team. The Royal Canadian Navy sent five destroyers, which were moored at Pier 91 and were available for tours.

STIRRING SOUNDS The highly anticipated Tattoo was scheduled for six performances beginning September 10. It was the first time a Canadian Tattoo had ever been presented outside Canada. Wind and rain marked the first Tattoo performances, knocking down the elaborate Fort Henry facsimile and forcing men and horses to perform in a sea of mud. Unwilling to allow the breathtaking spectacle to be rained out, fair officials quickly ordered asphalt for Memorial Field. Royal Canadian Engineers worked all night to repair Fort Henry. Men and horses were back in business on September 11, but the flybys were cancelled pending better weather.

above Canadian Tattoo program.

below left Seattle police officers kept the peace, Presley's handlers were strictly business, and for fans who made it close enough to snag the modest movie star's autograph, Elvis made the fair.

below right A young fairgoer adjusts a Canadian Tattoo participant's hat.

next two pages The magnificent Canadian Tattoo created an unforgettable spectacle.

above A ticket to the very popular Canadian Tattoo.

below Joseph Gandy and George Tsutakawa pose with large-scale models of the official Century 21 medallion.

The Canada Week excitement brought many local families back to the fair. Opening ceremonies were held Sunday, September 9, in front of the Canada Pavilion. Memorial Stadium's seats were jammed with 13,500 fairgoers, with another 2,000 packed into the aisles, entry tunnels, and backstage. Fairgoers loved the Canadian Tattoo. Bending to public demand, world's fair brass added an extra performance to make up for the one rained out on September 10.

Fair officials braced happily for the September 15–16 weekend. The weather was balmy, the Canadian Tattoo was happening each night, and local residents were beginning to realize that the wonderful world's fair would soon be just a memory.

On Saturday, the 74-acre fairgrounds filled to bursting with more than 106,000 patrons. Traffic snarled, people jostled for parking, and fair staff — reduced in number as college-age employees had headed back to school in recent weeks — worked harder than ever to attend to every detail. An extra matinee of the Canadian Tattoo was added for Sunday, and Joseph Gandy called the production, "the greatest and most thrilling spectacle of the Seattle World's Fair." Some 150,000 fairgoers saw the Tattoo over its seven performances.

STAMPS AND SOUVENIRS Two new United Nations memorial stamps were issued at the fair on September 17, which was designated United Nations Philatelic Day. The stamps, in 5-cent and 15-cent denominations, were postmarked at the United Nations post office in New York, and they also bore the Space Needle, Seattle, postmark. Ceremonies on the International Mall included a tribute to UN Secretary General Dag Hammarskjold, who had been killed in a plane crash one year previously, and to others who had given their lives in service to the United Nations.

GEORGE TSUTAKAWA'S OFFICIAL MEDAL

Internationally recognized as a painter, sculptor, and designer of fountains, Seattleite George Tsutakawa (1910–1997) designed Century 21's official medal. The coins were struck at the U.S. Mint in Philadelphia and were marketed as "the world's first United States space age coin."

One side of the coin featured imagery of the Space Needle, the Coliseum's hyperbolic parabola roofline, the official Century 21 "man in space" logo, and the legend "Century 21 Exposition, Seattle, Washington, U.S.A. 1962." On the flip side were abstract interlocking ovoid forms that Tsutakawa called "an image of the little known outer space, with all its vastness, richness and complexity of rhythm and motion of the stars and the moons and their planets which man hopes to penetrate by perfection of science and technology."

Later that day, Mayor Gordon Clinton proposed that Ewen Dingwall be appointed director of Seattle Center. With the fair's final day drawing ever closer, the need to appoint someone to oversee the conversion from fairgrounds to civic center was pressing. The new director, Clinton explained, would make recommendations for the use of buildings and would also oversee event scheduling over the crucial first year after the fair.

A long-awaited milestone was reached the same day: Century 21 sold its nine-millionth ticket. Nearly eight million people had visited the fair — the unused tickets were most likely from the presale, and those ticket holders would need to hurry in order to ensure they didn't go to waste.

Many of the foreign exhibitors were thinking ahead — a stroll through the foreign pavilions revealed many fixtures for sale, available for pickup after the fair closed. White marble, lava stone, and amber glass from the Mexico Pavilion; textiles, rugs, crafts, and even antique jewelry from the United Arab Republic Pavilion; gold leaf and art from the Thailand Pavilion; the sugar mural, salt mural, Kapiz-shell chandeliers, and other items from the Philippines Pavilion — almost anything fairgoers had admired during their visits to the fair could now be purchased and eventually carted home. "Everything moveable in the United Nations Pavilion, down to the light fixtures, has to be sold," the pavilion's manager, John Hampshire, told *The Seattle Times*.

All of this selling kept John McNeil, the fair's customs and immigration administrator, hopping. McNeil was charged with keeping track of every foreign item that had been included on a customs form when it was shipped to the fair for display. Foreign participants who decided to sell these items had to pay duty on them before the fair ended. Items that were declared to have no value had to be destroyed in the presence of customs employees. "Everything — everything — has to be accounted for," McNeil told *The Seattle Times*. "Those customs officers are going to be mighty busy around here for awhile."

left Massive shell lanterns hung in the Philippines Pavilion.

right Crowds on closing day looked for their favorite fair food and last-minute shopping bargains.

FOR THE BIRDS On September 20, 75 pigeons were launched off the top of the Space Needle for the World's Fair Unlimited Pigeon Rally (a publicity stunt dreamed up in attempt to capture waning press attention). Christa Speck, the human hostess in *Les Poupées de Paris* on Show Street, and Al Rochester toasted the birds with champagne. The honorary title "Miss Pigeon Rally" was bestowed upon Speck.

The birds were supposed to race 1,225 miles to Minneapolis–St. Paul, and their legs were banded with Century 21 information and numbered so that sponsors (mostly radio deejays, newspaper columnists, and other media personalities) could have bragging rights over which one arrived in the Twin Cities first. A course pigeon had been launched from Woodland Park Zoo the day before; the rallying pigeons were supposed to follow that bird's lead. Instead, the pigeons circled the Needle and then headed toward Pioneer Square in downtown Seattle. Homeward bound or not, the pigeons had served their public relations purpose.

FRESH SCENTS On September 21, for the final time, Georgia Gellert poured a new Revlon scent into the freshly scrubbed perfumed pool in the Fashion Pavilion. The scent, called "Intimate," was a return engagement — it had been the first perfume to scent the waters. It was brought back (or so the press was told) by popular demand. The perfume in the pool had been changed on the 21st of each month; one month after "Intimate" was poured, the fair would close.

Despite an autumnal sense that Century 21 was winding down, there were still thousands of things to see and hundreds of things to do each day. Fairgoers could watch the *Vogue* fashion show presented four times daily above the perfumed pool, and the Polynesian show that happened eight times daily in the Islands of Hawaii Pavilion. They could enjoy the pearl divers, flower arranging, and tea ceremonies in the Japanese Village. Spanish dancers and La Tuna musicians continued their popular performances in the Spanish Village Fiesta. There was film — from space-age *Friendship 7* in the NASA Pavilion to classic favorites like Fred Astaire and Ginger Rogers in *Flying Down to Rio* in the Playhouse. All of that, plus more Special Days, world-class performers in the Opera House, lectures in the United Nations Pavilion, fair food to savor, Show Street to enjoy, and the Gayway — always good for thrills.

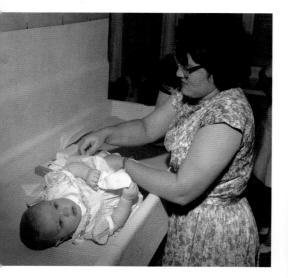

left Seattle's Baby Diaper Service provided free wet-for-dry exchange of the cloth diapers sported by virtually all infant fairgoers.

right Flight to Mars ride on the Gayway.

DISNEY AND DING Famous visitors continued to arrive. On September 21, Walt Disney and his family toured the grounds. Disney's approval meant a lot: His Disneyland had taught fair planners many important lessons about how to keep a public venue like the fairgrounds shipshape, even under heavy use. The fair had also boosted Disneyland's attendance as families on car vacations made the grand circuit.

On September 22, it was official: Ewen Dingwall would head the new Seattle Center. Other fair staffers were likely to be tapped, the city council said, in order to take advantage of the leadership and experience developed during the fair. The city council also prepared a resolution calling for the appointment of an 11-person nonsalaried Seattle Center Commission. And in Olympia, state legislators made it clear that the World's Fair Commission would under no circumstances be permitted to dissolve Century 21 Exposition, Inc., or distribute any of its assets until a satisfactory audit was produced.

Teen heartthrob Ricky Nelson brought his comedic variety show to the Arena on September 21 and 22. The singer was the younger son of Ozzie and Harriet Nelson and was well known to radio and television audiences from their long-running series *The Adventures of Ozzie and Harriet*, in which he played himself. Nelson, 22, had a younger fan base than Elvis Presley, and his fans were even less inclined to restrain themselves. Whenever they caught sight of the star, they shrieked and clutched one another.

ASTRONAUTS AND AUTOMAKERS On September 22, NASA research pilot Milton Thompson (a 1953 University of Washington graduate who had worked for Boeing before joining NASA) and newly designated astronaut Neil Armstrong made an appearance in the NASA Pavilion. The men, along with X-15 rocket plane pilots Stanley Butchart and William Dana, participated in the dedication of an X-15 display.

Henry Ford II also visited the fair that day, paying special attention to the popular Ford Motor Company Pavilion. Ford was the son of Edsel Ford and grandson of company founder Henry Ford, who had attended the Alaska-Yukon-Pacific Exposition.

During Henry Ford II's visit to Century 21, the Ford Pavilion welcomed its one-millionth visitor. Mary Ruth Jacobs, 27, of Bridgeton, Missouri, was the lucky one. She was given a 1963 Ford Falcon Futura, a car not yet available to the public. Jacobs and her husband David had driven to Seattle in, she admitted sheepishly, a 1961 Chevrolet. The couple caravanned both cars home to Bridgeton.

left: Chic runway models strutted above perfumed fountains, showing the latest fashions from *Vogue Magazine*.

right: Rail transport of the future, as imagined in 1962.

"CRANK" LETTERS

The fair's top brass got plenty of angry letters, many objecting to adult entertainment at Century 21, including some penned by a class of students from Grand Rapids, Michigan. These followed the same format: "Dear Sir: If the entertainment at the Seattle World's Fair is with nakedness as advertised, I as a young American citizen strongly object. That kind of stuff will ruin our country. Please change your program." Terry Pratt of Darlington, Wisconsin, went even further, calling Eddie Carlson "a traitor encouraging sick vulgar, sickening, indecent and impure shows at a World's Fair." Poor Carlson was chastised from Zillah, Washington, to Agana, Guam.

Writers received the standard reply: "All performances in the adult recreation center are in good taste, not obscene and conforming to national standards of first class theatrical productions. Practically all of the Fair, other than the Gayway section, is devoted to serious, scientific, and modern exhibits portraying the world of the future. These are produced by the United States Government, State of Washington, and some thirty five foreign nations and many of the leading industrial firms of America. Thank you for your interest in the Seattle World's Fair."

DWINDLING DOWN Dale Conner and Timothy Lee, 14-year-old pals from The Dalles, Oregon, managed to stretch out their summer adventure to the great world's fair longer than either of them imagined possible. They left The Dalles by bus on September 11, heading for Century 21. The boys soon ran out of money and thereafter slept each night under a different concession building. Two weeks later, tired and hungry, they phoned their families and then turned themselves over to the police. Their happy parents immediately arranged to get them home.

On September 30, Joan Baez, not yet a household name, gave a single evening performance of folk music in the Opera House. Baez, 21, had just released her third album, *Joan Baez in Concert*. Noting with some chagrin that Baez had kicked off her shoes before performing, *The Seattle Times* reviewer, Lou Guzzo, conceded that Baez "needs no gimmicks. With singular simplicity, her art finds its way directly to its target." Baez's earnest fan base, Guzzo opined, "already has assumed the status of a cult." Less than two months after her Opera House performance, Baez was the subject of a *Time* magazine cover story.

On the same day, Century 21 kicked off a weeklong tribute to India. India's ambassador to the United States, Braj Kumar Nerhu, and India's finance minister, Morarji Desai, toured the fairgrounds.

The wonderful world's fair was winding down. Seattleites made their final visits and remembered the glorious summer, knowing the days were slipping through their fingers. To the gratification of so many who had worked on Century 21 mainly for the civic center that would supersede it, the dream of a postfair Seattle Center would soon be a reality.

below The carousel on the Gayway was a spot of timeless fun within the fair's futuristic hustle.

oppotite Gracie Hansen, Barry Ashton, and their leggy showgirls brought real Las Vegas style to Seattle.

Chapter 9

October 1–21, 1962

Postfair planning accelerates, going-out-of-business sales abound, the Columbus Day Storm roars through the Pacific Northwest, crowds surge to enjoy final days, and Joe Gandy brings the fair to an emotional close.

O ctober began with a salute to Maine, the last of 50 states to be honored at the fair. Major General Edwin W. Heywood, state adjutant general, stood in representing Governor John H. Reed and presented a plaque to Governor Albert Rosellini, making him an honorary citizen of Maine. Heywood also presented personnel from Tacoma's KTNT TV with gift baskets, in thanks for their cooperation on a world's fair program with WABL TV of Bangor, Maine.

India Week celebrations began. Female members of the India Student Association at the University of Washington sang and danced at the Plaza of the States, wearing colorful saris. Indian documentary and feature films were presented in the Playhouse throughout the week, and Uday Shankar's group of 30 temple dancers settled into the Opera House for a week of performances. The dancers enjoyed the fair and were treated to a five-hour cruise on the yacht *Thea Foss*.

October 2 was Library Day, and as David Clift, executive secretary of the American Library Association, spoke to several hundred librarians in the Playhouse, the public address system failed. The audience, including those in the back, could still hear him

opposite Crowds fill the stands at Memorial Stadium for the world's fair closing ceremonies.

quite well, and Ken Prichard, assistant director of Special Events, later quipped to *Seattle Post-Intelligencer* columnist Jack Jarvis, "We did it on purpose to demonstrate the superb acoustics of our new Playhouse."

With only three weeks until the fair's end, Joe Gandy urged those who owned advance tickets and bonus books to "take full advantage of their investment." For those who had more tickets than they could use, Gandy announced the creation of the Youth to the Fair program, which, like the President's Club established by the Seattle City Council, would channel those extra tickets into the hands of underprivileged children.

BLASTING OFF   On October 3, a large crowd gathered in the NASA Pavilion to watch a television broadcast of astronaut Wally Schirra's blastoff from Cape Canaveral to orbit the earth. Many paused on their way to the viewing room to examine the model of John Glenn's *Friendship 7* capsule, twin to Schirra's vehicle. The model had replaced *Friendship 7* when the craft was moved to the Smithsonian Institution.

The mood was much calmer than when fairgoers had sweated through television coverage of Scott Carpenter's flight back in May. After a successful liftoff, Schirra spent the next nine hours performing engineering tests, while most in the pavilion wandered off to enjoy the fair. Later in the evening, there were tense moments during reentry, but after his six orbits Schirra splashed down in the Pacific without a hitch.

On October 5, the Seattle Center Advisory Commission held its first meeting to discuss plans for activity on center grounds the following summer. Ewen Dingwall emphasized the importance of immediate decisions on which fair buildings should be retained for Seattle Center use.

PIGEONS AND PURCHASES   While civic leaders pondered that weighty question, one of the pigeons launched from the Space Needle in September showed up in Minnesota after a 14-day, 1,225-mile flight. The tireless bird was sponsored by KVI disc jockey Dave Clarke. But sad news followed. Another pigeon, sponsored by KING disc jockey Frosty Fowler, had been shot by a hunter in Sioux Falls, South Dakota.

Fair attendance reached a new high on October 6, when 111,079 people passed through the gates. This was one of the last weekends to visit the fair. The weather was superb, and adding to the draw was a guaranteed crowd pleaser — bagpipers and highland dancers. The Royal Scots Greys and Argyll and Sutherland Highlanders played twice to packed audiences in the Arena.

Souvenir hunters found bargains galore, especially at the foreign exhibits. Bongos, silk ties, bamboo flutes, carved tchotchkes, and more were available for pennies on the dollar. Signs were plastered everywhere: End of Fair Special! Big Sale Today! Your Gain Is Our Loss!

Fairgoers had enjoyed patronizing the small shops lining Boulevards of the World. For many, it was a unique chance to shop for exotic imports not readily available in their habitual markets. Longtime local businesses like Uwajimaya, which offered Japanese housewares, gift items, and edible delicacies, gained exposure to new customers through their retail outposts at the fair and looked forward to serving that expanded clientele in their permanent establishments.

CHINA AND CHOCOLATE CAKE Republic of China Week opened on October 8 with a visit from Shu Kai Chow, personal representative of President Chiang Kai-shek and minister of Overseas Chinese Affairs for the Republic of China on Taiwan. Chow dedicated the fair's Republic of China Pavilion, joined by

below KOMO 4 TV's Art McDonald reports from Century 21.

opposite left India Pavilion brochure.

right Fairgoers examine the wares at the Space Needle souvenir shop.

FIRSTHAND MEMORIES OF TELEVISION AT THE FAIR

"I would go on the fairgrounds at 8 in the morning and be there until about 11 or 12 at night. We would get color because we'd shoot in the morning, and then we'd get it over to the lab. We were the only ones with color in the early days." — KOMO reporter Art McDonald

"We produced station IDs for hundreds of stations ... and a lot of them used them. Things like that you can't get unless someone thinks that it will do them real good to be associated with your name." — Public Relations Director Jay Rockey

above Young performers of the
Foo-Hsing Theater practice their
moves.

opposite Fairgoers enjoy the Gayway.

Senator Magnuson and Seattle City Councilman Wing Luke, the first Chinese American from a large mainland city to hold such an office. Mai Mon Wai, Seattle's Miss Chinese Community, cut the ribbon at the entrance of the pavilion.

The Foo-Hsing Theater — child and teenaged performers from Taiwan — arrived at the Opera House for a week of performances. It was the troupe's first stop on a tour that would take them along the western coast of the United States and Canada. Seattle's Chinese American community provided a bus for touring the city and organized parties and other social occasions. Members of the fair's Hospitality Committee took the children on walking tours of Seattle supermarkets and shops.

With less than two weeks to go before the fair ended, Senator Magnuson announced good news: President Kennedy would indeed visit the fair on October 21 and would take part in the closing ceremonies. Details of Kennedy's visit were still being worked out, but it was hoped that he would send a message to the *Mariner 2* spacecraft on its way to Venus, and that the space vehicle would send a signal back to earth, heralding the end of Century 21.

Joe Gandy's birthday was celebrated in the NASA Pavilion on October 9, along with that of NASA itself, which had been established four years earlier on October 1. Bob Button, press officer for the NASA exhibit, was responsible for the big bash. He had a large cake on hand for the space agency and a small one for Joe. Gandy commended all the NASA people for having "one of the most exciting and imaginative exhibits at the Fair."

ON THE HORIZON Fair employees braced for another successful weekend, maybe the biggest yet. Besides being the last full weekend before the fair closed, an exciting logging show was scheduled to open an eight-day run in Memorial Stadium — perfect fare for Pacific Northwesterners. But on Thursday, October 11, the skies darkened as a storm front moved in.

A major storm system extended from southern British Columbia to Northern California, but the brunt of the bad weather bypassed Seattle. Until the next day.

BUON GUSTO Seattleites, accustomed inclement weather, poured through the gates on October 12 to take in a variety of Columbus Day events. At noon, a large crowd gathered at the Plaza of the States to kick off festivities. Special guests included Dr. Paolo Rota, Italian consul in Seattle, and Brooke Hays, special assistant to President Kennedy. Governor Rosellini, a proud Italian American, was in his element as he introduced the speakers to an audience filled with many of Italian descent.

The Italian flag was raised to a position of honor, and afterward accordions played while Italian folk dancers stepped and whirled. Victor Rosellini, chairman of the fair's Plaza of the States committee, received a distinguished service award from his cousin, the governor. All in all, it started out as a nice day.

HEAVY WINDS As fairgoers roamed the grounds — taking in the exhibits, munching on snacks, enjoying a few rides on the Gayway — the winds returned. By midafternoon it was blustery. By 6 p.m. the gusts were strong enough to knock people down. And then it got worse. At 7:30, fair officials closed the Coliseum, worried that the glass windows might blow out. Throughout the fair, loudspeakers blared that winds up to 80 miles per hour were expected shortly.

The Space Needle closed lines for the elevators, but diners in the Eye of the Needle were allowed to finish their meals. People began leaving the fairgrounds, many using umbrellas to guard their faces from flying debris. Some folks decided to stay and flocked to the Food Circus, listening to weather reports on their transistor radios.

All around the grounds, trees snapped, banners ripped, signs were torn apart. The United States Science Pavilion's Gothic spires swayed noticeably. Assistant Special Events Director Ken Prichard recalled many years later that he had rushed to the fairgrounds, fearful that foreign exhibits in open pavilions would be devastated. His greatest concern was the Philippines Pavilion, which featured massive shells suspended above the exhibit space.

"The staff at the Philippine exhibit were just beside themselves," Prichard remembered. "So — this will illustrate the beauty of the Seattle World's Fair, and how it was organized — I was able to simply pick up the phone and call the garage and say do you have someone who can come over with a fork lift, a big one? And within, it seemed like, seconds, there they were. We tied one of the young men from the exhibit to it, and they lifted it up, and he was able to grab hold of one of those shells, and I threw him a rope, and one by one we were able to tie them." The shells, safely lassoed and secured, survived the howling gale.

By 9 p.m., the Space Needle was empty of guests, as gusts reached up to 60 miles per hour. At 9:15, officials closed the exposition but allowed those in the Food Circus to stay put if they lived south of Seattle, where storm damage was much worse. Power outages were reported everywhere, except at the fairgrounds.

STORM OF THE CENTURY Cyclone-level winds of more than 150 miles per hour first battered the coast, felling 11 billion board feet of timber in Washington, Oregon, and California. As the storm moved inland, most towns lost power. Trees toppled. More than 60 people were killed in the three states, nine in Washington. Worst hit was Oregon, where the Columbus Day Storm remains the deadliest natural disaster in that state's history.

Damage in Seattle was severe, but few injuries were reported. Repair crews worked around the clock to restore power in neighborhoods throughout the city. Many people, rather than sit around a darkened home all day, had the same idea: Let's go to the fair!

Storm damage on the grounds was easily fixed, and 75,855 people streamed through the gates. Saturday's big attraction was the lumberjack show, and crowds cheered the tree toppers, log choppers, and log rollers. The show ran twice, and in between local firefighters held exciting demonstrations.

The next day, 93,344 people showed up. Fair officials gathered at the North Gate, waiting to honor the nine-millionth visitor. Just before 2 p.m., 6-year-old Paula Dean walked through with her family and was greeted with cheers and hurrahs. Al Rochester handed her a big sign with the number 9,000,000 on it. She also received one of the fair's huge stuffed poodles. It was purple and almost twice her size. Joe Gandy presented her with a large bouquet of roses and a kiss on the cheek. Governor Rosellini gave her a transistor radio and other gifts.

APPROACHING THE FINISH LINE Rosellini was overseeing Governor's Appreciation Day, thanking many of the people who worked to make the fair a great success. The governor thanked all 8,000 Boy Scouts who raised 50 state flags during state day programs and helped out at other important events. Joe Gandy thanked all of the fair employees. "The heritage of this fair will be the spirit of those who served it," he predicted. Eddie Carlson presented Rosellini with a Century 21 Leadership Award.

The final week of the fair drew enormous crowds every day, everyone hoping to squeeze out the last drop of fun before it all shut down. Some families, like that of fair artist Robert Godden, his wife, Jean, and their two young sons, took ride after ride on the Gayway so that the carnival ride coupons that came with their advance-sale tickets would not go to waste. A summary of Gayway tickets during the fair's final week shows that 1,255,906 were sold. The biggest draws were the Wild Mouse and the Space Wheel.

The World's Fair Commission had already opened bids for the first phase of demolition, which included razing the Boulevards of the World, Show Street, all the concession kiosks, and some of the temporary buildings.

below Screaming world's fair fun.

opposite Microsoft cofounder Bill Gates counts the Wild Mouse as one of his favorite fair memories.

Another indication that Century 21 was moving into its postfair era occurred on October 16, when the Seattle Symphony Orchestra held the first concert of its regular season in the Opera House. To open the performance, Mayor Gordon Clinton appeared on stage and handed conductor Milton Katims a silver baton. To everyone's surprise, Katims handed it back, inviting the mayor to lead the "The Star Spangled Banner." Clinton conducted with aplomb and nearly brought down the house.

FINAL DAYS Thailand was honored on October 18. The next day, United Nations Day celebrated the 17th anniversary of the United Nations' founding in 1945. These were the last two international days at the fair.

Wrap-up continued as large numbers of people enjoyed their last visits. On the Gayway, 19-year-old Larry Roth and his girlfriend Gale Williamson cleaned up at one of the coin-tossing games, walking away with 23 giant stuffed animals valued at more than $600 retail. Over at the Belgian Waffle House, a strawberry shortage led the proprietor to start serving the treats with pineapple. No matter which fruit was ladled on, people still gobbled the waffles down.

Crowds continued to grow: 70,000 on both Wednesday and Thursday; more than 90,000 on Friday; and on Saturday more than 128,000 people came through the gates. This was the largest single-day attendance since the fair began.

WHITHER KENNEDY? Anticipation for President Kennedy's visit on the fair's final day was running high, but the White House kept shifting plans, making it hard for people to know exactly when Kennedy would arrive and how long he would stay.

Kennedy's press secretary, Pierre Salinger, noted that before Kennedy traveled to the fairgrounds he would attend a special breakfast at the Olympic Hotel. More than 2,000 tickets had already been sent out for this event, but the plans abruptly changed. First the breakfast was cancelled, and then it was announced that Kennedy would briefly visit the fairgrounds on Sunday, but only to attend the ceremony transferring the United States Science Pavilion from federal ownership to the Pacific Science Center Foundation.

The plans continued shifting until Saturday, when fair officials learned that the president wouldn't appear at all. According to Kennedy's doctors, the president had a severe cold. Senator Magnuson contacted Vice President Lyndon Johnson to see if he could take Kennedy's place at the fair, but Johnson said that he, too, had a cold and could not attend.

Fairgoers and fair staffers alike were disappointed that the president of the United States never visited Seattle's World Fair, except for a quick drive-through during its construction. But with or without him, the final day of the fair would be one to remember.

FINAL GATHERING On October 21, people began lining up early in the morning, just as they had on opening day. This crowd was more than twice as large. Throughout the day, 124,470 visitors made their way in for the very last time. Among them was Earl Addis, who was lucky enough to be designated the fair's ten-millionth visitor, after officials added

unused advance tickets to the total when they realized that actual attendance would fall a few thousand short. Addis and his family received armloads of gifts, including a pet dog.

Also seen on the grounds was Mrs. Ethel Lyons — the Space Needle Lady — who had befriended the Needle's ironworkers during construction. Lyon had visited the fair almost every day, and she proudly wore her signed hardhat. She told the *Seattle Post-Intelligencer* that her next project was gathering the addresses of all of her construction pals so she could send them Christmas cards.

Souvenir hounds swarmed the concession booths. Knowing that prices would be drastically marked down, many of them brought their own shopping bags, which they filled to the brim.

Lines were long everywhere as people visited many of their old favorites or exhibits that they had somehow not yet seen. Youngsters and oldsters alike crowded the Gayway to scream and laugh on rides that would soon be gone. Men crowded Show Street for one last look at a little ooh la la. And even though the Space Needle would remain long after the fair was closed, thousands made their way to the top to have one last overview of Century 21.

ORATIONS AND OVATIONS Senator Magnuson presided over the United States Science Pavilion's transfer ceremony in lieu of President Kennedy. After pressing a button that sent a signal to *Mariner 2* on its way to Venus, Magnuson handed the building's lease to Eddie Carlson, who accepted it for the Pacific Science Center Foundation.

In the afternoon, Carl Sandburg presented an anthology of his works in the Opera House. A near-capacity audience listened attentively to the man many considered to be the unofficial poet laureate of the United States. The 84-year-old Sandburg received two standing ovations, one when he walked on stage and the other after he finished his marathon reading.

BEGINNING OF THE END As evening drew near, many fairgoers made their way to Memorial Stadium. News reporters had already been given scripts of the closing ceremonies, written by Public Relations Director Jay Rockey and Special Events Assistant C. David Hughbanks. On headsets, Hughbanks and Operations and Services Assistant Mindy Kobbervig began issuing directions to the backstage crew. Live television coverage was starting, even before sundown. Soon 13,000 people filled the grandstands, and thousands more watched from the small hill west of the stadium. At 5 o'clock, the World's Fair Band, led by Jackie Souders, took to the field.

The Seattle Police Department drill team performed precision maneuvers. Then came the marching bands of every high school in the city, drum majors strutting and twirlers tossing their batons into the darkening sky.

Dignitaries representing the fair, city, state, congressional delegation, and every nation that had participated in Century 21 were ferried onto the field in Electricabs (electric pedicabs), and they gathered on a platform at the west end of the field. Metropolitan Opera star and Spokane native Patrice Munsel sang "Around the World in 80 Days."

COMMITTED TO HISTORY Joe Gandy stepped to the microphone and told of the great achievement that was now ending, noting that although the fair would fade into memory, it resulted in "a new cause, a new era of great

below Joseph Gandy, center, prepares to close Century 21 while, from left, Senator Warren Magnuson, Mayor Gordon Clinton, Governor Albert Rosellini, and Edward Carlson look on.

opposite above Jack Gordon, left, who directed all Plaza of the States events, with World's Fair Commission Vice Chairman Victor Rosellini.

below left During the last days of the fair, visitors swarmed the souvenir stands looking for bargains.

below right Earl Addis was the fair's ten-millionth visitor.

next page Numerous celebrations and entertainments were held at the Plaza of the States.

 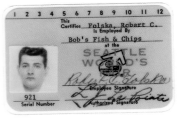

dreams and great realities for our Pacific Northwest." The audience joined in silent prayer. Mayor Clinton then spoke of the city's pride in taking part in the closing ceremonies of "our world's fair." At the east end of the field, a bank of fireworks displaying Mount Rainer, a fir tree, and the Century 21 logo lit up.

Stunning fireworks displays separated speeches, and each pyrotechnic fantasia was more elaborate than the ones that had come before. They were set pieces — firework charges set into framework that, when ignited, formed glowing pictures. Stagehands, dressed in black and barely visible, brought motion to the pictures, carrying smaller glowing pictures toward or away from the main imagery.

Edward Carlson spoke next, saluting the people of Seattle and the state of Washington for their encouragement. Governor Rosellini followed, emphasizing the pleasure that the fair had brought to the entire world. "In future days," he said, "we will look back in pride upon this great civic effort." The fireworks bank lit up again with a giant United Nations flag and six-foot-high figures of children from around the world.

Bagpipers piped, and the crowd responded warmly. Senator Magnuson, representing the entire congressional delegation, spoke next. The fireworks panel depicted an astronaut, a rocket, and a capsule orbiting the earth. Patrice Munsel sang "And This Is My Beloved," while young people who had worked at the fair ringed the stadium. As spotlights shone down on them, the ticket sellers, busboys, concessionaires, janitors, and cooks rushed onto the field and joined hands.

More fireworks! The Coliseum and United States Science Pavilion blazed, the Monorail glided smoothly, the glowing Space Needle's restaurant revolved and elevators descended. Joe Gandy took the podium again: "We dedicate this ceremony to Century 21, to the world of tomorrow, and to the men and women who will strive with abundant desire to make it a better world for all. This is the theme of the Century 21 Exposition. And this is our charge to the future. To you, the youth of today, we give you the 21st Century!"

below Young workers at the fair clasp hands and run out onto the field during closing ceremonies.

opposite left A variety of pyrotechnic displays, such as this one of the Space Needle, were ignited during evening ceremonies on closing day.

above right Mount Rainier and the Century 21 logo ignite as fireworks light up the sky.

below right All fair employees carried color-coded badges.

Aerial bombs and fireworks rockets lit the sky. The bands, playing together, whipped into the finale of Tchaikovsky's *1812 Overture* as the Space Needle Carillon bells clanged. After the crescendo, Gandy strode to the microphone flanked by Mayor Clinton and Governor Rosellini. The crowd went silent as Gandy's voice echoed through the stadium: "I now officially commit the Seattle World's Fair to history." He rapped a gavel on the rostrum once — a 21-gun salute boomed out — and it was over.

Almost. The World's Fair Band softly began playing "Auld Lang Syne," and Munsel began to sing. Quietly, the audience joined in, but increasing in volume. Soon the song boomed throughout the stadium. When the song ended, the stadium lights were doused and the crowd went silent. A few seconds later, the lights came back on, and fairgoers filed out of the stadium, tears streaming down many cheeks.

ONE LAST LOOK Most headed for home, but there were some who wanted to embrace every last minute. Even after the exhibits closed at 9 p.m., more than 28,000 people wandered the fairgrounds, many lost in thought. One by one, the pavilions went dark. The stragglers drifted away, until only the Gayway was open, still filled with people wanting one last ride on the carousel or the Ferris wheel.

Just before midnight, it began to drizzle. The Space Needle Carillon played its last song of the day, and then a voice boomed out over the loudspeakers, "Ladies and Gentlemen, the Seattle's World's Fair is closed!" The carnival music faded as the last of the fairgoers walked sadly out into the night rain. Behind them, the brightly colored lights flickered off.

A lone bagpiper played through the fair's final moments by the International Fountain, his last notes hanging softly in the air until midnight, when the fountain's lights went dark.

Chapter 10

Back to Century 20

Seattle returns from Century 21 to the present, the fair site begins its transformation into a cohesive civic center, Seattle Center evolves and grows, and the new Seattle Center Foundation begins raising money to help facilitate the center's development.

The fair was over. The grounds were silent and dark. The lights that had illuminated the grounds day and night were extinguished. The trees, which had retained their golden leaves due to the brilliance and warmth of artificial light, dropped their foliage overnight. The few fair employees who remained made their way past Gayway rides already being crated, and through crumpled waffle wrappers and discarded ticket booklets littering the formerly pristine grounds. The fair was over. It was a ghost town.

As Seattle paused to draw a breath, the world learned the real reason President Kennedy had missed Century 21's closing ceremonies: the Cuban Missile Crisis. On October 16, 1962, Kennedy had been shown photographic evidence, taken by U-2 reconnaissance planes, of Soviet Union missile sites in Cuba. Some had ballistic missiles on launchpads. The president and his closest advisors grappled with the unfolding crisis over the next six days, as the world teetered on the brink of nuclear war. It was a cautionary coda to a fair

opposite The Experience Music Project's architecture undulates on the site where the Velare Wheel once spun, and the Space Needle's halo shines on.

whose message had been scientific progress, nations working together, and the critically important need for peaceful use of space technology.

FOCUSING FORWARD Century 21 had succeeded brilliantly. Seattleites knew it — and so did the world. The fair was over, though, and the national spotlight moved on from the site of the fair's so-recent triumph. City Councilmember J. D. "Dorm" Braman's 1961 declaration that the fair was advancing civic center planning by 25 years had proven correct. But now programming, funding, marketing, and growth were needed. What was Seattle Center? What did Seattle want Seattle Center to be?

Over the next five decades, these questions would be answered, restated, and answered anew as the center evolved with the changing city.

Thanks to the foresight of those who made the fair, some anchors for the new center were in place in the fall of 1962, ready for their roles to be defined. The United States Science Pavilion had been transferred to the newly formed not-for-profit Pacific Science Center — its doors were open and dedication ceremonies were conducted the day after the fair closed. The Playhouse, Opera House, and Seattle Center Exhibition Hall (the fair's Fine Arts Pavilion) also stood ready. The Space Needle closed briefly to retool the menu, recostume the waitresses, and remove some of the restaurant seating, and then it reopened with fanfare. The Monorail was owned by Century 21 Exposition, Inc., and its fate for the moment remained undecided.

MOVING OUT Temporary buildings were removed by John M. McFarland House Wrecking, which had demolished many of the houses on the fairgrounds site before the fair. The company cleared away the Spanish Village Fiesta, parts of Show Street, and many other structures. "Certain structures have to be torn down when they are in the way of something good for the future," McFarland told *The Seattle Times*. "You can't be too sentimental — but you can't be indifferent either."

The Ellensburg Rodeo scooped up ticket booths, Bassetti & Morse's mod totem poles were dispersed across the county, and Gracie Hansen's building was trucked to Ravensdale Park in south King County. The massive Ford Motor Company Pavilion was dismantled, moved to Edmonds, and rebuilt on the waterfront to house a boat dealership.

The Washington State National Guard, which had moved operations to Pier 91 to make way for the fair, agreed to lease the old armory building to Seattle Center, as it had been leased to Century 21. The city finally bought the building in 1972 at Ewen Dingwall's urging.

By late December, plans were in place to convert the Coliseum into a sports and convention arena, including a flexible seating plan that could accommodate different configurations for hockey, basketball, wrestling, and other uses.

At midnight on December 31, 1962, the lease held by Century 21 Exposition, Inc., on the 74-acre site expired, and the land, enriched with buildings valued at up to $50 million, reverted to the City of Seattle.

GOODWILL TOUR   On January 16, 1963, Joe Gandy addressed the Seattle Rotary, many of whose members — Eddie Carlson, Michael Dederer, Jim Douglas, and Willis Camp among them — had greatly contributed to the fair's success. Gandy emphasized how they had volunteered their time in leadership positions on the executive committee, and he paid tribute to the "magnificent and talented" staff that worked beside them. He reminded the Rotarians forcefully that the group's real accomplishment lay not in the past with the fair, grand and successful as it had been, but in the future potential for Seattle Center. "Why did these men volunteer themselves for this tremendous community responsibility?" Gandy asked. "I think I can tell you that the fair alone would not have captured their interest or their effort. What they envisioned was that out of this fair would come something of value as a heritage to the City. ... We had studied and had seen that other world's fairs the world over left no physical heritage from the vast fortunes spent, and we were determined not to let that happen here."

We felt and still feel that it is economically immoral to spend vast fortunes of somebody's

money and have nothing left but memories."

JOSEPH GANDY, 1963

opposite left Gayway rides were removed after the fair, but thrill seekers did not have to wait long for the return of carnival-style pleasure — the Fun Forest opened in 1963.

right Like teenage girls around the world, this crowd in the Coliseum was thrilled to see The Beatles at their 1964 Seattle appearance.

A few weeks later, Joe and Laurene Gandy and their daughter Marilyn began a three-month trip around the world. Traveling at their own expense, the Gandys visited the countries that had participated in the fair, thanking each for its contributions to the success of Century 21.

The final fair business — closing the books — would not be finished until June 28, 1966, when Century 21 Exposition liquidators announced that the fair's books were closing with a profit. The state auditor had completed his ninth — and final — examination of the records and fiscal affairs of the liquidation of trustees for Century 21 Exposition, Inc. The trustees issued state treasurer Robert S. O'Brien a check for $99,508.67.

FAMILIAR FACES Ewen Dingwall, so crucial to the fair's success, took over — briefly, as it turned out — as executive director of Century 21 Center, Inc., which was the new nonprofit organization set up to stimulate permanent year-round use of the Seattle Center campus. As it turned out, Century 21 Center, Inc., lasted only until early 1965. "Our job is to create a program generating enough revenue to support all center activities, from arts to amusements. We want to work across the entire community," Dingwall said.

By January 1963, other former fair staffers working for Century 21 Center included former Exhibits Director Donald Foster, former legal officer Robert Ashley, former Special Events staffer C. David Hughbanks, former Foods Director Nick Jorgensen, former Special Site Projects Assistant Director Fred Christensen, former Exhibits Assistant Georgia Gellert, and former Controller Division staffer David Bergman.

FINDING A PATH In early 1963, Century 21 Center signed a five-year contract with the city to manage and promote half of Seattle Center campus, and the group immediately began a $2 million underwriting campaign, targeting Seattle's business community. Money quickly emerged as a major concern. Century 21 Center began operations with a debt load: It owed Century 21 Exposition, Inc., $60,000 for salary advances received during its formation period and for supplies and equipment purchased from the fair. The contract excluded management of almost all income-producing properties, including the Opera House, Playhouse, parking garage, Exhibition Hall, Arena, and the Coliseum, all being managed by the city. Century 21 Center was seeking organizations that could provide short-term programming and special events in parts of the center it was managing — mainly open and pavilion shells. Century 21 Center was to receive income from concessions and merchandise. In order for any of this to work financially, many people would have to come to the center for events and purchase food, drink, and merchandise. Another key factor would have to be a swift and successful fund-raising drive.

Desperate for immediate cash, Ewen Dingwall and landscape architect Lawrence Halprin (who was overseeing the conversion from fairgrounds to Seattle Center) quickly introduced the notion of another Gayway-type amusement park area. "We want fine arts, repertory theater, and all the rest in the center," Dingwall said, "but we have to have revenue-producers to help those things that are not income-producing themselves." Civic Center Advisory Commission Chairman Harold Shefelman was "shocked" at the idea of an amusement park, *The Seattle Times* reported, and considered that it would intrude on the setting of the Pacific Science Center. Shefelman soon tempered his views: "We all ought to realize that this (amusement park) plan is not the ideal plan — but the ideal plan is one that never will be in existence anywhere."

Seattle architect Roland Terry named the amusement area Fun Forest, envisioning carnival rides in a sylvan setting, widely spaced and surrounded by garlands of lights and groves of illuminated trees. The generous landscaping — Terry's plan called for more than 500 new trees and 30 miniature fountains — was planned to curtain the Fun Forest from the rest of Seattle Center. But very little of the plan was implemented because of money constraints.

LIQUIDATING THE FAIR

When the appointment of Edward Carlson, state Senator Michael Gallagher, and state Representative Ray Olsen to serve as the Century 21 Exposition, Inc., liquidators drew criticism from some state legislators, Carlson asked the legislature to appoint three neutral people to liquidate the assets. "We are not looking for bouquets or accolades," Carlson told *The Seattle Times*, "but some of us have given a lot of years for the fair and unjust criticism now wears us down."

Governor Dan Evans agreed, and Seattle certified public accountant Edward P. Tremper, Everett attorney Clarence Coleman, and Walla Walla businessman Donald Sherwood were named liquidators in March 1963. (Seattle accountant Arthur Cooperstien succeeded Coleman, who died on December 31, 1964.)

The fair's financial situation at the close was complicated. To name a few of the issues: some assets were jointly held, others needed fair value assigned before they could be accounted for and sold, portions of the grounds were leased from the City of Seattle and resolving this debt required deft negotiation, some doubtful accounts receivable (such as that of the Spanish Village Fiesta) were uncollectible and required write-off, and some taxes due the City of Seattle were in dispute. That the books were finally closed with a profit can almost certainly be credited to the meticulous determination with which the liquidating trustees apparently negotiated the best settlement possible in every instance. However, state Auditor Robert V. Graham's final report states, "From examination of the records of the World's Fair/Century 21 Exposition, Inc., it appears the City of Seattle, among others, benefited at the expense of the State of Washington."

this page Seattle Opera Association board members Kayla Skinner, Albert Foster, and Helen Jensen announce the newly formed association's 1964–1965 season.

opposite above The Arena's events have spanned the gamut from hockey to rock shows to (temporarily) ballet.

below Seattle Repretory Theatre logo.

SEATTLE OPERA

Founded in 1963 by Glynn Ross, Seattle Opera grew directly from the wealth of performing artistry nurtured by the Seattle World's Fair. In 1975, Seattle Opera gave its first complete cycle of Richard Wagner's four-opera *Ring des Nibelungen* in one week, an event that had not happened in the United States since 1939 and the first such American production outside of New York. This *Ring* festival continued for nine consecutive summers until 1984, becoming one of the company's signature events.

In 1983, Speight Jenkins succeeded Ross. Under his leadership Seattle Opera has created a wealth of original productions. Seattle Opera is one of the leading opera companies in the United States and is recognized throughout the world as the pre-eminent presenter of Wagner's *Ring* cycle in this country.

COURTING THE COMMUNITY The first major event at Seattle Center, the Seattle National Boat Show, held February 16–24, 1963, at the Coliseum, breathed a little life back into the dormant fairgrounds. The Coliseum won high marks from organizers, who were pleased to have a venue with ceilings high enough to display even the largest sailboats.

Dingwall organized a Seattle Center Booster Squadron. Local residents were asked to join and help promote the city and state. "One of the major reasons for the outstanding success of the Seattle World's Fair was the great promotional effort put forth by the people of Seattle and the state of Washington. ... We have every bit as much to 'sell' today, even though the fair is gone," he explained.

The Food Circus reopened, featuring expanded seating, more restaurants, and lower prices. The Seattle Art Museum welcomed visitors in its modern art pavilion. The International Fountain's dramatic punch was improved by the addition of 100 more water nozzles. Local folk musicians drew large crowds at weekly Seattle Center hootenannies, first outdoors and then in the Food Circus. Seattleites embraced their new Seattle Center and its largely free programming — but the bills continued to pile up.

The city helped, appropriating $125,000 to aid the struggling fledgling in October 1963, but visitors to the center did not spend much money, and the underwriting campaign was yielding less than expected. One bright spot for the city was that the auditorium facilities along Mercer Street were enjoying active rental schedules.

SETTING THE STAGE One bright and promising moment during this period was the creation of the Seattle Repertory Theatre, whose first production opened in the Playhouse on November 13, 1963. Seattle businessman and arts patron Bagley Wright led the efforts of an influential group of theater aficionados.

"I was in charge of finding tenants for the buildings," Wright remembered many years later. "That's how the Rep, really, was born. We needed somebody to go in the Playhouse. Century 21 Center funded the theater in the early days ... and then we began to raise money independently."

In December 1963, Ewen Dingwall resigned as executive director of Century 21 Center, Inc. Ding was offered a new role as executive director of the HemisFair, a world's fair to take place in San Antonio, Texas, in 1968. Donald Foster replaced him as acting director but chose not to stay on. On May 1, 1964, former Seattle World's Fair Operations Director Maxwell Burland became executive director of Century 21 Center, Inc.

Developing the level of visitor traffic — and spending — that the center needed was proving difficult. Maybe a new name would help? The Seattle Center Advisory Commission summoned eight public relations and advertising firms and tossed them the challenge. Their top choice, Puget Gardens, was quickly heaped with public scorn. How about Queen City Center, one local wondered? Needleland? Space Center? Pleasure Island? Kennedy Park? Pacifica? Space Needle Park, some agreed, or Seattle Tivoli, a nod to Denmark's famous Tivoli Gardens. In the end, the name "Seattle Center," already in use, stuck. The naming question got people talking, though, and that was beneficial.

Maxwell Burland resigned as director of Century 21 Center in late August 1964 after less than four months on the job. Robert J. Williams, a loaned executive from Northwest Bell Telephone, replaced him.

SEATTLE STEPS IN By fall of 1964, Century 21 Center, Inc., told the Seattle City Council that it simply could not make ends meet. If Century 21 Center went bust, could the city take over the Monorail, the Fun Forest contracts, and existing food and merchandise concessions. The city was already operating the Playhouse, Opera House, Exhibition Hall, Arena, Coliseum, and the parking garage. Yes, the council felt, the city could take over.

The City of Seattle was Century 21 Center's largest creditor. After the city purchased its assets for $700,000, in spring of 1965, Century 21 Center paid off its other creditors and placed the rest of the money in a trust, from which their underwriters were to be repaid over several years. Century 21 Center's contracts

SEATTLE REPERTORY THEATRE

Founded in 1963 and originally housed in the Seattle World's Fair Playhouse (now home to Intiman Theatre), the Seattle Repertory Theatre is Seattle's flagship professional theater company. Over the course of the theater's long history, millions of Seattle Rep audience members have attended more than 300 different productions, including the debuts of almost 100 new works.

The company moved to the 842-seat Bagley Wright Theatre (named for its founding board member) in 1983, adding a second venue, the 282-seat Leo Kreielsheimer Theatre (the "Leo K") in 1996. Highly respected nationally for its artistic excellence and leadership in the theatrical field, Seattle Repertory Theatre was honored with a Tony Award for Outstanding Regional Theatre in 1990.

STUART VAUGHAN, *Artistic Director* • WILLIAM S. TAYLOR, *General Manager*

NORTHWEST FOLKLIFE FESTIVAL

One of the largest folklife celebrations in North America, Northwest Folklife Festival was founded in 1972 and was the second postfair event (after Bumbershoot) to utilize the entire Seattle Center campus. Blanketing the campus with color, music, exhibits, films, crafts, and delicious tastes each Memorial Day weekend, Northwest Folklife celebrates folk culture with help from 7,000 participants in more than 1,000 performances on 27 indoor and outdoor stages.

Northwest Folklife philosophy considers that everyone is a bearer of folk arts and believes it is as important to participate in the arts as to observe them. A beloved tradition for people of all ages, Northwest Folklife encourages individuals and communities to celebrate, share, and sustain the vitality of folk, ethnic, and traditional arts for the present and the future.

with the city were relinquished, as were its agreements with concessionaires and other operators. The city hired consultants to manage the transition and empowered Greater Seattle, Inc., to take over Seattle Center promotional activities.

With the city's financial backing, Seattle Center settled in for the long haul with former auditorium manager Don Johnston as director and began the work of balancing the needs of Seattle's increasingly diverse constituency. From this point on, the name "Seattle Center" was used for both the physical site and its business operations.

Special Events Director Louis Larsen was hired as a consultant to help generate interest in the new Seattle Center, and he planned some spectacular events: a firefighter show with magnesium fire and screaming women being rescued; a week of Nordic events, including a ski jump off the Coliseum roof that drew a crowd of 50,000.

A NEW DECADE In fall 1970, Mayor Wes Uhlman appointed Jack Fearey, former KING 5 TV program director, to replace Don Johnston as the center's executive director.

Seattle Center greatly benefited from a $2.4 million federal economic development grant in 1972. The grant facilitated some much-needed redevelopment of fair-era buildings, making them suitable for year-round programming.

But the federal grant met only a fraction of the center's needs. In 1973, the Seattle Center Advisory Commission sent Mayor Uhlman and the city council a report stating that buildings at Seattle Center had reached a "desperate state of deterioration." The center needed money to make repairs and needed it quickly, because ordinary preventive maintenance had gone unfunded and thus neglected for so long. "The commission wishes to bring to your attention and to the attention of the public," commission Chair Dr. James L. Wilson told the mayor and the council, "the urgency to reverse the erosion of the Center before it collapses."

The Food Circus in the old armory was remodeled in 1974, reopening as Seattle Center House. Part of the building was converted for use as a conference center. A new ventilation system was installed, new skylights brightened the atrium space, and ramps and new floor surfaces improved access. Concession stands were remodeled, new sit-down restaurants were created, and a covered walkway from the Monorail terminal to the Center House and the three-block walkway from the Center House to the Mercer Street theaters was constructed.

SHOWING ITS AGE In 1975, Seattle voters passed a $5.6 million tax levy to finance the repair and ongoing maintenance of all major buildings on the Seattle Center campus, the first of several occasions when Seattleites opened their wallets in support. Improvements included replacing the Coliseum's deteriorating concrete roof; repairing the area surrounding the International Fountain; replacing the flooring of the Exhibition Hall; making repairs in the Fun Forest area; updating electrical, ventilation, and plumbing systems; recarpeting and reupholstering in the Opera House; installing new seats in the Playhouse; repairing leaks to many buildings; repairing the ice-making machinery in the Arena; and many other much-needed refurbishments throughout the site.

These repairs helped, but the decade-plus of deferred maintenance continued to take a toll. Fifteen years after the fair, in a September 1977 election, the Seattle City Council asked voters to approve a $19 million bond issue for capital improvements to upgrade and complete the center. "The Center is the

ROCKIN' THE COLISEUM

Rock 'n' roll may not have had much of a presence at Century 21, but two years after the fair ended the Seattle Center Coliseum welcomed its first major rock concert, a visit from The Beatles. On August 24, 1964, the lads from Liverpool played in front of 14,300 screaming fans. The Fab Four returned in 1966 for two more shows in the venue, bringing in a gross take of $118,071, at the time the largest single-day's gross income for any entertainment show in Seattle history.

Over the years, the Coliseum — and later KeyArena — has hosted numerous bands and musicians, including The Who, Led Zeppelin, the Rolling Stones, Jimi Hendrix, James Brown, Elvis Presley, Linda Ronstadt, David Bowie, Pink Floyd, the Grateful Dead, Queen, Heart, Van Halen, Bruce Springsteen, Metallica, and Pearl Jam.

SEATTLE SUPERSONICS

When the Washington State Coliseum was built for the world's fair, Seattle had never had a major league sports team. But hopes were high that one day it would and that the new arena would become the team's home. Those dreams came true in 1967 after the National Basketball Association decided to expand into eight new cities.

Team owners named their new franchise after the supersonic transport — a fast and high-flying jet plane of the future that was then under development at Boeing. But whereas the SST never left the runway, the SuperSonics (as they were soon called) took off and soared to great heights, eventually winning the NBA Championship in 1979.

Ownership changed over the years, until the team ended up in the hands of a consortium led by Oklahoma City businessman Clay Bennett, who moved the SuperSonics to that city in 2008 and renamed the team the Oklahoma City Thunder.

BUMBERSHOOT

Founded in 1971, Bumbershoot is North America's largest urban arts festival, drawing more than 150,000 visitors to Seattle Center each year over the Labor Day weekend. It was the first event to utilize the entire Seattle Center campus since the close of the Seattle World's Fair. Known first simply as Festival '71 and Festival '72, the event was christened Bumbershoot in 1973.

Bumbershoot showcases musicians, artists, actors, acrobats, and all manner of other performers on 20 unique indoor and outdoor stages across the Seattle Center campus. For many Seattleites, Bumbershoot is a favorite way to end the summer.

Anniversaries and Observances

During its first 50 years, Seattle Center observed anniversaries and evolved as a public gathering place during times of joy and grief. Here are some highlights:

1968 On April 7, 1968, more than 8,000 people, including Governor Dan Evans, march from the Central Area to Memorial Stadium to mourn the April 4 assassination in Memphis, Tennessee, of civil rights leader Martin Luther King.

1977 Seattle Center hosts a four-day celebration of the 15th anniversary of the fair, complete with films from 1962, exhibits of fair memorabilia, and free lessons teaching teens more accustomed to doing the bump and the hustle how to swivel their hips and do the Twist.

1982 Seattle Center Foundation and the Seattle Center Advisory Commission observe the fair's 20th anniversary by instituting a yearly recognition of volunteers whose work contributed significantly to the success of the world's fair or Seattle Center. The first three recipients are the late Joe Gandy, Civic Center Advisory Commission Director Harold Shefelman, and the late J. D. "Dorm" Braman, Seattle's mayor from 1964 to 1969.

1983 It's the 21st anniversary of Century 21 — and the 21st birthday of Jamie Williams, who was born just after midnight on April 21, 1962, leading the *Seattle Post-Intelligencer* to dub her "Seattle's Century 21 Baby." Jamie and her family celebrate as guests of the Space Needle restaurant, where Jamie blows out candles on a huge cake.

1987 World's fair public relations mastermind Jay Rockey and Unico Properties Director Don Covey cochair a six-month series of events to celebrate the 25th anniversary of Century 21.

1992 By the fair's 30th anniversary, many projects it seeded — from cultural institutions to festivals to the Monorail and the Space Needle to Seattle Center itself — have become civic icons, part of how Seattle defines itself and how the world defines Seattle.

1994 Since the earliest days of Seattle Center, area residents have been drawn to the site as a public gathering place in times of joy and in times of sorrow. When the body of Aberdeen native and grunge rock legend Kurt Cobain is discovered in his Madrona neighborhood home on April 8, 1994, a suicide, thousands of fans gather for a memorial vigil at Seattle Center.

1999 On April 21, 1999, the 37th anniversary of Century 21 Exposition's opening day, the Space Needle is named an official City of Seattle historic landmark. It is the first structure approved for landmark status on the basis of all six possible designation criteria, ranging from architectural merit to historical and physical prominence.

2001 A memorial service following the September 11 terrorist attacks, scheduled for three hours, became a five-day outpouring of grief in which 75,000 visitors laid more than one million flowers at the International Fountain.

Pacific Northwest's finest outdoor-indoor family rec room," one Seattle Center official told *The Seattle Times*. "Imagine what your family rec room would look like if over three million people went through it every year for over a decade."

Seattle voters agreed. The funding facilitated major improvements: the purchase of the Nile Temple, the construction of the Seattle Repertory Theatre facility, and the addition of a performance space in the Center House basement, among many other renovations and repairs.

After the bond measure was approved, but before construction started, Seattle Center hosted the Treasures of Tutankhamen exhibition, which not only drew droves of Washington residents but helped put the old fairgrounds back on the national map of travel destinations. Seattle was one of only six American cities chosen to show the landmark exhibition of artifacts from the tomb of Tutankhamen, Egypt's boy king. King Tut also brought a familiar face back to Seattle Center grounds: Ewen Dingwall managed the exhibition. During its four-month stay in 1978, the King Tut exhibition drew 1.3 million visitors. This was the largest crowd to attend a single postfair attraction at Seattle Center.

BUILDING A FOUNDATION   As part of the 15th anniversary observance, Seattle Center Foundation was incorporated on May 6, 1977, as a nonprofit organization by Century 21 veterans Laurene Gandy, Edward Carlson, C. David Hughbanks, and longtime civic arts activist Patricia Stewart Phelps. Seattle Center Foundation's purpose is to promote and funnel foundation, governmental, and public contributions to the center and to encourage support for the center through public gifts and bequests.

In 1982, as the world's fair marked its 20th anniversary, Seattle Center Foundation and the Seattle Center Advisory Commission instituted an annual recognition of volunteers whose work had contributed significantly to the success of the world's fair or of Seattle Center. The first three Seattle Center Legion of Honor Award recipients were the late Joe Gandy, Civic Center Advisory Commission Director Harold Shefelman, and the late J. D. "Dorm" Braman, Seattle's mayor from 1964 to 1969. Braman had served on the Washington World's Fair Commission and had been instrumental in getting the Space Needle built and in developing solutions for legal questions surrounding remodeling the Civic Auditorium into the Opera House. As mayor during the earliest days of Seattle Center, Braman had resolved numerous issues in the transition from fairgrounds to civic center.

By August 1982, the center was facing an $850,000 cash shortage. Revenue depended heavily on good summer weather to stimulate outdoor crowds, but a gloomy wet season had kept crowds low, and this came on

The Seattle Art Museum's King Tut exhibition at Seattle Center in 1978 drew more visitors than any event since the fair.

PACIFIC NORTHWEST BALLET

The Pacific Northwest Dance Association, originally an offshoot of the Seattle Opera, was founded in 1972 and had its own first independent season in the Opera House in 1973. The company became an independent organization in 1977 and was renamed Pacific Northwest Ballet in 1978. In 1977 Kent Stowell and Francia Russell joined the company as artistic directors, guiding the company for the next 28 years. During their tenure, Pacific Northwest Ballet and its professional training school built a highly respected international reputation. The 45-member company's reputation for excellence has continued under the artistic leadership of Peter Boal.

top of a national recession. Mayor Charles Royer and his staff pulled together a $1 million rescue plan: unpaid furloughs for most employees, some layoffs, shorter operating hours on the Monorail, and an emergency $500,000 appropriation by the city council. Union members affected by the plan agreed to its stipulations, which covered union and nonunion employees and managers from Seattle Center Director Jack Fearey on down.

The city council approved only $50,000 of the appropriation amount and undertook an immediate retreat to examine Seattle Center budgeting problems in detail.

DINGWALL RETURNS In November, Fearey tendered his resignation after a 12-year tenure, telling *The Seattle Times*, "It's time for a new leader." Steady hands were ready: Ewen Dingwall agreed to serve as interim director of Seattle Center. His position quickly became permanent.

Dingwall's daughter, Emily Easton, remembered her father's pleasure at being asked by Mayor Royer to assume the job: "He really enjoyed being back and working at the center, where his heart really was."

Dingwall reorganized top management, began the lengthy process of replacing the aged phone system that served the buildings, and brought everything from floor wax to light bulbs to programming under his fiscal lens. He brought seasoned city finance manager Kathy Scanlan as his assistant director.

The news media, Ding said, had overstated fiscal troubles and conditions at the center. "I'm tired of the apocalyptic headlines," he told the *Seattle Post-Intelligencer*. "We are busy selling the idea that the Seattle Center is a healthy place."

STRATEGIZING PARTNERSHIPS Dingwall rejected the very notion that Seattle Center could be self-supporting. One significant reason for this was that major nonprofit building tenants received rent discounts, which functioned as indirect city support for the arts. Many merchants in the Center House owed back rent, the Fun Forest needed overhaul, and the underused Memorial Stadium remained an obstacle to full site utilization. Most other Seattle Center buildings — especially the Arena, Exhibition Hall, conference rooms, and State Flag Plaza (the Plaza of the States during the world's fair) — were underutilized and thus were hurting the bottom line. The two most lucrative enterprises on center grounds — the Pacific Science Center and the Space Needle — were privately owned.

On the plus side, the Seattle Rep's new Bagley Wright Theatre was drawing crowds, and the Seattle Opera, the Seattle Symphony, and the Pacific Northwest Ballet — all Opera House tenants — had strong support.

In May 1984, Seattle's public broadcast television station, KCTS Channel 9, announced plans to build its headquarters on the old Show Street site at the corner of Mercer Street and 5th Avenue N. Built with funding that included a major gift from the Seattle Rotary Club Number 4, the new facility allowed KCTS to unify offices, which previously had been scattered across the University of Washington campus.

THE IMAGINEERS The search for an enduring, more financially stable vision for Seattle Center led in 1986 to an unusual chapter in the site's postfair development. That year, Seattle Center leaders began preliminary discussions with Walt Disney Imagineering, Inc. The Imagineers were a team of architects, landscape architects, artists, animators, engineers, sculptors, and planners assembled by Walt Disney in 1952 to develop Disneyland. Until 1984, when Disney came under new corporate ownership, the Imagineers' work had been confined to projects directly related to Disney parks in Anaheim, Orlando, and Tokyo. Their new direction was to pursue non-Disney projects — and Seattle Center was to be the first.

Despite critics who decried the move as "Mickey Mouse," the city council hired Disney and its financial consultant, Harrison Price, to produce a complete study of the Seattle Center site and programming, design concepts, facility utilization, circulation patterns and entrances, the market for various concepts, and economic feasibility.

While the Imagineers were at work, the milestone 25th anniversary of the Seattle World's Fair focused much additional attention on the center, its purpose in the civic scheme, and its future.

COMING OF AGE On April 6, 1987, just as anniversary celebrations were about to begin, the Seattle City Council adopted a list of general policies and goals for the redevelopment of Seattle Center. Affirming the old fairgrounds' role as the city's civic center, the goals stated that it should also be the focal point for public art, culture, and education; that it should be an integral part of Seattle's parks, recreation, and entertainment

opposite Bumbershoot (seen here in 1976) has been the Pacific Northwest's annual goodbye to summer since 1971.

INTIMAN THEATRE

From its inception in 1972 in a tiny 70-seat theater in Kirkland to its present operation in the 480-seat Playhouse Theatre, Intiman (the name is an approximation of the Swedish word intim, meaning "intimate") has steadily grown into one of the nation's leading regional theaters. It has developed innovative programs that forge increasingly strong connections within the larger Puget Sound community and that encourage dialogue about the role of the theatrical experience in American life, helping the public recognize the narrative line between past and present. In 2006 Intiman Theatre was awarded the Regional Theatre Tony Award, the highest awards honor an American regional theater can attain.

below Groundbreaking ceremonies
for KCTS 9.

attractions; and that it should be accessible to people of all ages, backgrounds, and physical conditions. It was a solid set of goals, heartfelt and attainable — a good beginning — and a fitting tribute to the energy and dedication of the men and women who had worked so hard to make the Seattle World's Fair/Seattle Center project a reality.

A statewide committee, cochaired by Century 21 public relations wizard Jay Rockey and Unico Properties Chief Executive Officer Donald Covey, organized the 25th anniversary celebration, which took place across the entire Seattle Center campus over six months. Hundreds of volunteers, donations from local companies, and thoughtful leadership from fair veterans like Eddie Carlson, Laurene Gandy, Ewen Dingwall, Clayton Young, Willis Camp, Marlene Jones, and Louis Larsen and the center's special events staff members contributed to the commemoration's success.

On April 1, 1988, Ewen Dingwall retired as Seattle Center director. Now 75 years old, Ding had guided the joint fair/civic center, and later Seattle Center, through crucial years, putting his permanent mark on the place. In his honor, the courtyard outside the Intiman Theatre (built as the world's fair Playhouse) was renamed the Dingwall Courtyard.

OF MOUSE AND MEN Mayor Charles Royer asked longtime fair and Seattle Center player C. David Hughbanks to shoulder Seattle Center acting director duties, assisted by deputy mayor Carol Lewis. From February to September, Hughbanks and Lewis oversaw the difficult process of dealing with Disney, trying to prod the organization into producing a finished product. These were very difficult months — so much uncertainty was making staff, Center-based organizations, and city officials unsettled and uneasy.

In May, the Imagineers presented the Seattle City Council with three plans, the result of their $500,000 study. Plan one called for leaving the center basically as it was. Plan two suggested that it be transformed into a regional family entertainment center. Plan three mandated passive programming — in other words, a park. None of the plans included hard cost estimates or explored economic justifications. Seattle was distinctly underwhelmed.

KCTS 9

KCTS 9, the Pacific Northwest's first educational television station, went on the air on December 7, 1954, broadcasting from the University of Washington campus. In 1970 the station affiliated with the Public Broadcasting System. KCTS 9 built studios on the Seattle Center campus in 1986, ending its affiliation with the University of Washington the following year. KCTS is viewer-supported, receiving contributions from throughout Washington State and from across Canada. KCTS 9's mission is "to improve the quality of life in the communities we serve by providing meaningful programming on air, online and in the community that informs, involves and inspires."

"What has happened here in Seattle is the crown jewel as far as I'm concerned. Nothing I've ever been involved with anyplace else compares to this one."

EWEN DINGWALL ON CENTURY 21 AND SEATTLE CENTER

The city council added strong language to the second phase of Disney's contract, requiring revenue projections and financial analysis for the many proposed changes. As that phase was beginning, word came that (since the contract for Euro Disney, near Paris, had recently been signed) Disney would no longer serve outside clients, although it would complete projects already under contract. When Disney turned in its final reimagining, the estimated price tag was an unrealistic $270 million to $335 million.

ENTER VIRGINIA ANDERSON At this critical juncture, in June 1988, Mayor Charles Royer named Seattle Housing Authority Board of Commissioners Chair Virginia Anderson as the new Seattle Center director. It was an inspired choice — Anderson would prove herself a steady visionary during the center's next 18 years, a leader who listened. Anderson's first task was to develop alternatives to the Disney plans, and in April 1989 she revealed three possible options for Seattle Center development over the next 25 to 30 years.

Like her predecessors, Anderson stressed the critical need to update and improve infrastructure on the 74-acre campus. "No matter what plan is adopted," she told the *Seattle Post-Intelligencer*, "it's the unseen things about the Seattle Center that really need addressing." As in the past, Seattleites remained active, vocal contributors to the planning process, even floating various ideas of their own. "Everyone has an idea about what the Seattle Center is," Anderson told the *Weekly*. "Seattle Center is hallowed ground. ... The Center is Seattle. The image of a city is its public spaces — the Pike Place Market, the waterfront, Seattle Center. What these spaces are says a lot about who you are."

MASTER PLAN The Seattle Center 2000 Master Plan, a $167 million makeover, debuted in spring 1990. The plan retained most of the center's existing buildings; added a Children's Complex, concert hall, remodeled Center House, and upgraded Memorial Stadium; improved facilities for the Intiman Theatre, Pacific Northwest Ballet offices and studios, Pottery Northwest, and the Seattle Repertory Theatre; and relocated the Fun Forest to the old Metro bus-barn property, among other changes.

Public involvement in the development of the master plan was extensive, including a detailed display at the music and arts fair Bumbershoot staffed by Seattle Center employees ready to answer questions, a questionnaire completed by more than 500 people, a detailed display in the Municipal Building, a two-week fully staffed open house at Center House, and breakfast meetings with business leaders.

THE CHILDREN'S MUSEUM, SEATTLE

The Children's Museum, Seattle, opened in a storefront in Pioneer Square in 1981, moved to the Center House in 1985, expanded in 1989, and expanded again in 1995. Children and their parents and caregivers enjoy 32,000 square feet of kid-sized learning environments — a Mexican restaurant, a theater and box office, exhibits demonstrating hands-on health and scientific principles, and traveling exhibits. Discovery Bay, an environment designed to stimulate the very youngest visitors; Cog City, a maze of lifts, levels, and tubes that teach cause and effect; an art studio; and a global village and mountain forest are among the Children's Museum's many family-friendly offerings.

GIANT MAGNET

Founded in 1986 Giant Magnet's International Children's Festival (formerly known as Seattle International Children's Festival) delighted fans for more than two decades. More than 750,000 children from schools across Washington, Oregon, and Western Canada saw some of the world's finest performing artists. They learned about culture and geography, history and humanity, and about one another. In a world of differences, Giant Magnet helped to advance cultural awareness and understanding through the magic of the performing arts. Giant Magnet's 25th festival in 2011 was its farewell gift to the community.

From this process, center staff (including the Seattle Center Employee Advisory Committee), the Seattle Center Advisory Commission, and the Seattle Design Advisory Commission learned that diversity was the center's hallmark strength, that Seattle Center was an active urban place whose outdoor and indoor spaces combine to celebrate the region, and that it was the combined energy of center organizations, activities, facilities, and public spaces that made the center the region's premier gathering place.

The Seattle Center 2000 plan clearly articulated the deliberation with which its authors sought to maintain "the Center's role as providing opportunities for our diverse and creative communities. ... It stems from the recognition that at the inception of Seattle Center, even our most visionary community leaders could not have guessed what we would become. Likewise, it is not up to us to dictate the limits of the Center's growth, but to nurture a vital, exciting web of activities for our community in the future."

FINDING FUNDING Seattle and King County officials patched together a pair of property-tax levies totaling $143.2 million to pay for Seattle Center renovations and to repair five Seattle neighborhood community centers. When the levy vote was finally taken on May 28, 1991, Seattle voters approved their share of the renovation, but King County voters rejected their measure, which included the lion's share of capital improvements. It was another bandage — not the desperately needed major surgery.

The state pitched in another $8.5 million out of capital funds, but center officials still faced a mountain of difficulty — with so many repairs needed, which were the top priorities? Refurbishing the Opera House alone would cost $8 million — inspections of exterior mortar had revealed a rear wall in such bad shape that bricks were actually falling down. Repairs to the Mercer Street garage were penciling out to twice the initial estimates.

The roof on the old Blue Spruce (still providing office space) leaked badly; replacing it would cost $90,000. The Northwest Rooms needed renovating. The Coliseum's $2.2 million in repairs were already scheduled. The Seattle Children's Theatre was ready to break ground for its new facility, but some of the funding was to have come from the county levy. Pacific Northwest Ballet, already well along with converting the upper portion of the Exhibition Hall into studios and office space, had also counted on the county levy and was scrambling to raise funds from private sources.

TURNING POINTS The demolition of the fair's Domestic Commerce and Industry Pavilion strikingly opened the campus along Broad Street, allowing for the creation of Broad Street Green, stimulating privately funded projects, and improving one of the center's most visible entry portals. This was a major turning point in the campus's evolution from a constrained property to a more fluid, cohesive series of indoor and outdoor rooms linked by the site's grid — the ghostly whisper of former city streets.

By 1993, the Pacific Northwest Ballet project was complete and was lauded nationwide as a premier facility for dance. Seattle Children's Theatre's building also opened to praise. The Seattle City Council approved plans to make over the Coliseum — a $104 million project. And, with the approval of the Seattle City Council, Microsoft Corporation cofounder Paul Allen had announced plans to build a museum on center grounds dedicated to preserving the memory of rock icon and Seattle native Jimi Hendrix. The Experience Music Project's mission eventually expanded to include all Northwest rock music.

In October 1995, Seattle applauded the $198 million worth of renovations throughout the center — the first results of the Seattle Center 2000 Master Plan. The rebuilt KeyArena — essentially a new building

above left Alexander Leiberman's *Olympic Iliad* (1984) provides a striking focal point on the Broad Street Green.

above right Virginia Anderson, Seattle Center director from 1988 to April 2006, shepherded the organization through a period of tremendous growth.

opposite International Fountain, Fisher Pavilion, and north Seattle Center campus, as pictured in an architectural illustration by Stephen Bower.

opposite left The Fun Forest hugged the base of the Space Needle from just after the fair until 2011.

above right Ice skating on the rink created inside the Fisher Pavilion is a (rainless) winter treat.

below right The Police played KeyArena in 2007, part of their reunion concert tour.

within the Coliseum that retained the iconic roofline — welcomed sports and concert fans and improved the aesthetics and flow around the building. The greatly expanded Seattle Children's Museum invited kids and their parents. Center House food concessions on the floor above the museum had been spiffed up.

There was more. The completely rebuilt International Fountain provided both accessible interactive water play and a perch for contemplative respite. Even the Fun Forest had been cleaned up and now offered new rides. A third of the overall budget had been contributed by the private sector — a heartening signal of a growing public understanding that public/private/nonprofit partnerships would be key to future Seattle Center growth. *The Seattle Times* summed up the changes: "With strong direction from the passionate and driven zeal of Director Virginia Anderson and a variety of organizations and institutions, Seattle Center has come alive. It is fun and lively. Like a fine old piece of familiar furniture that has been lovingly restored and embellished, the place simply shines."

GROWING PAINS Still, there was much to be done. In 1996, a major assessment of the aging Opera House placed a $95 million price tag on full repair and seismic retrofits. Cramped backstage areas, fire safety issues, rusty pipes, inadequate restroom facilities, and earthquake worries: The Opera House's laundry list of problems led Corporate Council for the Arts Director Peter Donnelly to quip that perhaps the dim lighting in the venue's lobby was a plus, since it hid the tape patching the vast expanse of shabby, worn-out carpet.

Although public funding was critical to survival, by now Seattle Center was attracting equally important contributions from foundations and private donors. The Seattle area was experiencing a huge growth spurt of innovation marked by the arrival of such iconic companies as Microsoft Corporation, Amazon.com, McCaw Cellular Communications, Inc. (later AT&T Wireless), and Starbucks Coffee Company, and the corresponding creation of enormous private wealth. By 1997, fully half the building money spent on center projects during the decade had come from foundations and private donors. "Every project has come together differently," Virginia Anderson told *The Seattle Times*. "In several cases it helped to have the public portion (of funding) figured out first so when we approached private sources they knew how much government was participating."

The Pacific Science Center's 400-seat Boeing IMAX Theater and Ackerley Family Exhibit Gallery opened in 1998. The glass-walled gallery and futuristic frosted-white bubble transformed the building's Broad Street facade, adding a lush tropical butterfly house, exhibit space, and a state-of-the-art film venue to the Science Center's many attractions.

The Space Needle added a two-story glass structure surrounding the lower portion of its three support legs. This provided entrances designed to protect crowds from inclement weather, check-in facilities for the restaurant, and commodious retail space.

PRODUCTIVE PARTNERSHIPS In 1999, Seattle voters renewed the 1991 Seattle Center levy. Some of the money was earmarked for Opera House renovations. These public funds were greatly enhanced by Seattle Center Foundation's first major fund-raising effort, which resulted in a stunning new campus treasure for the Seattle Opera and Pacific Northwest Ballet: Marion Oliver McCaw Hall. Other marriages of public and private funds facilitated the replacement of the fair-era Plaza of the States with the sleek multiuse Fisher Pavilion; a reconfigured Mercer Arena; the addition of the playful,

Burning an enormous papier-mâché egg stuffed with New Year's wishes provided a dramatic climax to "At the Crossroads: A Fire Ceremony," and welcomed the new millennium with a physical embodiment of transformation.

peaceful Kreielsheimer Promenade as an enhanced entry portal to the campus; and development of further green space. Seattle Center was poised for major evolution, moving into the maturity of its long-held role as Seattle's beloved civic living room.

On April 21, 1999, the 37th anniversary of the Century 21 Exposition's opening day, the Space Needle was named an official City of Seattle historic landmark. It was the first structure approved for landmark status on the basis of all six possible designation criteria, ranging from architectural merit to historical and physical prominence.

ENTER CENTURY 21 As the decade drew to a close, violent clashes during protests against the World Trade Organization ministerial conference in Seattle in December 1999 combined with the threat of terrorism to put a damper on millennium celebrations planned at Seattle Center. Mayor Paul Schell and city police were still reeling from the WTO, which had given Seattle an international black eye, when a 35-year-old Algerian named Ahmed Ressam was arrested at Port Angeles as he tried to enter the United States from Canada with what authorities said were bomb components (he later was imprisoned for engaging in terrorist activities in association with Islamic extremist Osama bin Laden). Ressam reportedly had made a reservation at a motel near Seattle Center. Schell decided to take no chances. He cancelled the scheduled December 31 millennium party.

Although the new millennium did not officially begin until January 1, 2001, most people marked December 31, 1999, as the final day of the twentieth century. Seattleites and their Seattle Center stood at last on the brink of the future the Seattle World's Fair had heralded: Century 21.

To the world, Seattle now meant computers and the rapid technological transformation associated with them. It meant exciting music, from grunge to classical. It meant groundbreaking new theater, dazzling operatic productions, high-caliber classical and modern dance, and world-class art. It meant coffee, rain, salmon, books, green countryside, tall mountains — easily identifiable icons of the Pacific Northwest. Much of what made the city "Seattle" was celebrated, performed, contemplated, cogitated, or appreciated at Seattle Center.

City of Seattle Historic Landmarks at Seattle Center

Center House

Kobe Bell

Seattle Center Monorail

The city was long past its raucous gold rush childhood and long past its starry optimistic adolescence. It now faced maturity. How its citizens would meet this transition, how they in their great diversity would interact and find common ground for civic good, would be the twenty-first century's real challenge.

Like an odometer rolling over, the calendars changed from 1999 to 2000. On March 19, more than 12,000 people gathered at Seattle Center to watch artist Carl Smool ignite 17 giant sculptures — an event originally planned for the 1999 New Year's Eve festivities. Smool's burn was inspired by Las Fallas, a Valencian spring-welcoming festival. The festival titled At the Crossroads: A Fire Ceremony, involved incineration of large papier-mâché figures including a 16-foot-tall Four Horsemen of the Apocalypse and 12 animals from around the world. The centerpiece was a giant egg stuffed with thousands of slips of paper bearing New Year's wishes submitted by people who had passed through Seattle Center. The entire menagerie went up in flames, a glowing symbol of transformation.

ROCK AND ROLL Nearby, the finishing touches were being added to another harbinger of change, this time architectural: Paul Allen's Experience Music Project — EMP. Designed by celebrated architect Frank Gehry, the museum's undulating exterior featured an ensemble of bright multicolored reflective surfaces. To some, the building's crumpled appearance summoned images of a smashed guitar or a discarded cigarette package. To one journalist, the Space Needle had dropped her dress. Designed with the aid of aerospace

"Seattle is incredible in the competence of its volunteer community. I think there's been a very high standard set, and our project helped to set a high standard. It's a very, very different place."

EWEN DINGWALL ON SEATTLE

Seattle Mural

Pacific Science Center

Space Needle

software, the building's innovative construction techniques forced its materials to behave in ways beyond the bounds of any other structure to date.

The building garnered mixed reviews, but some critics thought the jangly mass of colors and forms was a perfect setting for a museum devoted to rock and roll music. When the EMP opened on June 23, 2000, visitors enjoyed an extensive collection of rock memorabilia, primarily focused on musicians from the Northwest, including Jimi Hendrix, the Kingsmen, Heart, Nirvana, and Pearl Jam. The museum also boasted a bevy of high-tech multimedia displays.

The real twenty-first century arrived on January 1, 2001, and huge crowds gathered at Seattle Center to officially welcome the new millennium. The Space Needle, happy to renew the annual New Year's Eve tradition after the previous year's cancellation, lit the night sky with a record 2,000 fireworks.

9/11 Over the years, Seattle Center has clearly been the region's nexus for joyful celebration. In times of grief, the civic center has provided solace and a place to gather for community solidarity. In the days following the terrorist attacks on September 11, 2001, a three-hour memorial flower vigil was scheduled at the International Fountain.

Crowds spontaneously arrived a day early to share their collective grief, and by Saturday more than 30,000 people had come to lay flowers within the fountain's basin. The numbers kept growing and Seattle Center extended the vigil, which eventually lasted five days. During that time more than 75,000 people brought one million flowers to this historic event. Afterward, the flowers were composted as a symbol of hope and renewal. Bags of the mulch were given away on the one-year anniversary of the event, and half were used in a memorial garden at the center.

The twenty-first century was beginning quite differently than Century 21 fairgoers had imagined. As the Pacific Northwest community faced an uncertain future, a Seattle Center discovery yielded an intriguing view of the past.

BURIED TREASURES During the Civic Auditorium's prefair conversion into the Opera House, construction workers discovered a small time capsule that had been interred behind a plaque within its walls just before the auditorium opened in 1928. The box contained items related to Seattle's history — some dating as far back as the 1800s. Then, on or around April 9, 1962, world's fair officials had added another box, filled with new items pertaining to Century 21. The original time capsule was once again sealed behind the plaque, along with its new partner.

In 2002, prior to the $127 million transformation of the Opera House into what would become Marion Oliver McCaw Hall, the time capsules were discovered again. The contents were unveiled as part of the groundbreaking ceremonies for the hall's reconstruction on January 17, 2002.

Some of the 75-year-old items included rare sweetbriar rose seeds from the garden of Louisa Boren Denny, who with her husband, David Denny, helped found Seattle and had owned the future Seattle Center property; an original 1889 plat map of Denny family land donated to the city; and Seattle newspapers dated May 18, 1928. The 1962 artifacts included newspapers, an invitation to the Opera House grand opening, and an envelope containing one world's fair trade dollar. And there was a folder containing letters dated 1962 from each department of the City of Seattle, in which the department heads wrote of their hopes for the future.

THE CURTAIN RISES AGAIN Thus grounded in history, work began on the hall's next incarnation. In 1999 Seattle voters had approved a levy dedicating $29 million toward the refurbishment, to which the city council added $9 million in bonds. Craig McCaw of McCaw Cellular Communications and his brothers Bruce, John, and Keith gave $20 million in honor of their mother's lifelong support of arts in the community. At the time, this was the largest arts or cultural capital gift ever made in the region, and it also was linked to Century 21: the brothers' late father, J. Elroy McCaw, had been one of the fair's vice presidents. The McCaw gift was supplemented by the Kreielsheimer Foundation's substantial gift of $10 million.

left Bruce and Jolene McCaw during a celebration held in the Marion Oliver McCaw Hall construction site.

right The Space Needle floats benevolently over Marion Oliver McCaw Hall's glass facade.

Designed by LMN Architects, the new structure saved about 30 percent of the original building, including the auditorium ceiling. Staggered seats and a more steeply raked auditorium improved sight lines, and the hall's sidewalls were moved 30 feet closer, creating intimacy while preserving the acoustics of the old building.

Other improvements included a five-story lobby with a floor-to-ceiling curved glass wall, state-of-the-art backstage technology, a better backstage and orchestra pit, a new lecture hall, a coat check, a gift shop, and café. The new building included the latest in seismic safety and was fully accessible to patrons with disabilities.

Marion Oliver McCaw Hall opened on June 28, 2003, with a gala "The Curtain Rises" party, which included performances by the major resident organizations: Pacific Northwest Ballet and its orchestra and the Seattle Opera. The following day, McCaw Hall welcomed the public with free performances by local musicians and dancers.

GOING GREEN   Another new building on the campus also received accolades in 2003: the American Institute of Architects named Fisher Pavilion at Seattle Center one of the Top Ten Green Projects of the year.

Fisher Pavilion opened in September 2002, and replaced Century 21's last "temporary" structure — the Plaza of the States — which had outlasted its original six-month life span by 39 years. Designed by the Miller/Hull Partnership, the 21,000-square-foot exhibition hall is buried on three sides, allowing for 19,000 square feet of usable roof plaza.

Its innovative design made Fisher Pavilion a centerpiece for Seattle's green building program. Because the building is below ground, and was built using high-mass concrete, the heating savings were considerable — more than 13,000 BTUs per square foot per year. The building also boasted low-demand plumbing fixtures as well as a highly efficient irrigation system, which optimized flow to garden areas by monitoring a central automated weather station.

The building's footprint also opened up a major view corridor, connecting the Charlotte Martin Theatre (of the Seattle Children's Theatre) to the International Fountain, the Seattle Center theater district, and to vistas of the city and Queen Anne Hill beyond.

CHANGING TIMES But as Seattle Center welcomed bold new changes to its campus, it also faced challenges. By 2004, the center was again struggling with a mounting deficit, primarily due to sagging attendance at SuperSonics games in KeyArena, especially the luxury-suite rentals. At the same time, a steep interest payment was coming due on McCaw Hall.

To cushion against the deficit, in 2005 two Seattle Center parking lots were sold to housing developers for $7.6 million. The City of Seattle also sold a 12-acre Seattle Center parking lot on 5th Avenue N to the Bill & Melinda Gates Foundation, netting $27 million and a new underground parking garage as part of the deal. The foundation's mission of promoting global health and education would make them an excellent neighbor once they moved in next to Seattle Center in 2011.

Director Virginia Anderson announced her resignation effective April 3, 2006. Over a span of 18 years, Anderson brought about dramatic changes to the center by preserving the best aspects of the 1962 world's fair, developing many new arts, sports, and recreational facilities, broadening the center's ethnic programs, and uniting a strong constituency of groups and individuals in support of Seattle Center.

Hubert G. Locke — former dean of the Daniel J. Evans School of Public Affairs at the University of Washington — summed up the passion Anderson brought to her stewardship of Seattle Center in a column for the *Seattle Post-Intelligencer*: "That we have, in the heart of the city, this unique urban oasis where the elderly dance, children romp in the fountain or the Fun Forest, sports lovers cheer their favorites, theater goers enjoy good drama, with dance and musical offerings from rock to grand opera within a stone's

MONORAIL DREAMS

In 1962, the Seattle World's Fair Monorail was touted as the transportation solution for the upcoming century. Beginning in 1997, Seattle voters who remembered this dream threw their support behind a citywide monorail system. In 2002, planning began on the first stage of the system, a 14-mile Green Line that would run between Crown Hill and West Seattle, passing through Seattle Center.

The project had the support of many prominent community members and political figures, but as financial troubles grew so did its detractors. In 2005, following cost overruns and revenue shortfalls, Seattle voters killed the Seattle monorail project they had supported in four earlier votes.

FUN FOREST

The Fun Forest amusement park opened on the Gayway site soon after Century 21 ended. The rides were initially owned by Century 21 Center, Inc., the nonprofit organization that managed Seattle Center. Jerry and Beverly Mackey and their partners, Bill and Stella Aubin, secured the contract to operate the Fun Forest, purchasing the rides from Century 21 Center when that organization dissolved in late 1965. The Aubins' teenage daughter Stella helped out with the family business, as did her boyfriend, Steve Robertson, whom she later married. Robertson became the amusement park's manager in 1976.

Originally, the Fun Forest included three rides from the Gayway: the Wild Mouse roller coaster, the carousel, and the Space Wheel. A new Wild Mouse roller coaster and Ferris wheel opened in 1965, by which time 20 rides were in operation. Over the years, fun seekers welcomed other additions, such as the Galaxie roller coaster, the Rainbow Chaser, the Round Up, the Matterhorn, the Windstorm, and the Flight to Mars.

Even with updates and modernizations, by the start of the twenty-first century the Fun Forest was showing its age and had plenty of competition for leisure dollars. Ticket sales dropped, and the hours of operation were scaled back. In 2009, the amusement park's lease — which was initially set to expire in 2014 — was shortened in exchange for reduced rent, and the amusement park closed the following year.

above Fun Forest.

left: Eva Stejer, Marion Stejer, and Jeremy Korkikian-Hinklin experience sculpture joyfully atop the bronze whale that is part of Gloria Bornstein's *Neototems* (1995).

center Camille Little (20), Abby Bishop (2), Sue Bird (10), Lauren Jackson (15), and Svetlana Abrosimova (25) and their 2010 Seattle Storm teammates swept to victory as WNBA champions for the second time in franchise history.

right Native American storyteller Gene Tagaban, His Holiness the 14th Dalai Lama, and translator Thupten Jinpa at Children and Youth Day, April 11, 2008, at KeyArena, during a five-day citywide Seeds of Compassion conference.

throw of each other — much of this can be credited to the extraordinary leadership and managerial skill of a distinguished public servant who has presided over the Center for almost two decades."

During her tenure, Anderson oversaw creation and implementation of the Seattle Center 2000 Master Plan, which helped propel the center into the twenty-first century, especially through the construction or redevelopment of many of the center's iconic elements. But with the new century came new challenges, and a new longer-term plan was needed to accommodate dramatic neighborhood and regional changes, increased demands for environmental sustainability, and changing entertainment and market trends.

Seattle Mayor Greg Nickels appointed Seattle native Robert Nellams to fill Anderson's position. Nellams had joined Seattle Center in 1996 as director of patron services and was promoted to deputy director in 1998, a position he filled until he was named acting director. Nellams aimed to modernize the campus and increase its relevance to teenagers and young adults. He would be the driving force behind the Century 21 Master Plan that charted the center's future.

VOX POPULI In November 2006, Mayor Nickels appointed a 17-member citizens' committee to chart Seattle Center development for the next 20 years. Through a series of public meetings and online discussions, the aptly named Century 21 Committee first gathered input from Seattle citizens, community organizations, Seattle Center employees and resident organizations, commissions, and elected officials to determine what the public might want for the center's future.

The committee heard calls for more open space, more programs for young adults and children, more for the growing residential and working populations neighboring Seattle Center, and more amenities to make the center a place to visit often. The committee sought ways to unify the physical space and the center's purpose as an arts, recreational, and civic center at the core of the community. And it also took on the issue of Memorial Stadium, the missing piece in the center of the campus.

GAME OVER Work on the plan continued over the next year and a half, during which a new challenge arose with the loss of the SuperSonics, the center's anchor tenant. Trouble began after an ownership group led by Oklahoma businessman Clay Bennett purchased the team in 2006. Bennett claimed he wanted to keep the SuperSonics in Seattle — if a new modern arena was built and the state or city footed most of the bill.

In April 2007, after Governor Christine Gregoire refused to call a special legislative session to consider funding a new $500 million arena, Bennett immediately announced that the 2007–2008 basketball season would likely be the team's last in Seattle. The City of Seattle took Bennett to court, forcing him to honor the last two years of the team's lease with KeyArena, but Bennett wriggled out of the lease by agreeing to pay the city $45 million.

Since his appointment as Seattle Center director in 2006, Robert Nellams has worked to broaden the center's appeal to young people, who will help shape its mission in the coming decades.

The Century 21 Master Plan transforms Seattle Center campus from an occasional destination to Seattle's first option for activities of every kind, setting out a future that is vibrant with activity, flexible in order to accommodate change, open and welcoming, and sustainable in construction and design.

The Century 21 Master Plan sets these goals for Seattle Center, the City of Seattle, and the region:

- Enhance the position of Seattle Center as the nation's best gathering place
- Dramatically increase open space
- Connect Seattle Center facilities into a synergistic whole
- Provide capacity for existing and future arts, cultural, and recreational programs to be nurtured, grown, and developed

- Create program and design that captivates and attracts private funding partners
- Build on the history of Seattle Center while creating the flexible framework to provide for the needs of the future
- Integrate environmental sustainability in design, construction and operations to reduce energy demands and serve as a model for sustainable development
- Enrich and connect to the fabric of adjacent neighborhoods through welcoming design, programming and operations
- Increase accessibility to the center of the grounds for all users
- Encourage greater mass transit use and easier non-motorized connections
- Improve pedestrian safety
- Provide the programs and destinations to attract a larger and increasingly diverse audience

CENTURY 21 MASTER PLAN

The Century 21 Master Plan is characterized by reclaiming and unifying open space at the heart of the campus and making connections — connections between buildings on the periphery and open spaces at the center; connections through the campus to growing neighborhoods on the center's edges; connections between the center's historic past and its dynamic future — all the while connecting the center's patrons to vibrant programming in world-class facilities.

Open space at Seattle Center is the green canvas — the free, public space that is the connective tissue of Seattle Center. The Century 21 Master Plan adds 10 acres of public open space, connecting the people and activities that were once isolated at its edges.

HIGHLIGHTS OF THE PLAN

The Century 21 Master Plan reinforces the City of Seattle's bold, ongoing commitment to sustainable design and takes its cues from the land itself, looking at the whole site from the ground up. Four strategies complement the strong emphasis on open space and connections in the master plan, targeting:

1 ECOLOGICAL SYSTEMS allowing the landscape and waterscape to work together

2 CARBON FOOTPRINT REDUCTION through energy conservation measures

3 GREEN BUILDING TECHNOLOGY LEED certification of Silver or better for all buildings and open spaces

4 PUBLIC EDUCATION OPPORTUNITIES making evident these strategies to Seattle Center's visitors through exhibits, signage, and tours

The Century 21 Master Plan calls for increasing the mode and frequency of transit, improving pedestrian connections to and through the campus, and making it easier and safer to access the center from a vehicle, by bike, or on foot.

This is a bold, comprehensive plan that charts the direction for the growth of Seattle Center over 20 years. It retains flexibility for change and is not intended to be fully funded or constructed in one piece. Rather, each element will be developed when demand, opportunity and resources converge. Public funding can be the catalyst that spurs private investment. Seattle Center has a proven track history for this approach.

Above: Mass enjoyment at Bumbershoot.

Opposite: Artist's concept rendering of repurposed Memorial Stadium site.

left Festal cultural festivals draw visitors with many different cultural heritage traditions to share and celebrate.

right Experience Music Project sponsors Sound Off, a battle of underage (too young to drink) bands.

CHARTING A CLEAR COURSE Undeterred by this upheaval, the Century 21 Committee in 2008 presented a bold new direction for Seattle Center. The Seattle Center Century 21 Master Plan reenvisioned the campus from its center to its perimeters, using open space and landscaping to unify diverse architecture, and created cohesion for the physical and programmatic elements that made Seattle Center one of the nation's best gathering places. The Seattle City Council adopted the master plan in August 2008, clearing the way for further development.

A PLACE FOR ALL To complement the master plan, Seattle Center developed a Public Programming Strategic Plan to create opportunities that help people find renewal and sustenance through human connection. These programs celebrate and connect diverse cultures, generations and classes; create learning through engagement; welcome guests with art, entertainment and creativity; and showcase participant communities who demonstrate their talents and interests.

The Center also serves as a significant event producer by bringing commercial programs to campus venues such as KeyArena and Marion Oliver McCaw Hall — and by developing its own programs to interest and entertain audiences of all ages and walks of life. As the Century 21 Master Plan renovates the grounds and facilities, the programming at Seattle Center creates the daily vibrancy envisioned for this civic center since the Seattle World's Fair.

CENTURY 21 TAKES SHAPE Even in tight budget years, Seattle Center moved forward on the Century 21 Master Plan and completed several projects, including campuswide signage, the Broad Street Green, the Seattle Center Skatepark, and Theater Commons.

Broad Street Green, completed in March 2008, dramatically opened up the southern edge of Seattle Center where the Interiors, Fashion, and Commerce Pavilion building once created an imposing wall. Now the green welcomes visitors to the center with an expansive lawn, outdoor art, landscaping and a seat wall.

Seattle Center Skatepark, completed in July 2009, features state-of-the-art skating elements; a flowing street plaza with ledges, stairs, and transitions for all skill levels and abilities; structural glass riding surfaces; compelling skateable sculptures; and cutting edge design. The Skatepark draws active teens and young adults, exemplifying Seattle Center's aim of expanding campus use in exciting, unconventional ways.

In June 2010, Seattle Center celebrated the grand opening of Theater Commons. Located between the Seattle Repertory Theatre and Intiman Theatre, this 1.6-acre parcel was redeveloped to open and beautify the north entry to the campus. The central feature of the space, Donnelly Gardens, was dedicated to honor longtime arts leader Peter Donnelly, who died in March 2009.

A GLASS ACT As the 50th anniversary of the 1962 fair drew near, agreements were announced on new Seattle Center attractions both temporary and permanent. On December 15, 2010, after several months of civic discussion, Seattle Mayor Mike McGinn proposed a multielement plan for new development at Seattle Center. On the now-vacant site of the fair's Gayway (and later the Fun Forest), about 59,000 square feet of land was to be transformed to present the first long-term exhibition featuring the work of renowned artist Dale Chihuly. The Chihuly Garden Exhibition was to boast a comprehensive exploration of the artist's work presented in both interior and exterior spaces, including an exterior art garden and unique stand-alone glass house featuring a site-specific installation. The Chihuly Garden Exhibition was to be privately funded by Center Arts LLC, a partnership between the Space Needle Corporation and Chihuly Studio.

As part of the agreement, Center Arts committed to provide $1 million to create a family play area at the center. In addition, Seattle radio station KEXP planned to permanently move its studios into Seattle Center's Northwest Rooms. "We've listened, and we've worked hard to bring forward a set of proposals to make Seattle Center more vibrant, more kid-friendly, and more financially stable," McGinn said. The city council unanimously approved the plan on April 25, 2011. The Chihuly Garden Exhibition was expected to open for the 50th anniversary of the fair's opening on April 21, 2012.

ON TO THE NEXT FIFTY Seattle Center and Seattle Center Foundation also announced big plans for the 50th anniversary of the fair — a six-month celebration from April 21 to October 21, 2012, called The Next Fifty. Like the fair it commemorated, The Next Fifty's focus was to be the future, with imagination, innovation, and involvement at the core of the programming. Hundreds of community volunteers donated their time to plan events, exhibitions, and discussions that would once again showcase Seattle Center as the place where our shared future is explored.

Seattle's civic center had come full circle. In 1962, a geographically isolated town, little-known beyond its region, invited our nation to dream big. Fifty years later, a newly minted global city asked the world to dream big again. Seattle Center had matured to embody the dream of the fair's founders: a cultural hub for the Pacific Northwest and a gathering place for people of all backgrounds. The moon is not a common destination yet, but Seattle Center has become one: a living reminder of the dedication, passion, and vision of those who brought us the Century 21 Exposition — and launched Seattle's future.

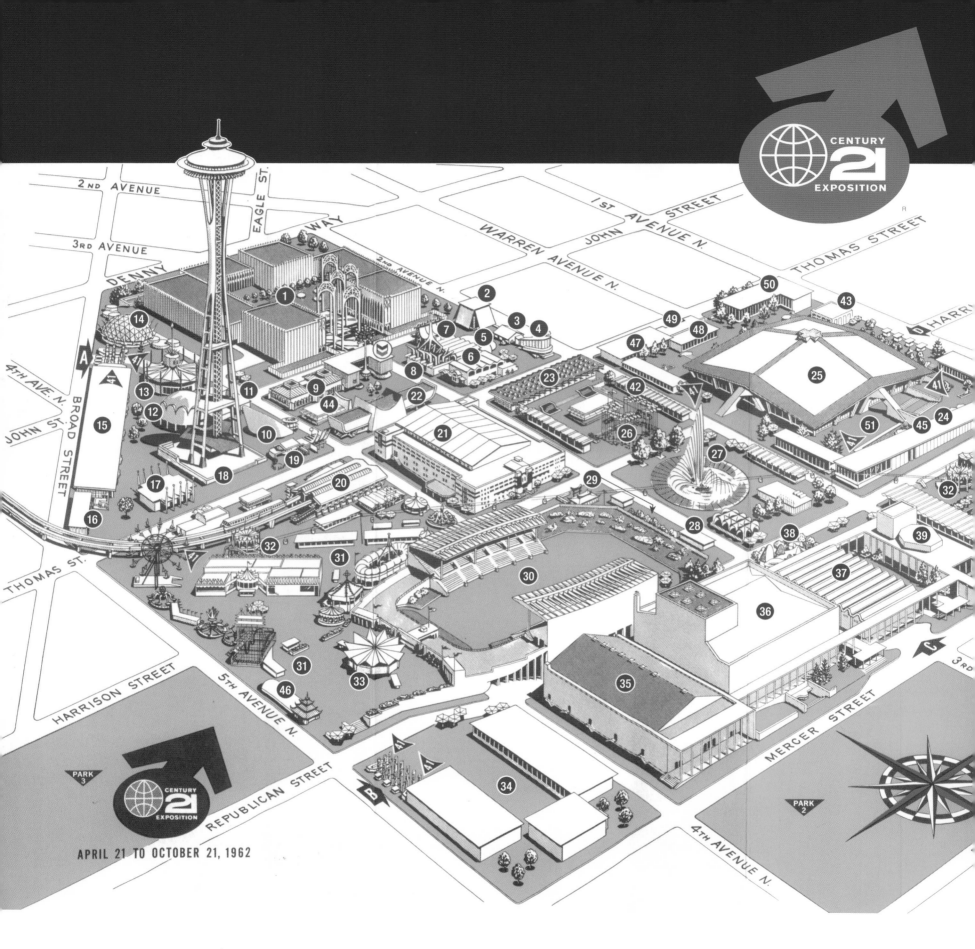

CENTURY 21 EXPOSITION

2ND AVENUE
3RD AVENUE
DENNY
EAGLE ST.
2ND AVENUE N.
WARREN AVENUE N.
JOHN
1 ST AVENUE N. STREET
THOMAS STREET
HARRI
4TH AVE. N. ST.
JOHN ST.
BROAD STREET
THOMAS ST.
HARRISON STREET
5TH AVENUE N.
REPUBLIC STREET
MERCER STREET
4TH AVENUE N.
3RD

PARK 3
CENTURY 21 EXPOSITION
APRIL 21 TO OCTOBER 21, 1962

PARK 2

The Buildings of Century 21 Exposition

Standard Oil Exhibit
⊘ United States Science Pavilion
2. Seattle-First International Bank
3. U.S. Plywood Association American Home of the Immediate Future
4. Sermons from Science Pavilion
5. Nalley's Space Age Theater
6. Club 21
7. Official Information Center
8. Christian Witness Pavilion
9. IBM Pavilion
10. Hydro-Electric Utilities Exhibit
11. Transport 21
12. Alaska Exhibit
13. Gas Industries Pavilion
14. Ford Motor Company Pavilion
15. Domestic Commerce And Industry Building #55
16. Christian Science Pavilion
17. Forest Industries Exhibit
18. Space Needle
19. General Electric Living Exhibit
20. Monorail Terminal
21. Food Circus
22. Bell Telephone Systems Exhibit
23. Domestic Commerce And Industry Building (Hall of Industry)
24. International Commerce and Industry Buildings
25. Washington State Coliseum

26. Plaza of States
27. International Fountain
28. Press Building
29. Spanish Village Fiesta
30. Stadium
31. Gayway
32. Sky Ride
33. Islands of Hawaii Pavilion
34. Show Street Complex
35. Arena
36. Opera House
37. Exhibition Hall
38. Home of Living Light
39. Playhouse
40. International Mall
41. Restrooms
42. Boulevards of the World
43. Fair Headquarters
44. Seattle Mural
45. Fountain of Creation
46. Japanese Village
47. Great Britain Pavilion
48. Republic of China Pavilion
49. Administration Building/Blue Spruce
50. NASA Pavilion
51. International Plaza
A — South Entrance (Broad Street)
B — East Entrance (5th Avenue North)
C — North Entrance (Mercer Street)
D — West Entrance (1st Avenue North)

Administration Building (Blue Spruce)

Architect: George Bolotin (1956)

Acquired by Century 21 Exposition, Inc. (building predated fair)

On-site now: Blue Spruce (still used by Seattle Center)

The modest Blue Spruce apartment building served as much-needed office space for fair staffers before and during the exposition.

Alaska Exhibit

Architect: Mandeville & Berge

Funded by National Bank of Commerce of Seattle

On-site now: Open space

Alaska had free space within the National Bank of Commerce Pavilion. Visitors entered the building via a ramp, passing images and relics documenting the 49th state's past, present, and future. A facsimile of Mount McKinley towered over everything, a northern lights display radiating above it toward the domed ceiling.

Postfair, the building housing the Alaska exhibit was demolished.

above, from left Fair Headquarters; Alaska exhibit.

opposite Century 21 Exposition transformed Seattle city blocks into a great world's fair.

Arena

Architect: Redesign by Bassetti & Morse of existing Ice Arena, Schack, Young & Myers (1928)

Interior reconfigured by LMN Architects (Loschky Marquardt & Nesholm) (2001)

Funded by City of Seattle

On-site now: Building still exists as Mercer Arts Arena

Bassetti & Morse's renovation of the Ice Arena converted some restrooms into dressing rooms, added an insulation cover over the ice surface, improved heating and ventilation systems, and added a portable stage platform. The Arena, the Civic Auditorium/Opera House, and the Fine Arts Pavilion/Exhibition Hall shared brick exterior cladding and colonnades, providing visual harmony.

Renamed Mercer Arena in 1995 and Mercer Arts Arena in 2001, the facility hosted Seattle Opera and Pacific Northwest Ballet performances during construction of Marion Oliver McCaw Hall. In 2008 the Seattle Opera signed a long-term lease on Mercer Arts Arena, enabling the company to bring together all of its operational departments.

Armory — see Food Circus

Bell Telephone Systems Exhibit

Architect: Raymond Loewy — William Snaith, Inc.

Architect-engineer: John Graham & Co.

Funded by Pacific Northwest Bell Telephone

On-site now: Mural Amphitheatre

The Bell Systems exhibit featured a full-sized model of the satellite *Vanguard 1*, the newly developed Bellboy paging system, a telephone that dialed automatically when a coded punch card was fed through a console, a model solar battery like those developed by Bell Systems for use in satellites, and Bell's new push-button dialing system, including a side-by-side comparison with rotary dialing.

The Bell Systems exhibit building was demolished after the fair.

Blue Spruce — see Administration Building

Boulevards of the World

Architect: Naramore, Bain, Brady & Johanson (international clients)

Roland Terry & Associates (domestic clients)

Funded by Century 21 Exposition, Inc.

On-site now: South Fountain Lawn and open space around International Fountain

Boulevards of the World was the main shopping area at Century 21, with multiple structures housing retail operations. Many foreign nations participating in the fair had commercial counterparts on Boulevards of the World that offered then-unusual imported items. Traditional souvenirs, toys, film, and a wide array of licensed items using the Century 21 logo were available. In addition, Canadian Pacific Airlines, the Port of Seattle, the States of Oregon and Arizona, the Washington State International Trade Fair, and the Western Washington Corporation of Seventh Day Adventists had exhibits on Boulevards of the World.

Postfair, the various buildings' roof panels were used by a Bainbridge Island shopping center. Most of the buildings were demolished immediately, although the Fiesta Cafe, the Hofbrau/Tivoli Gardens, and the Plaza Restaurant remained in business briefly. Smitty's Pancake House was relocated to Pacific Highway South, and the Hofbrau/Tivoli Gardens ended up at Northgate Mall.

Center House — see Food Circus

Christian Science Pavilion

Architect: Young, Richardson & Carleton

Funded by Churches and Societies of Christ, Scientist of Washington

On-site now: Broad Street Green

The Christian Science Pavilion showed film strips extolling the benefits of studying the Bible and the teachings of Christian Science, and an exhibit showed recorded news summaries from Christian Science Monitor reporters around the globe.

The Christian Science Pavilion was presented to the city after the fair. The pavilion became the Exhibition Gallery/Cascade Gallery and was demolished in 1981.

Christian Witness Pavilion

Architect: Durham, Anderson & Freed

Funded by 19 Protestant denominations and 14 Christian-centered agencies

On-site now: Children's Garden

Two-thirds of the Christian Witness Pavilion was devoted to a children's center, where children aged 3 to 7 got childcare mixed with evangelism. A 40-foot stained glass window in the building's facade was a major focal point, as was a 16-foot mosaic of 60,000 wooden blocks designed by Stanley Kloth. The adult portion of the exhibit consisted of a small theater where visitors experienced a 10-minute sacred sound and light exhibition that employed a rocket launch countdown as metaphor for the journey through life.

The Christian Witness Pavilion was demolished after the fair. The wooden block mosaic was moved to Gethsemane Lutheran Church at 911 Stewart Street in downtown Seattle, where it is displayed in the narthex. St. Leo's Catholic Church in St. Paul, Minnesota, purchased the stained glass window.

Club 21 (Nile Temple)

Architect: Samuel Morrison (1956)

Funded by Nile Temple Holding Corporation (leased by Century 21 Exposition, Inc.)

On-site now: Building still exists as part of Seattle Children's Theatre (Charlotte Martin Theatre, Eve Alvord Theatre, Allen Family Technical Pavilion)

Club 21 was a private club for top fair brass, Seattle businessmen and their wives, and high-ranking visitors and exhibitors. Members enjoyed dining facilities, meeting rooms, showers and barbershop; switchboard, paging, and stenographic services; and nightly entertainment.

The Nile Temple was used as the gift shop for the 1978 King Tut exhibit. The city purchased the building the following year. It housed the Pacific Arts Center and, beginning in 1987, some operations of the Seattle Children's Theatre (then performing at the PONCHO Theatre at Woodland Park Zoo). In 1993 it was renovated and became part of the Seattle Children's Theatre complex (built 1993, expanded 1995).

above, from left Arena (Interior); Boulevards of the World; Canadian Pacific; Club 21.
below, from left Bell Telephone Systems Exhibit; Christian Science Pavilion; Christian Witness Pavilion.

Commerce Pavilion — see Domestic Commerce and Industry Building #55

Concession Stands

Architect: Wendell H. Lovett & Ted Bower

Funded by Century 21 Exposition, Inc.

The concession stands were located throughout the grounds and were sold and/or demolished after the fair.

Domestic Commerce and Industry Building
(Hall of Industry)

Architect: Robert Billsborough Price

Funded by Century 21 Exposition, Inc.

On-site now: Fisher Pavilion

Colorful plastic pyramids projecting up from the Hall of Industry roof and down from the ceiling into the building served as decorative skylights. A glass wall along the north side of the block-long building overlooked the Plaza of the States and Boulevards of the World. Displays included:

• National Cash Register, featuring advanced models of cash registers, computers, and record tabulators; paper impregnated with perfume; and a film lounge.

• Rohr Aircraft Company, where visitors could operate a simulated satellite tracking station.

• United Air Lines, where visitors could test their memory and speed against a computerized reservations machine.

• Bekins Moving and Storage, which told the story of moving day in the year 2000.

• Carnation Company, where an animated mechanical cow labeled the "marvelous milk machine" demonstrated how "she" made milk.

• H. J. Heinz Company, relating Heinz's food-source procurement in the Pacific Northwest.

• Northwest Airlines, where recorded jet engine sounds, a mock-up of an airplane cabin, and a rotating photographic display of cities served by Northwest allowed fairgoers to experience "flights of the future today."

• REA Express

• S. C. Johnson Company

After the fair, the building became known as the Flag Pavilion. After a remodel, the Flag Pavilion hosted the King Tut exhibition's 1978 visit to Seattle. The pavilion was demolished in 2001 to make way for Fisher Pavilion.

Domestic Commerce and Industry Building #55
(Commerce Pavilion, Fashion Pavilion, Interiors Pavilion)

Architect: Waldron & Dietz

Funded by Century 21 Exposition, Inc.

On-site now: Broad Street Green

Exhibits in this 500-foot-long building heralded up-to-the-minute developments in fashion and interior design, along with industrial and commercial displays. One of the most popular was the Mobil Economy Run, a game that tested driving skills. In the fashion exhibit, *Vogue Magazine* sponsored "The Miracle of Modern American Fashion" shows at 2, 4, 6, and 8 p.m. These shows were staged around a 26- by 40-foot pool scented with a changing array of Revlon perfumes. The American Institute of Interior Design and its council of furnishing manufacturers sponsored the interior design exhibit, featuring design, materials, and decoration trends by 32 leading American firms.

Postfair, the building housed the Fun Circus, an indoor amusement facility for very young children. It was demolished in late 1989–early 1990.

Entrance Gates

Architect: Bassetti & Morse

Funded by State of Washington

East Gate (5th Avenue N), multicolored totem poles by Bassetti & Morse

On-site now: Open area near KCTS 9

Presidential Gate/North Gate (Mercer Street)

On-site now: Intiman Theatre, Fountain Court entrance, Exhibition Hall

South Gate (Broad Street), multicolored totem poles by Bassetti & Morse

On-site now: Broad Street Green

West Gate (1st Avenue N)

On-site now: Plaza west of KeyArena

With the exception of the gate at the west entrance of the Playhouse Courtyard, outside of Intiman Theatre, all entrance gates were moved or demolished after the fair.

Exhibition Hall (Fine Arts Pavilion)

Architect: Kirk, Wallace, McKinley & Associates

Funded by City of Seattle

On-site now: Building still exists, with Pacific Northwest Ballet upstairs and Exhibition Hall downstairs

The Exhibition Hall contained five main galleries. In 1993 the upper level of the Exhibition Hall was remodeled to house Pacific Northwest Ballet's studios, offices, and ballet school, and it reopened as the Phelps Center.

Fair Headquarters

Architect: Not available

Remodeled for Century 21 use by Tucker & Shields (1960)

Purchase funded by State of Washington

On-site now: Building still exists as West Court Building, housing Ticketmaster and KeyArena box office

This modest office building preexisted the Seattle World's Fair and was within the footprint of the fairgrounds. Instead of demolishing it, fair planners repurposed it to serve as exposition headquarters before and during the fair.

Fashion Pavilion — see Domestic Commerce and Industry Building #55

Fine Arts Pavilion — see Exhibition Hall

Flag Pavilion — see Domestic Commerce and Industry Building

Food Circus (Washington State National Guard Armory)

Architect: Original armory by Floyd Naramore and Arrigo M. Young (1939)

Revisions to armory by Durham, Anderson & Freed (1962)

Original construction funded by State of Washington and Public Works Administration grant

Revisions funded by State of Washington

On-site now: Building still exists as Center House (Center High School, Center House Theatre, Center House Food Court, Children's Museum, Conference Center, Seattle Center Administrative Offices)

Fifty-two food concessions were arrayed throughout the Food Circus, and in the center towered a 39-foot-high, 12.5-ton fruitcake.

After the fair, the Bubbleator was moved from the Coliseum to the Food Circus, where it carried passengers between the first and second floors in the area now used for the Children's Museum forest trail exhibit. The Bubbleator was removed in 1980.

The Food Circus was remodeled according to plans by Roland Terry & Associates, given skylights, and renamed the Center House in 1974. In 1993–1994 Van Horne & Van Horne Architects renovated the food court area. The building was designated a City of Seattle landmark in 2004.

above, from left Domestic Commerce and Industry Building (Hall of Industry); Domestic Commerce and Industry Building #55; South Entrance (Broad Street); Exhibition Hall (foreground) and Opera House.
below, from left Concession stand near Washington State Coliseum; Administration Building/Blue Spruce; Food Circus (interior).

Ford Motor Company Pavilion

Architect: Paul Thiry

Funded by Ford Motor Company

On-site now: Broad Street Green

Ford Motor Company Pavilion's white and gold dome featured "An Adventure in Outer Space," a simulated flight past celestial bodies and beeping satellites. Futuristic cars, consumer products of the future, and a Century 21 farm were also on display.

Postfair, the Ford Pavilion was moved to Edmonds, Washington, and served as the Surf & Sand Marina until its eventual demise.

Forest Industries Exhibit (Forest Products Theater)

Architect: Robert Billsborough Price

Funded by Century 21 Forest Industries Committee, Inc. (Weyerhaeuser Corporation)

On-site now: Broad Street Green

The Forest Industries exhibit celebrated all things wooden. A locally produced film starring Jacqueline Holt, William Benedict, and Dick Wilson played in the Forest Products Theater. The film's wacky space-age storyline called for Holt, a "suburban-type dreamboat," to land her family rocket on Mars while looking for a uranium service station. The curious Martians hook her up to a "grazarius loaded with crodneys," a device that allows them to examine her "lovely thinkpiece" and see the sights of Earth via her Forest Products thoughts: the felling of trees, the process of creating shingles, the manufacturing of plywood, and the building of new homes.

Postfair, the building became the Piccoli Theatre, a venue for puppet shows. It was demolished in 1981.

Gas Industries Pavilion

Architect: Floats, Inc., in association with Herb Rosenthal

Funded by Western Oil & Gas Association

On-site now: Peace Garden near Space Needle valet parking

Natural gas torches formed the support pillars for the roof of the Gas Industries Pavilion. Exhibits explained the history of gas sources, the uses of gas, its distribution from Greek times to the present, and its projected use in the year 2001. A gas-powered clock on the pavilion's roof told time according to the number of gas torches lit.

Postfair, the Gas Industries Pavilion foundation was used as the site of the Fun Forest carousel, which.

It was demolished in 1996.

Gayway

Design: John C. Ray Jr.

Attractions: Antique Car Ride, Broadway Trip, Bubble Bounce, Cake Walk, Calypso, Carousel, Century 21 for Fun, Flying Coaster, Giant Wheel, Hot Rods, Laff on the Farm, Meteor, Monster, Olympia Bobs, Quick Draw Theater, Rotor, Skooter, Space Wheel, Flight to Mars, Wild Mouse

Funded by Century 21 Exposition, Inc.

On-site now: Experience Music Project (eastern portion), newly envisioned Center Square (formerly Fun Forest, western portion)

The Gayway occupied a two-block stretch immediately east of the Food Circus and encompassed the fair's Monorail terminal and the eastern terminal of the Sky Ride. Most of the rides cost 25 cents, a few were 35 cents, and the Ferris

wheel was priced at 50 cents. The Gayway rides were removed after the fair, except for the Wild Mouse, Space Wheel, and carousel. Most Fun Forest rides were not those used in the Gayway. As of 2010, the only Gayway survivor is the small structure that was used as Quick Draw Theater during the fair. The upper portion of this modest structure now houses Monorail offices, and the lower portion houses the Frontier Gallery.

General Electric Living Exhibit (General Electric Home of the Future)

Architect: John Graham & Co.

Funded by General Electric Corporation

On-site now: Fun Forest Arcade Pavilion

The General Electric Home of the Future featured all-electric living: color television projected on wall surfaces, an electronic home library, push-button sink, bakery drawer, clothes-conditioning closet, and a wall-sized home computer.

The General Electric Living exhibit building was demolished after the fair.

Hall of Industry — see Domestic Commerce and Industry Building

Home of Living Light (Century 21 Plywood Home of Living Light)

Architect: Liddle & Jones

Funded by Douglas Fir Plywood Association

On-site now: Open space

In response to projected overpopulation in the future, the Home of Living Light was designed to provide private refuge on small, scarce building lots.

Walls of wood paneling, rigid in one direction and flexible in the other, could take any shape while supporting the required roof loads. Four conical sky-lights located over each major area of the house and could be turned toward or away from the sun to adjust the level of natural lighting.

Postfair, the Home of Living Light was barged to Olympia. One half became the Jacaranda Restaurant (later the Ebb Tide) and the other served as a golf course clubroom until destroyed in an explosion in 1967.

Horiuchi Mural — see Seattle Mural

Hydro-Electric Utilities Exhibit (Pavilion of Electric Power)

Architect: Jack N. Bryant

Funded by a consortium of public and private hydroelectric utilities in the state of Washington

On-site now: Fun Forest Arcade Pavilion

The Pavilion of Electric Power featured a working dam replica with six spillways over which 3,000 gallons of water flowed each minute. Visitors entered through a large tunnel in the dam's face. A ramp led to a map showing Washington's dams, and a large relief map of the state lit up to show transmission networks.

The Hydro-Electric Utilities exhibit building was demolished after the fair.

above, from left Gayway; Gas Industries Pavilion; Home of Living Light (Century 21 Plywood Home of Living Light).

below, from left Ford Motor Company Pavilion; General Electric Living Exhibit (General Electric Home of the Future); Hydro-Electric Utilities Exhibit (Pavilion of Electric Power).

IBM Pavilion

Architect: Carreiro Sklaroff Design Associates

Consulting architect: Charles E. Broudy

Landscape architect: Karl Linn

Funded by International Business Machines, Inc.

On-site now: Mural Amphitheatre

Silver poplar trees formed exterior walls of the IBM Pavilion, which was divided into three "gardens of learning." One garden described human's mastery of technology, from early tool use to artistic expressions. Another featured a children's maze designed to provoke comparisons between the children's decision-making process at the junctures of the maze and the working of a computer. The third garden detailed current and future uses for computers — as libraries for vast quantities of information, as language translators, and as controllers of physical processes. Visitors could type souvenir postcards on the new IBM Selectric typewriter.

Postfair, the IBM Pavilion became an outdoor screened café, and later the shell for a miniature golf course. It was demolished in 1996.

Interiors Pavilion — see Domestic Commerce and Industry Building #55

INTERNATIONAL COMMERCE AND INDUSTRY BUILDINGS*

Surrounding the International Mall:

* India and Korea Pavilions Building

Architect: Walker & McGough

Funded by State of Washington

On-site now: Seattle Repertory Theatre (Bagley Wright Theatre, PONCHO Forum, Leo Kreielsheimer Theatre)

In accordance with Bureau of International Exposition rules stipulating that participating nations be provided free space that was protected from the elements, Walker & McGough created two overarching structures resembling rigid umbrellas or sails against a window-wall of glass set into a zigzag retaining wall to protect the various free-standing pavilions within. All of the international pavilions were demolished after the fair, but the zigzag retaining wall was incorporated into the Bagley Wright Theatre.

The India Pavilion emphasized modern India's resurgence since 1947, when the country gained independence from Great Britain. Examples of traditional Indian industries such as silk and cotton fabric production, tea, coffee and jute production, and handcrafts were displayed beside modern industrial goods.

The Korea Pavilion displayed traditional lacquerware, brass serving vessels, and more than 800 agricultural, mineral, and industrial products.

The building was demolished in late 1981.

* United Nations, African Nations, Thailand, and Philippines Pavilions Building

Architect: Walker & McGough

Funded by State of Washington

On-site now: Seattle Repertory Theatre (Bagley Wright Theatre, PONCHO Forum, Leo Kreielsheimer Theatre)

The United Nations Pavilion had a film center and lounge where visitors could talk with officials and representatives of United Nations member countries.

The African Nations Pavilion featured artifacts and handcrafts from the nations of Africa, many of

which had only recently achieved independence. Participants included Cameroon, Central African Republic, Republic of Chad, Republic of Congo (Leopoldville) (now Democratic Republic of the Congo-Kinshasa), Republic of Congo (Brazzaville), Dahomey (now Republic of Benin), Ethiopia, Gabon, Ghana, Guinea, Ivory Coast, Liberia, Libya, Malagasy Republic (now Madagascar), Mali, Mauritania, Morocco, Niger, Senegal, Sierra Leone, Somali Republic (now Somalia), Republic of South Africa, Sudan, Tanganyika (now Tanzania), Togo, Tunisia, and Upper Volta (now Burkina Faso).

The Thailand Pavilion featured a film theater; a seating area with Thai furniture and an inlaid parquet floor; display cases filled with rubber, tin, rice, grain, fruits, tobacco, silk, and tropical furniture woods; and a three-dimensional abstract temple.

The Philippines Pavilion entry was clad in Philippine ebony and served as the background for a white marble information desk. An ornamental reflecting pool along the side of the pavilion culminated in a fountain of giant Philippine shells that was designed by Manila sculptor N. Veloso Abueva. The Philippines Pavilion was a joint project of the Philippine government and the Seattle Filipino business community.

The building was demolished in 1981.

* San Marino, Peace Corps, and City of Berlin Pavilions Building

Architect: Walker & McGough

Funded by State of Washington

On-site now: Open space

The San Marino Pavilion featured examples of the tiny country's two main industries: art pottery and the San Marino government's issuance of stamps.

The Peace Corps Pavilion offered the first public presentation of the work of the U.S. Peace Corps, officially established by President Kennedy on March 1, 1961.

The City of Berlin Pavilion used audiovisual displays to tell the story of divided Berlin, especially the lives of West Berliners whose homes were encircled by the then-makeshift Berlin Wall recently erected by communist East Germany.

The building was demolished in late 1981.

Surrounding the International Plaza, within which the Washington State Coliseum was the central feature:

* United Arab Republic, Brazil, European Economic Community, Japan, Mexico, Canada, Denmark Pavilions Building

Architect: Paul Thiry

Funded by King County

On-site now: Building still exists as Northwest Rooms

Thiry's building was an overarching protective structure for the various free-standing pavilions within and was fully enclosed after the fair to enable its use as a conference and meeting facility.

The United Arab Republic Pavilion featured photographs, films, and displays about Egyptian life.

The Brazil Pavilion featured Brazilian-grown coffee and tea, brewed on-site and served to visitors. Brazilian dancers, singers, musicians, painters, sculptors, and others presented performances and demonstrations highlighting life in Brazil.

The European Economic Community Pavilion allowed visitors to listen to recorded messages from the leaders of Belgium, France, the Federal Republic of Germany, Italy, Luxembourg, and The Netherlands.

The Japan Pavilion featured a miniature Japanese garden and a Japanese room where activities of daily life were demonstrated. Cases were filled with samples of silks, pottery, and carved miniatures. Modern Japanese industry was exemplified by a display of motorcycles and by scale models of tankers produced by Japanese shipyards.

The Denmark Pavilion featured the very popular Danish modern furniture, along with silverware, porcelain, textiles, and decorative items.

The Mexico Pavilion portrayed Mexico's advancement in social, economic, and cultural fields.

The Canada Pavilion featured Canada's first satellite, the S-27 *Topside Sounder*, displayed at the fair prior to its launch, and information about Canada's research into the peaceful use of atomic energy.

above, from left IBM Pavilion; International Commerce and Industry Buildings surrounding the International Mall; United Nations Pavilion; African Nations Pavilion; United Arab Republic Pavilion.

below, from left IBM Pavilion (interior); City of Berlin Pavilion.

* Sweden Pavilion

Architect: Paul Thiry

Funded by King County

On-site now: Building still exists

The Sweden Pavilion included a lounge furnished with modern Swedish furniture; a shop where Swedish glass, ceramics, flatware, textiles, books, and records were sold; and an exhibit recounting the salvage of the seventeenth century man-of-war, the *Vasa*.

* Republic of China Taiwan Pavilion

Architect: Paul Thiry

Funded by King County

On-site now: Seattle Center Pavilion (a relocated portion of NASA Pavilion)

The Republic of China (Taiwan) Pavilion highlighted the island nation's textile industry, ceramic and silver manufacturing, and "Chinese Modern" furniture manufacturing — an adaptation of Mandarin furniture featuring silk and brocaded upholstery.

The Republic of China (Taiwan) Pavilion was demolished in 1995 during the redevelopment of the Coliseum/KeyArena.

* Great Britain Pavilion

Architect: Paul Thiry

Funded by King County

On-site now: Seattle Center Skatepark

The Great Britain Pavilion featured animated demonstrations of scientific advances and exhibits highlighting the projects of scientists in the United Kingdom.

The Great Britain Pavilion was retained after the fair, becoming a branch of the Seattle Art Museum from 1964 until 1987. It was demolished in early 2009 to make way for Seattle Center Skatepark.

Fountain of Creation

Designed by: Everett DuPen

Funded by Century 21 Exposition, Inc.

On-site now: Fountain still exists, refurbished in 2003

University of Washington professor Everett DuPen's fountain in the International Plaza, near the former Canada Pavilion site, consists of a large shallow pool from which rise three abstract bronze sculptures depicting the evolution of human life from a single cell to the conquest of space.

International Fountain

Architect: Kazuyuki Matsushita and Hideki Shimizu, with Seattle Associate Architects John D. Phillips and Harry S. Rich

Redesign by Nakano-Dennis, with TRA (1995)

Funded by City of Seattle

On-site now: Fountain still exists, with substantial renovation and redesign in 1995

Designed to shoot water into sculptural forms as much as 150 feet high, the central portion of the fountain was compared to a sunflower, with "seed" nozzles. Machinery deep underground facilitated changes in colored lighting patterns and spray shapes. Taped carillon music accompanied the sprays.

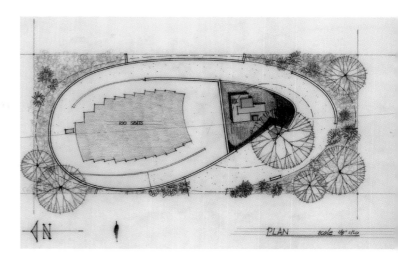

A 1995 renovation replaced the central fountain apparatus while retaining the spray pattern, raised the bowl floor, replaced sharp rocks with aggregate concrete paving, and added a gently sloping spiral ramp that provides wheelchair access and enables water play. The surrounding plaza was redesigned at the same time.

Islands of Hawaii Pavilion (Polynesian Playhouse)

Architect: John Graham & Co.

Funded by Hawaii-Seattle World's Fair Pavilion, Inc.

On-site now: Parking lot

When the Hawaiian state government did not appropriate funds for an official exhibit at Century 21, a group of Honolulu businesspeople stepped in and funded the Islands of Hawaii Pavilion as a commercial venture. Dole Food pineapple products were for sale inside.

Postfair, the Islands of Hawaii Pavilion housed a penny arcade and then a Fun Forest refreshment stand. It was demolished in the late 1990s.

Japanese Village

Architect: Not available

Funded by Naico, Inc. (Masaka Yashiro and Stanley Omija)

On-site now: Parking lot

The Japanese Village consisted of six structures, including a temple housing 24 scale models of shrines from Japan's Nikko National Park and 1,000 costumed dolls. One area was devoted to sumo wrestling, and female pearl divers demonstrated their skills in a glass-walled tank.

The Japanese Village was demolished after the fair.

Monorail Terminals (fairgrounds and Westlake Park)

Architect: Adrian Wilson & Associates

Funded by Alweg Rapid Transit Systems

On-site now: Fairgrounds terminal still exists, Westlake terminal replaced

Plastic-roofed track-level terminals on either end of the 1.2 mile Monorail line protected riders from the

elements as they boarded the train. Inclined moving sidewalks transported riders to the ground.

The Westlake terminal was demolished, and a new loading platform constructed, during Westlake Center construction in 1986. The Monorail itself was designated a City of Seattle landmark in 2003.

Nalley's Space Age Theater (Nalley's Pavilion)

Architect: Paul Thiry

Funded by Nalley's, Inc.

On-site now: Seattle Children's Theatre (Charlotte Martin Theatre, Eve Alvord Theatre, Allen Family Technical Pavilion)

Nalley Foods, a Tacoma producer of potato chips, chili, and other products, highlighted food's journey from field to table. The exterior of Nalley's Pavilion was all flowing curves, and the interior featured a combination "space-age theater" and exhibit.

Nalley's Pavilion was demolished after the fair.

above, from left Sweden Pavilion (foreground), Denmark Pavilion (background); Great Britain Pavilion; International Fountain; Westlake Park Monorail Terminal; Nalley's Space Age Theater (Nalley's Pavilion). below, from left Republic of China Pavilion; Canada Pavilion; Islands of Hawaii Pavilion (Polynesian Playhouse); Japanese Village.

NASA Pavilion

Architect: Paul Thiry

Funded by King County

On-site now: Portion still exists, in different location, as Seattle Center Pavilion

NASA's $2 million exhibit was the agency's first large-scale attempt to tell the story of the U.S. space program. After the federal government's science exhibit, NASA's was the largest exhibit at the fair. Fairgoers saw models of satellites launched by the United States, including *Explorer 1*, *Vanguard 1*, *Pioneer*, *Ranger*, *Mariner 2*, and the Canadian *Topside Sounder*. Actual rockets and scaled-down models were also featured. These were joined by John Glenn's *Friendship 7* midway through the fair. A large display explained NASA's progress toward developing three-man space vehicles for orbital and moon flight. A small theater screened films about space exploration, astronomy, and rocketry.

Part of the building was relocated to Pavilion B in 1995, during construction of the loading dock as part of the Coliseum's renovation into KeyArena, and is now called Seattle Center Pavilion. The portion that remains is designated "NASA" and is used for Seattle Center facilities maintenance equipment.

Nile Temple — see Club 21

Official Information Center (General Insurance Company Information Center)

Architect: C. B. Whitmore, the Austin Company

Funded by General Insurance Company of America

On-site now: Children's Garden

The information center was an open-sided structure featuring a tangerine-colored nylon roof. Female guides inside could answer any fair-related question and offer advice about activities throughout the Pacific Northwest.

Postfair, the information center was used as a picnic shelter. It was torn down in 1981.

Opera House

Architect: Redesign by James B. Chiarelli & B. Marcus Priteca of existing Civic Auditorium, Schack, Young & Myers (1928)

Funded by City of Seattle

On-site now: Marion Oliver McCaw Hall, Nesholm Family Lecture Hall, SIFF Cinema

Chiarelli and Priteca's redesign took the interior of the Civic Auditorium down to its structural foundations (columns and beams). Retaining the exterior shell, they rebuilt the interior within it and then clad the exterior.

The Opera House was extensively renovated in 2002–2003 following a design by LMN Architects, which retained 30 percent of the old structure. It reopened as Marion Oliver McCaw Hall in 2003.

Playhouse

Architect: Kirk, Wallace, McKinley & Associates

Funded by City of Seattle

On-site now: Building still exists as Intiman Theatre

The Playhouse was constructed in just 34 days. In 1963 it became home to the newly formed Seattle Repertory Theatre. Seattle Rep moved to the new Bagley Wright Theatre in 1982, and in 1987 the heavily renovated Playhouse reopened as home to the Intiman Theatre.

Plaza of the States (State Flag Plaza)

Architect: Richard Bouillon

Funded by State of Washington

On-site now: South Fountain Lawn

The Plaza of the States served as a formal venue for ceremonies honoring visiting U.S. governors and highlighting their states. Each state was represented by its flag, each flying atop a 33-foot pole, and by a plaque. Many civic groups, high school and college bands, and other boosters participated in celebrations and entertainments at the Plaza of the States.

The plaza was demolished in 2001 to make way for Fisher Pavilion.

Press Building (VFW, Veterans Hall)

Architect: Schack, Young & Myers (1928)

Funded by Veterans of Foreign Wars (leased by Century 21 Exposition, Inc.)

On-site now: Open space

The modest VFW building housed the fair's busy press department. After the fair the building reverted to VFW use. It was demolished in 2002, in conjunction with the construction of the central utilities plant that serves Seattle Center.

Seattle Center Pavilion — see NASA Pavilion

Seattle-First International Bank

Architect: Paul Thiry

Funded by Seattle-First National Bank

On-site now: Seattle Children's Theatre (Charlotte Martin Theatre, Eve Alvord Theatre, Allen Family Technical Pavilion)

Fairgoers could enjoy all of the usual bank services, plus greatly extended hours. A display of coin banks, a state-of-the-art coin and cash packaging machine, and an exhibit of Pacific Northwest sculpture were featured.

The building was demolished after the fair.

above, from left NASA Pavilion; Official Information Center; Playhouse; Seattle-First International Bank. below, from left Opera House (interior); Plaza of the States (State Flag Plaza); Press Building (VFW, Veterans Hall).

Seattle Mural

Design: Paul Horiuchi, mounted on parabolic support structure by Paul Thiry

Funded by Century 21 Exposition, Inc., grounds development funds

On-site now: Mural still exists

Century 21 Exposition, Inc., commissioned the glass tile mural as a gift to Seattle. Heralded at its April 21, 1962, unveiling as "the largest work of art in the Pacific Northwest," it was Horiuchi's first (and only) work of public art. The Seattle Landmarks Preservation Board granted the Seattle Mural landmark status in 2004.

Sermons from Science Pavilion (Moody Institute Pavilion)

Architect: Harold J. Nesland, for Nesland

Funded by Moody Institute of Science under sponsorship of Christ for the World Committee

On-site now: Seattle Children's Theatre (Charlotte Martin Theatre, Eve Alvord Theatre, Allen Family Technical Pavilion)

Dr. George Speake gave two sermons a day and showed films designed to soften the unchurched (who were presumed to be open to science but closed to religion) for future evangelism. Speake's sermons concluded with a dramatic "Million Volt Demonstration," in which he stood on an Oudin resonator and allowed one million volts of electricity to pass through his body and ignite a board held in his hands.

The Sermons from Science Pavilion's prefabricated brick panel construction made relocation simple, and after the fair it was given to the U.S. Air Force and moved to Everett's Paine Air Force Base, where it was used as a chapel.

SHOW STREET COMPLEX*

Building for *Backstage U.S.A.*, **Bavarian Tavern**, *Girls of the Galaxy*, **Gay Nineties Review, Antique Car Show, Diamond Horseshoe, Flor de Mexico, Indian Village/TeePee Salmon Barbeque, Cellier de Pigalle, Stella**

Architect: Paul Thiry

Funded by Century 21 Exposition, Inc.

On-site now: KCTS 9

Backstage U.S.A. featured 36 showgirls in their dressing room, in various stages of undress. In another part of the exhibit, female performers danced onstage. *Girls of the Galaxy* featured young women in space-age costumes on a revolving stage.

The building was moved to the King County fairgrounds in Enumclaw after the fair.

* Gracie Hansen's Paradise International

Architect: Howard Dong and Associates

Funded by Century 21 Exposition, Inc.

On-site now: Open space near KCTS 9

Producer Barry Ashton described the Paradise International revue that Gracie Hansen hired him to produce as "a smart night-club show glamorizing the American woman," but in Seattle the topless show-girls shocked as much as they dazzled.

After the fair, a portion of the building was moved to Ravensdale Park in south King County, becoming the Gracie Hansen Community Center.

* Le Petit Theatre

Architect: Roland Terry

Funded by Century 21 Exposition, Inc.

On-site now: Open space near KCTS 9

Le Petit Theatre was home to *Les Poupées de Paris*, a nighttime adults-only puppet show modeled after the famous *Folies Bergère* and Lido Club shows in Paris, featured two male puppeteers operating 70 (mostly female) puppets — showgirls, jugglers, tightrope walkers, and a full puppet orchestra. Les Poupées was the brainchild of Sid and Marty Krofft, brothers who would later make a splash in Saturday morning television with *The Banana Splits* and *H.R. Pufnstuf*. During the day, Roland Terry's innovative design rotated the seating area so that daytime audiences viewed a magic show on a separate stage. The Paris Spectacular wax museum shared the building.

The building was demolished after the fair.

Sky Ride (Union 76 Sky Ride)

Architect for terminals: Tucker & Shields

Funded by Trams, Inc., and Century 21 Exposition, Inc., sponsored by Union Oil Works

Sky Ride terminals resembled giant inverted umbrellas and provided shielded turnaround and loading points. One terminal was located near the Monorail terminal on the eastern side of the fairgrounds; the other was near the San Marino Pavilion on the International Mall. The Sky Ride was built by Von Roll Iron Works of Switzerland.

The Sky Ride was purchased by the city after the fair. It was dismantled in 1981 during construction of the Bagley Wright Theatre, and it now operates at the Western Washington Fair in Puyallup.

Space Needle

Architect: John Graham & Co. (some sources credit Victor Steinbrueck with design assistance)

Structural consultant: John K. Minasian

General contractor: Howard S. Wright Company

Structural steel frame fabrication and erection: Pacific Car & Foundry Co.

Funded by Pentagram Corporation (Bagley Wright, Ned Skinner, Norton Clapp, John Graham, and Howard S. Wright)

On-site now: Building still exists

The privately owned 605-foot Space Needle galvanized global attention during construction, becoming the symbol of the Seattle World's Fair and Seattle's icon. The steel beam sections, curved into shape at Pacific Car & Foundry's Seattle plant, were hoisted individually and welded into place by teams of master welders working 12 hours a day. When the Space Needle was completed, it wrested the title of "Seattle's tallest building" away from the 522-foot Smith Tower, which was built in 1914.

For years the Smith Tower was heralded by many as the "tallest building west of the Mississippi," even though a Kansas City skyscraper topped it by 19 feet in 1931. The 605-foot Space Needle held the crown for only eight years, after which it was topped by the 630-foot Seattle-First National Bank Building — which many referred to as "the box the Space Needle came in."

During the fair, the Space Needle was home to the Schulmerich Carillon Americana, featuring 538 bells. The Schulmerich carillon was removed in the 1970s.

In 1982 the Skyline Banquet Facility was added at the 100-foot level. In 2000 the base area was redesigned, creating an enclosed retail pavilion. The Space Needle was designated a City of Seattle landmark in 1999.

above, from left Seattle Mural; Sermons from Science Pavilion (Moody Institute Pavilion); Gracie Hansen's Paradise International; Le Petit Theatre; Skyride (Union 76 Sky Ride).

below, from left This way to Show Street; During the fair, the Space Needle's pagoda roof was painted glowing orange, a shade officially known as Galaxy Gold. The Needle's halo was Re-entry Red, its core was Orbital Olive, and the legs were Astronaut White.

Spanish Village Fiesta

Architect: Julio Fernando Cavestany

Funded by Spanish Village Fiesta, Inc. (Dorwin Cook, George Bowden, and Associates), and later Century 21 Exposition, Inc.

On-site now: Open space

The Spanish Village Fiesta featured a popular restaurant that offered paella and other Spanish delicacies, flamenco dancing, and musical performances.

    The Spanish Village Fiesta was demolished after the fair.

Stadium (Memorial Stadium)

Architect: George Wellington Stoddard (1947)

Funded by Seattle Public Schools

On-site now: Building still exists, scheduled for removal

The stadium was built in 1947. A wall memorializing Seattle Public School students who'd lost their lives during World War II was added in 1951. The concourse under the stadium's north wing housed Exhibit Fair, a collection of concession kiosks. During the fair, the Tommy Bartlett water-ski show was a stadium feature, performing in a giant, specially built water track. As of 2011 the stadium is scheduled for removal under a joint agreement between Seattle Center and Seattle Public Schools.

Standard Oil Exhibit

Architect: Piero Patri for Patri, Patri, Patri

Funded by Standard Oil Company of California

On-site now: Mural Amphitheatre

A large model of an oil molecule revolving aloft a tall support staff marked the Standard Oil exhibit, and petroleum-based products were highlighted throughout the display — even the exhibit's walls were made of plastic.

After the fair, the Standard Oil exhibit building was dismantled, trucked to Mount Vernon, and reassembled to house Meyer Sign & Advertising.

State Flag Plaza — see Plaza of the States

Transport 21

Architect: Mandeville & Berge

Funded by Western Association of Railroads

On-site now: Open space

The Transport 21 exhibit showed rail transportation's history and predicted its future. A model of Ford Motor Company's Levatrain — a wheel-less vehicle that carried freight and passengers at speeds of up to 500 miles per hour on a cushion of air — was on display. Another exhibit presented a full-size model of a personal passenger capsule, a predicted popular method of space-age high-speed travel.

    Transport 21 was demolished after the fair.

United States Science Pavilion

Architect: Minoru Yamasaki and Naramore, Bain, Brady & Johanson

Landscape architecture: Lawrence Halprin

Funded by U.S. government

On-site now: Building still exists as Pacific Science Center

The United States Science Pavilion presented what the official guidebook called "the exciting story of science in a show unlike any ever seen before." Yamasaki's design clustered arching "space gothic" structures around a tranquil fountain, surrounding this peaceful refuge with six buildings housing the different "chapters" of the science story. In Area 1: *The House of Science*, an innovative film by Charles and Ray Eames, introduced science and the theme of the exhibits. In Area 2: The Development of Science, models and exhibits explained the growth of scientific knowledge. Area 3 was the Spacearium,

a space-age planetarium. Area 4: The Methods of Science, featured bright young science demonstrators recreating famous experiments. In Area 5: The Horizons of Science, the meaning of the whole exhibit and implications for the use of science in the future were summarized. Area 6 was a hands-on laboratory where young visitors between the ages of 8 and 13 could perform simple experiments.

The building and most of the exhibits were turned over to the newly formed nonprofit organization, the Pacific Science Center, immediately after the fair closed. The Seattle Landmarks Preservation Board granted the building official landmark status in 2010.

U.S. Plywood Association American Home of the Immediate Future (Living Research House)

Architect: Robert Martin Englebrecht

Funded by U.S. Plywood Corporation

On-site now: Seattle Children's Theatre (Charlotte Martin Theatre, Eve Alvord Theatre, Allen Family Technical Pavilion)

The low-cost American Home of the Immediate Future consisted of house sections prebuilt by the Panelbild Division of U.S. Plywood that were then bolted together at the lot, allowing for customization by adding or subtracting sections. Century 21's version featured three bedrooms, two baths, kitchen, service area, den, and living room. Heating, cooling, plumbing, and wiring systems were prebuilt into the 12-inch-deep floor area of each module.

After the fair, the American Home of the Immediate Future was immediately moved to Mercer Island. As of 2011, it is still in use.

VFW, Veteran's Hall — see Press Building

above, from left Spanish Village Fiesta; Standard Oil
Exhibit; U.S. Plywood Association American Home
Of The Immediate Future (Living Research Home);
Transport 21.
below, from left Stadium; United States Science
Pavilion.

Washington State Coliseum

Architect: Paul Thiry

Funded by State of Washington

On-site now: Building still exists, with substantial modification, as KeyArena

Heralded for its hyperbolic paraboloid roof suspended from a framework of concrete beams, the Washington State Coliseum housed Century 21's theme exhibit, the World of Tomorrow, a honeycomb-shaped "cloud" of 3,250 aluminum cubes 200 feet across and 60 feet high (as tall as a six-story building). Visitors accessed the cube structure in groups of 100 via the Plexiglas Bubbleator elevator. As they ascended, the Bubbleator operator gave the first speech of a 21-minute multisensory performance complete with imagery, taped dialogue, odors, dramatic music, and sound and lighting effects that the visitors would navigate. The show's official title was *The Threshold and the Threat* — the threat being, of course, nuclear annihilation, and the threshold being the present time.

The Coliseum housed:

• The American Library Association exhibit, containing a UNIVAC (universal automatic computer), a microfilm exhibit, and an array of electronic devices predicted to be of use in libraries of the future.

• The General Motors Corporation exhibit, including a Firebird III engineered for automatic guidance (i.e., it was driverless), a demonstration of the principles of ground-effect machinery that enabled heavy objects to move on a cushion of air, and a hands-on activity allowing visitors to shoot simulated solar guns and operate a simulated atomic reactor.

• The Pan American Airways exhibit, dominated by a huge revolving globe and a sculpture representing flight.

• The Washington Tourist Information Center.

• France's exhibit, which proposed greater reliance on the arts and the natural environment as a tonic for the loss of individual identity caused by technological innovations.

• The Cancer Research exhibit.

• The Radio Corporation of America exhibit, highlighting RCA-Victor's participation in space research.

After the fair, the City of Seattle purchased the Coliseum from the state and converted it into an all-purpose convention and sports facility based on plans by Paul Thiry. Between 1994 and 1995 the building was completely remodeled, including lowering the court 35 feet below street level. The architectural integrity of Thiry's roofline was maintained by using the existing steel trusses in combination with four new main diagonal trusses. As much of the wood, steel, and concrete as could be salvaged were used to construct the new structure. It reopened in 1995 as KeyArena.

OTHER STRUCTURES

Post office

Kobe Bell

Restaurants separate from the Food Circus. Some of these, such as the two Belgian Waffle shops, had distinctive facades.

Individual booths, such as Victor Steinbrueck's American Institute of Architects booth, Canadian Pacific arch, separate from covered exhibit spaces. Some, like Societe Candy's miniature candy factory by Durham, Anderson & Freed, featured demonstrations — in that case, saltwater taffy production. One, the Gems of the World building, was moved to St. Louise parish school in Bellevue after the fair. Some of the world's fair ticket booths were purchased by the Ellensburg Rodeo/Kittitas County Fair.

above left Hofbrau Haus Restaurant.

above right United States Post Office Space Needle Station.

below Japanese schoolchildren from Kobe, Seattle's sister city, raised funds for a one-ton temple bell that was dedicated during the fair.

opposite The Washington State Coliseum housed the fair's showcase exhibit, The World of Tomorrow.

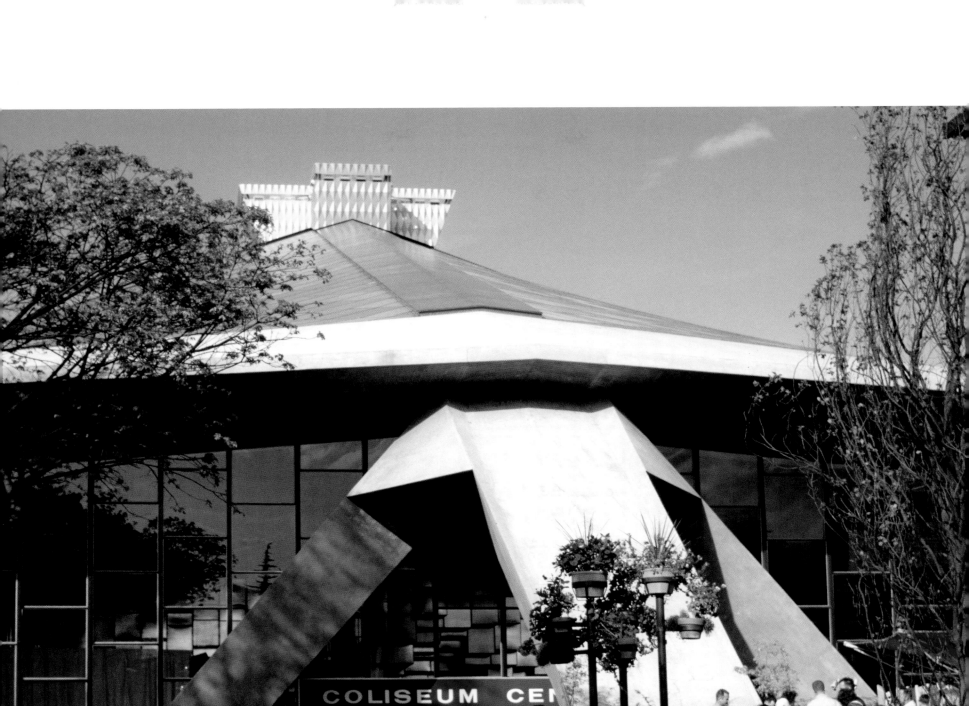

left Space Needle construction transfixed Seattle residents, then captured global attention.

opposite above left King County plat map of future Century 21 Exposition/Seattle Center site.

above right Plans for Seattle's Civic Field, Auditorium, and Ice Arena.

below: Opening day pass to the 1909 Alaska-Yukon-Pacific Exposition.

Chronology

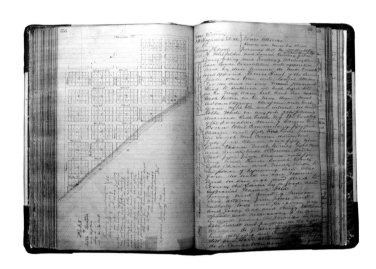

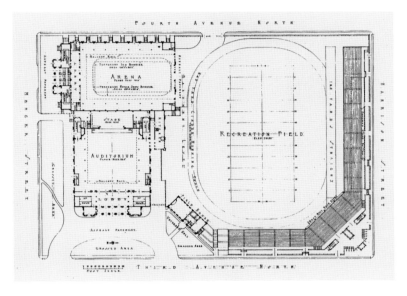

David Denny files a land claim on January 24, 1853, for a tract that more than a century later will become the site of Century 21.

Physical environment abutting future site of Century 21 is altered by second phase of the Denny Regrade between 1904 and 1911.

Alaska-Yukon-Pacific Exposition (A-Y-P) opens on June 1, 1909.

Alaska-Yukon-Pacific Exposition closes on October 16, 1909.

Civic Field (now Memorial Stadium) opens in 1927.

Civic Auditorium, Ice Arena, and Civic Field are dedicated on May 18, 1928.

Bureau of International Expositions is officially organized in Paris on November 22, 1928.

National Guard Armory, built to house the 146th Field Artillery, is dedicated on April 17, 1939.

Civic Field is renamed High School Memorial Stadium on November 27, 1947.

Albert Canwell's Legislative Fact-Finding Committee on Un-American Activities holds highly publicized hearings in the National Guard Armory in 1948 on alleged communist activities.

Memorial wall honoring 762 Seattle high school youth or alumni killed in World War II is dedicated outside Memorial Stadium on May 29, 1951.

City Councilmember Al Rochester begins suggesting in 1954 that Seattle host a "world's fair" to coincide with the 50th anniversary of the A-Y-P.

Seattle City Council drafts a memorial statement to the state legislature on January 27, 1955, recommending an investigation of the feasibility of a world's fair to be held in Seattle.

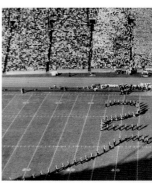

First printed mention of a proposed world's fair appears in the Seattle newspapers on January 30, 1955.

Seattle City Council formally adopts the memorial statement to the legislature on February 7, 1955.

Governor Arthur Langlie signs a bill authorizing a commission to study the feasibility of a world's fair in February 1955.

Washington World's Fair Commission, chaired by Edward Carlson, holds its first meeting at the Olympic Hotel on August 19, 1955.

Members of the World's Fair Commission take a daylong bus tour of proposed fair sites on March 22, 1956.

World's Fair Commission votes unanimously on July 6, 1956, to coordinate the fair program with the city effort to develop a civic center at and around the Civic Auditorium.

World's Fair Commission concludes in September 1956 that there is not time to produce a 1959 A-Y-P commemoration and recommends to the state legislature that a "Festival of the West" be held from July through October of both 1960 and 1961.

Seattle voters approve a $7.5 million bond issue on November 6, 1956, for buildings and land acquisition in the vicinity of the Civic Auditorium.

Seattle Civic Center Advisory Commission is created by the Seattle City Council in December 1956.

Washington Governor Albert Rosellini signs S.B. 45, which authorizes the World's Fair Commission to hold a fair in Seattle in 1960, on February 19, 1957.

Washington Legislature approves $7.5 million in March 1957 for world's fair funding.

Ewen Dingwall is appointed project director of the Seattle Civic Center Advisory Commission and Washington World's Fair Commission in April 1957, becoming the future fair's first paid employee.

Soviet Union launches the world's first space satellite, *Sputnik*, on October 4, 1957.

World's Fair Corporation of Washington, Inc., is incorporated on October 9, 1957.

Alarmed by empty coffers, key World's Fair Commission board members issue plea for $1,000 preliminary pledges to 30 wealthy board members

on December 3, 1957, and receive $25,000 within the next few weeks.

First meeting of Washington World's Fair, Inc., trustees is held on January 28, 1958.

Explorer 1, America's first satellite, is sent into orbit on January 31, 1958.

Ewen Dingwall, Eddie Carlson, and world's fair Public Relations Director Jim Faber meet with top U.S. scientists in Washington, D.C., in attempt to secure their support for focusing the fair on science, on March 15, 1958.

Expo 58, the Brussels World's Fair, opens on April 17, 1958.

Civic Auditorium vicinity is chosen as site for the world's fair, now referred to in the press as Century 21, on July 7, 1958.

The name "Century 21 Exposition" is officially approved by the World's Fair Corporation board of trustees on July 22, 1958.

First meeting of the National Science Planning Board is held in Seattle on August 6, 1958, to plan a science exhibit for Century 21.

Paul Thiry is selected as Century 21 principal architect on August 13, 1958.

CENTURY 21 EXPOSITION

Journey West for a glimpse of the century ahead

BRING THE WHOLE FAMILY!

CENTURY 21 EXPOSITION
SEATTLE, U.S.A. 1962

President Dwight D. Eisenhower signs Public Law 85-880 on August 28, 1958, to study the extent of federal participation in Century 21.

President Eisenhower, in Seattle to attend the Columbo Plan Conference, presses a red button to set the Century 21 electronic countdown chronometer in motion on November 10, 1958.

Demolition of buildings on fair site begins on November 12, 1958.

The name "World's Fair Corporation of Washington" is officially amended, becoming Century 21 Exposition, Inc., on November 20, 1958.

President Eisenhower forms the National Aeronautics and Space Administration on December 17, 1958.

On January 23, 1959, the Seattle City Council agrees to buy the planned Coliseum from the state and convert it to a sports pavilion and trade show facility after the close of the fair.

Seattle City Council passes Resolution 18952 in support of the Century 21 Exposition on March 2, 1959.

Century 21 Monorail plan is presented to the public on March 30, 1959.

Re-creation of the 1909 A-Y-P transcontinental auto race is celebrated before groundbreaking ceremonies at the fair site on June 23, 1959.

Edward Carlson steps down as president of Century 21 Exposition, Inc., and is replaced by Joseph Gandy on July 4, 1959.

David "Ned" Skinner and Greg MacDonald chair an underwriting committee that raises $4.5 million beginning on July 27, 1959, to finance Century 21 operations during the prefair period.

U.S. House of Representatives approves bill authorizing federal participation in Century 21 on August 13, 1959.

U.S. Senate approves bill authorizing federal participation in Century 21 on August 21, 1959.

Federal government appropriates $9 million to construct the United States Science Pavilion at Century 21 on September 15, 1959, later bolstered with an additional $900,000.

Seattle voters approve a proposition on September 29, 1959, to remodel the Civic Auditorium into the Opera House.

above, from left Washington Governor Arthur B. Langlie; Aerial view of Memorial Stadium, Civic Auditorium, and Arena, ca. 1958; House demolition was a necessary prelude to the fair; 1958 Seattle city planning commissioners, including (sitting, left to right) Paul Thiry, Harold Shefelman, Robert Cotter, Gilbert Mandeville, Paul Brown, Roy Morse, (standing, left to right) John Spaeth, F. E. Huggard, Merlin Brown, and Fred McCoy visit fair offices prior to Thiry's appointment as the exposition's chief architect; University of Washington marching band saluted Century 21 at the 1961 Rose Bowl half-time show, while Husky fans participated in a memorable card stunt up in the stands; Senator Warren Magnuson (center), Century 21 Exposition, Inc., President Edward Carlson (next right), and vice presidents (counterclockwise from behind Carlson) Lee Moran, Otto Brandt, Robert Colwell, Edward Tremper, Fred Paulsell (treasurer), James B. Davis, and Iver Cederwell; The fair's font was clean and clear; One promotional brochure used the old exhortation, "Go West!"; Monorail prototype; Promotional brochures ranged from folksy to futuristic. below NASA signified the future in space, validating the fair's premise.

Washington World's Fair Commission and Century 21 Exposition, Inc., agree to postpone the opening of the exposition from 1961 to spring 1962, on October 2, 1959.

U.S. State Department sends invitations to 84 nations with whom the United States has diplomatic relations on November 10, 1959, urging them to participate in Century 21.

Century 21 begins a worldwide campaign for participation on January 10, 1960.

Expo Lodging, Inc., a private venture by the Seattle area housing industry, is incorporated on April 21, 1960.

Century 21 is certified by the Bureau of International Expositions, the international sanctioning organization for world's fairs, on May 5, 1960.

Coliseum construction begins on May 12, 1960.

First Boeing 707 jet to enter service on the Pacific Coast is christened the Century 21, on June 1, 1960.

Senator Warren Magnuson secures $70,000 in further federal appropriations to fund Library 21; a Health, Education, and Welfare Department Learning Center; and a NASA exhibit.

Century 21 adopts a new name on July 22, 1960: Century 21 Exposition — America's Space Age World's Fair.

A 550-foot observation tower is proposed for the fair on September 12, 1960.

Bureau of International Expositions recognizes Century 21 as an official world's fair on November 12, 1960.

John Kennedy takes the presidential oath on January 20, 1961, becoming the first U.S. president born in the twentieth century.

Civic center is renamed Seattle Center on February 28, 1961.

State senate approves an additional $3 million to fund construction of Coliseum and state theme exhibit for Century 21 on March 5, 1961.

International Fountain design, by Hideki Shimizu and Kazuvuki Matsushita, is chosen on March 13, 1961.

Monorail construction contract between Century 21 and Alweg Rapid Transit Systems is signed on March 13, 1961.

Edward Carlson steps down as chairman of Century 21 Exposition, Inc., and is replaced by William Street on March 17, 1961.

Groundbreaking ceremonies for Monorail are held on April 6, 1961.

Soviet cosmonaut Yuri Gagarin completes one full orbit around the earth on April 12, 1961, the first human to do so.

Groundbreaking ceremonies for the Space Needle are held on April 17, 1961.

Twenty-one 21-year-old women, holding letters that spell out "Century 21 World's Fair," pose for a publicity photo in front of the Coliseum construction on April 21, 1961.

Space Needle gets okay from Federal Aviation Agency on May 2, 1961, as long as the tower is lighted per FAA regulations.

First continuous concrete pour for the Space Needle foundation begins on May 22, 1961.

President Kennedy tells Congress on May 25, 1961, "I believe this nation should commit itself

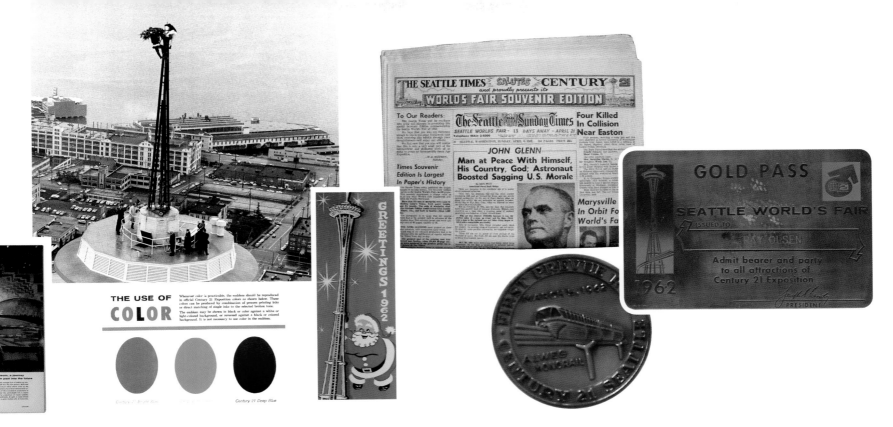

to achieving the goal, before this decade is out, of landing a man on the moon and returning him safely to Earth."

Dr. Athelstan Spilhaus is installed as the commissioner of the U.S. science exhibit on June 1, 1961.

Century 21 officials sign a $2 million contract for the Gayway on June 14, 1961.

Century 21 worker is killed in a crane accident at the Civic Auditorium on July 25, 1961.

Dahlia is named to official flower for Century 21 on August 30, 1961.

Eye of the Needle is chosen as the name of the Space Needle restaurant on October 16, 1961.

Gracie Hansen receives a contract on October 25, 1961, to operate a nightclub on Show Street.

Century 21 site is closed to the public on October 31, 1961, until opening day on April 21, 1962.

World's Fair Commission names the Coliseum the "Washington State Coliseum" on November 1, 1961.

Ford Motor Company agrees on December 5, 1961, to build a pavilion in Century 21's last open space.

Space Needle construction workers fly the American flag from the top of the Space Needle, signaling completion of the structure's highest point, on December 8, 1961.

LIFE magazine with cover featuring the Space Needle under construction is published on February 9, 1962.

Expo Lodging officially becomes a division of Century 21 on February 13, 1962.

American astronaut John Glenn orbits the earth on February 20, 1962.

World's fair East Gate collapses during construction on February 26, 1962.

Lee Moran, Century 21 vice president of exhibits, dies in a plane crash in New York on March 1, 1962.

Monorail depot roof collapses under heavy snow on March 1, 1962.

World's fair hospital treats its first patient on March 21, 1962.

Seattle Center is dedicated and two time capsules, dedicated to the citizens of Seattle in 2012, are sealed in a cornerstone of the Opera House on April 9, 1962.

Legislators' preview of Century 21 is held on April 15, 1962.

Monorail is christened on April 19, 1962.

above, from left Promoting participation in the fair was a round-the-world job; Northwest Airlines boosted the fair; Space Needle on the drawing board; Pin; No grown-up visit was complete without *A Night In Paradise;* Seattleites predicted that these items (horse, car, cigarettes) might be extinct by the year 2000; Coliseum construction; Rear-screen projection was a novel technique when utilized on the cubes in the fair's theme exhibit, *The Threshold and the Threat*; Santa atop the Space Needle (still under construction), December 1961; Century 21 Exposition's designated colors; Even 1961's Christmas cards promoted the upcoming fair; Both major Seattle papers produced World's Fair editions; Monorail preview ride medallion; Gold Passes gave high-ranking bearers carte blanche to the fair.

below Twenty-one 21-year-olds beckon visitors to Century 21.

Century 21 opens on April 21, 1962.

U.S. Air Force plane performing in opening day festivities crashes in a Mountlake Terrace neighborhood killing two people on April 21, 1962.

Easter services are held on April 22, 1962.

Wisconsin Day is held on April 23, 1962.

Idaho Day is held on April 24, 1962.

Texas Day is held on April 27, 1962.

Montana Day is held on April 28, 1962.

Portland Day and Arkansas Day are held on April 29, 1962.

Sweden Week is held beginning April 30, 1962.

Alabama Day and Law Day are held on May 1, 1962.

First naturalization ceremony for new U.S. citizens is held on the grounds on May 1, 1962.

Girl Scout Day is held on May 2, 1962.

LIFE magazine with cover featuring the Monorail and headlined "Century 21 Opens — Out of This World Fair in Seattle" is published on May 4, 1962.

San Francisco Day is held on May 4, 1962.

Camp Fire Girls Day is held on May 5, 1962.

Soviet cosmonaut Major Gherman Titov visits Century 21 on May 5, 1962.

Los Angeles Day is held on May 6, 1962.

Washington State Week is held beginning May 7, 1962.

New York Day is held on May 10, 1962.

John Glenn visits Century 21 on May 10, 1962.

State Beautification Day, Iowa Day, and School Patrol Day are held on May 12, 1962.

Mothers Day is held on May 13, 1962.

Fair officials close the *Girls of the Galaxy* show due to excessive nudity on May 15, 1962.

Kobe Day is held on May 16, 1962.

Denmark Day is held on May 17, 1962.

Boy Scout Day is held on May 19, 1962.

Vancouver, B.C., Day is held on May 21, 1962.

International Law Day and Nebraska Day are held on May 25, 1962.

Oregon Day is held on May 26, 1962.

British Week is held beginning May 27, 1962.

Memorial Day is observed on May 30, 1962.

Dominion Monarch arrives in Seattle to serve as a hotel ship on May 30, 1962.

American Waterworks Day is held on May 31, 1962.

HRH Prince Philip, Duke of Edinburgh, visits Century 21 on June 1, 1962.

Connecticut Day is held on June 2, 1962.

Wyoming Day and Architects Day are held on June 3, 1962.

Dr. Jonas Salk visits the fair and is honored at the United States Science Pavilion on June 4, 1962.

World's Fair Trade Dollar Days begin on June 4, 1962.

North Dakota Day and Hawaii Night are held on June 5, 1962.

Kansas Day is held on June 7, 1962.

Seattle Symphony debuts at Opera House with Verdi's *Aida* on June 7, 1962.

Indiana Day is held on June 8, 1962.

Georgia Day is held on June 9, 1962.

South Dakota Day is held on June 10, 1962.

Century 21 attendance passes two million on June 10, 1962.

Missouri Day and International Rotary Day are held on June 11, 1962.

Minnesota Day is held on June 12, 1962.

Nevada Day and Communications Day are held on June 13, 1962.

Flag Day is held on June 14, 1962.

California Day is held on June 15, 1962.

American-Norway Day is held on June 17, 1962.

Rhode Island Day is held on June 18, 1962.

Adlai Stevenson, U.S. ambassador to the United Nations, visits Century 21 on June 18, 1962.

United Nations Day and Michigan Day are held on June 19, 1962.

Illinois Day and West Virginia Night are held on June 20, 1962.

Colorado Day is held on June 21, 1962.

A-Y-P Exposition Day is held on June 22, 1962.

North Carolina Day is held on June 23, 1962.

International Jaycees Day is held on June 25, 1962

Florida Day is held on June 27, 1962.

above, from left Joseph Gandy and Gherman Titov help celebrate Camp Fire Girls Day; World's Fair postage stamp; Oregon's exhibit was a respite from fairground bustle; New York promoted its upcoming world's fair from a booth in the Interiors, Fashion, and Commerce Pavilion; Great Britain Pavilion brochure; Polio vaccine developer Dr. Jonas Salk; Citizenship ceremonies in the Flag Pavilion; Logo patch; Carol Channing helps George Burns light his cigar using a Space Needle lighter; Thomas MacGuire and Charles Feck (kneeling), Wallace Denhoff, Guy Bodor, and George Krusse of Reserve Anti-Submarine Squadron US-721 celebrate Illinois Day; Pianist Van Cliburn; Space Wheel on opening day.
center Ticket to Peaceful Uses of Space conference.
left World's Fair stamp First Day Cover envelope.

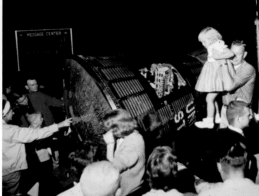

South Carolina Day is held on June 28, 1962.

Ohio Day is held on June 30, 1962.

U.S.A. Week is held beginning July 2, 1962.

Washington, D.C., Day is held on July 2, 1962.

Pennsylvania Day is held on July 3, 1962.

Independence Day is observed on July 4, 1962.

More than 2,000 mobile-home owners from around the world rally in Auburn on July 4, 1962.

Alaska Day is held on July 7, 1962.

Philippines Week is held beginning July 9, 1962.

Telstar 1, the world's first communications satellite capable of both sending and receiving signals, is launched from Cape Canaveral, Florida, on July 10, 1962.

Kiwanis Day is held July 11, 1962.

Korea Day is held on July 13, 1962.

New Mexico Day is held on July 14, 1962.

Children's Week is held beginning July 15, 1962.

Visit U.S.A. Day is held on July 15, 1962.

Mercury 7 astronauts John Glenn and Scott Carpenter appear before Congress to testify against the inclusion of women in the U.S. space program on July 18, 1962.

New Jersey Day is held on July 20, 1962.

Kentucky Day is held on July 21, 1962.

Japan Week is held beginning July 23, 1962.

The United States exchanges live television broadcasts (including one originating at Century 21) via *Telstar 1* with 14 European nations, including from Century 21, on July 23, 1962.

Seafair Day is held on July 29, 1962.

American Automobile Association Day and Fleet Day are held on July 31, 1962.

United Arab Republic Day and Delaware Day are held on August 1, 1962.

Marilyn Monroe dies in her home in Los Angeles, California, on August 5, 1962.

U.S. Attorney General Robert Kennedy visits Century 21 on August 6, 1962.

John Glenn's *Friendship 7* space capsule goes on display in the NASA Pavilion on August 6, 1962.

Miami Day is held on August 9, 1962.

Massachusetts Day and Lions International Day are held on August 12, 1962.

International Trails Day and Snipe Regatta Day are held on August 14, 1962.

Utah Day is held on August 16, 1962.

Patricia Ann Thearse Dzejachok is crowned Miss Century 21, World's Fairest, on August 18, 1962.

Flying Farmers Day is held on August 21, 1962.

Oklahoma Day and Babe Ruth–Little League Day are held on August 25, 1962.

Mexico Week is held beginning August 27, 1962.

Peace Corps Day is held on August 31, 1962.

Tennessee Day is held on September 1, 1962.

Labor Day is observed on September 3, 1962.

Brazil Week is held beginning September 5, 1962.

Virginia Day is held on September 5, 1962.

Elvis Presley arrives in Seattle on September 5, 1962, for 10 days of shooting for the film *Meet Me at the Fair* (released as *It Happened at the World's Fair*).

Mississippi Day is held on September 6, 1962.

Canada Week is held beginning September 10, 1962.

Elks Day is held on September 10, 1962.

Maryland Day is held on September 12, 1962.

Victoria, B.C., Day is held on September 15, 1962.

United Nations Philatelic Day is held on September 17, 1962.

European Community Week is held beginning September 23, 1962.

Louisiana Day is held on September 23, 1962.

International Downtown Executives Day is held on September 26, 1962.

Vermont Day is held on September 27, 1962.

Edward Carlson is honored as World's Fair First Citizen on a Special Day designated by Governor Albert Rosellini, September 27, 1962.

New Hampshire Day, State Host City Day, and Broadway High School Alumni Day are held on September 28, 1962.

India Week is held beginning September 30, 1962.

Maine Day is held on October 1, 1962.

Library Day is held on October 2, 1962.

Paul Thiry submits his plans and recommendations for the postfair Seattle Center to Mayor Gordon Clinton on October 4, 1962.

Mercer Island Day is held on October 7, 1962.

Republic of China Week is held beginning October 8, 1962.

Columbus Day is held on October 12, 1962.

above, from left This postcard featuring the International Fountain was also a playable recording of *The Summer of 1962*; Fairgrounds coaster; Hydrogen bomb "father" Dr. Edward Teller visited the fair and spoke at the National Advanced Technological Management conference; KING 5 TV cameras shot the fair from every angle, including from the Eye of the Needle; Coins worth $1 at participating Alaska businesses were fair giveaways to promote tourism; Fairgoers marveled at *Friendship 7* in the NASA Pavilion; Elvis Presley, Joan O'Brien, Jackie Souders, and the World's Fair Band shoot the film's finale; Smith Association card; Governor Albert Rosellini and Edward Carlson; Tape recorded Library of the Future; Circus Berlin aerialists; Count Basie and His Orchestra; Joseph Gandy and Richard Nixon.

below Thailand issued a Century 21 postage stamp.

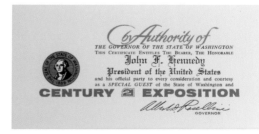

Governor's Appreciation Day and Fraternity-Sorority Day are held on October 14, 1962.

Thailand Day is held on October 18, 1962.

Century 21 closing ceremonies are held on October 21, 1962.

Cuban Missile Crisis becomes public on October 22, 1962.

United States Science Pavilion reopens as Pacific Science Center on October 22, 1962.

Space Needle reopens for business on October 26, 1962.

Seattle World Center Corporation, a nonprofit corporation to promote the full use of Seattle Center, is formed on October 29, 1962.

Seattle World Center is renamed Century 21 Center, Inc., on November 5, 1962.

Century 21 Exposition's lease ends and City of Seattle resumes possession of fairgrounds on January 1, 1963.

All assets and liabilities of Century 21 Exposition, Inc. are transferred to the liquidating trustees on March 8, 1963.

It Happened at the World's Fair opens in movie theaters on April 3, 1963.

Century 21 Center, Inc., announces plans to construct Fun Forest amusement area on May 5, 1963.

Century 21 Exposition fairgrounds reopen as Century 21 Center on June 1, 1963.

Soviet cosmonaut Valentina Tereshkova becomes the first woman in space on June 16, 1963.

Seattle Repertory Theatre opens in former Century 21 Playhouse on November 13, 1963.

President John Kennedy is assassinated in Dallas, Texas, on November 22, 1963.

President Lyndon Johnson signs the Civil Rights Act into law, including Title VII banning discrimination on the basis of race and sex, on July 22, 1964.

City of Seattle purchases the Monorail system from Century 21 Center, Inc., for $600,000 in 1965.

Century 21 Center, Inc. is dissolved in spring 1965.

Seattle Mayor J. D. Braman signs into law Ordinance 93769 establishing Seattle Center as a city department on April 8, 1965.

Century 21 Exposition liquidators announce that the fair's books are closing with a profit, on June 28, 1966.

U.S. astronaut Neil Armstrong becomes first person to set foot on the moon on July 20, 1969.

Festival '71, the first postfair event to utilize the entire Seattle Center campus, is held in mid-August 1971 and is repeated as Festival '72 the following August, becoming Bumbershoot (an annual event) in 1973.

Northwest Folklife Festival is held for the first time over Memorial Day weekend in May 1972, utilizing the entire Seattle Center campus and becoming an annual event.

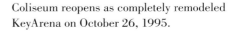

The nonprofit Seattle Center Foundation is incorporated to administer and encourage charitable gifts, grants, donations, bequests, and memorials to Seattle Center on May 6, 1977.

Seattle voters pass a $19 million bond measure for a wide variety of upgrades and improvements to Seattle Center in 1978.

King Tut Exhibition draws thousands of visitors to Seattle Center from July 16 to November 15, 1978.

The Sky Ride is moved to Western Washington Fair in Puyallup in 1979.

The Bubbleator is removed from its relocated position in the Center House, donated to Children's Hospital, and placed in storage in 1980.

Groundbreaking ceremonies for Seattle Repertory Theatre's Bagley Wright Theatre on the site of Century 21's International Mall buildings are held on December 29, 1981.

Space Needle's Skyline Level addition, housing kitchen and banquet facilities, opens in mid-July 1982.

Sally Ride, serving as mission specialist on the space shuttle Challenger becomes the first American woman in space on June 18, 1983.

Gene Achziger purchases disassembled Bubbleator, transports the pieces to his home in Redondo, and reconstructs it to use as a greenhouse in 1984.

Bite of Seattle outgrows its Green Lake location and moves to Seattle Center in 1986.

KCTS 9 moves broadcast operations to a new building on the site of Century 21's Show Street on October 5, 1986.

Playhouse Courtyard outside Intiman Theatre is dedicated to Ewen Dingwall in appreciation of his vision and enthusiasm for Seattle Center from 1957 to 1988 on June 27, 1989.

Gracie Hansen Community Center, formerly the Paradise International nightclub, is dedicated in Ravensdale Park in south King County on September 16, 1989.

Annual tradition of New Year's Eve fireworks display at the Space Needle begins on December 31, 1992.

Seattle Children's Theatre opens its Charlotte Martin Theatre on the sites of the Sermons from Science Pavilion, American Home Pavilion, Nalley's Pavilion, and Club 21 on September 20, 1993.

Coliseum reopens as completely remodeled KeyArena on October 26, 1995.

above, from left Souvenir of the fair's closing day; Official medallion; The United States Science Pavilion reopened immediately as Pacific Science Center; Festival '71 grew into Bumbershoot; Seattle Repertory staffers (from left) Ruth McCloy, press director, Norman Israel, business manager, and Barbara Tenneson, subscription director; Space Needle fireworks are a New Year's Eve tradition; Opening day at Seattle Children's Theatre Charlotte Martin Theatre; Gracie ran for governor of Oregon in 1970; Comcast Bite of Seattle; KeyArena opening day; Plaque in Intiman courtyard honoring Ewen Dingwall; Bumbershoot. below President Kennedy's guest pass for closing day was never presented due to the Cuban Missile Crisis.

Seattle Landmarks Preservation Board names the Space Needle an official city landmark on April 21, 1999.

Experience Music Project opens on the eastern portion of the Century 21 Gayway on June 23, 2000.

Space Needle's ground-level retail pavilion addition opens on June 15, 2000.

Seattle Shakespeare Company, founded in 1991, produces a season of works by Shakespeare and other classic playwrights in Seattle Center House Theatre and moves its administrative offices to Seattle Center House in summer 2000.

Book-It Repertory Theatre moves its administrative offices and performances to Seattle Center House in 2000.

Seattle Public Schools opens the Center School, a small public high school with a focus on the arts and community engagement, in Seattle Center House in September 2001.

Marion Oliver McCaw Hall opens on the site of the former Civic Auditorium/Opera House on June 28, 2003.

Seattle Landmarks Preservation Board names the Monorail an official city landmark on August 4, 2003.

Seattle Landmarks Preservation Board names Kobe Bell, Seattle Mural, and Seattle Center House official city landmarks on September 15, 2004.

The VERA Project, an all-ages volunteer-powered music and arts organization, moves from downtown to a custom-designed venue in the Northwest Rooms at Seattle Center in February 2007.

Seattle International Film Festival opens a year-long programming venue, SIFF Cinema, in McCaw Hall's Nesholm Family Lecture Hall, in March 2007.

Seattle Center Century 21 Master Plan is adopted in August 2008.

Seattle Center issues Century 21 Design Guidelines, Century 21 Architectural Design Guidelines, and Century 21 Public Art Plan and Guidelines in 2009.

Seattle Center issues strategic plan "Destination 2012" in May 2010.

Seattle Landmarks Preservation Board names Pacific Science Center an official city landmark on July 21, 2010.

clockwise from left Craig McCaw, Korynne Wright, Seattle Mayor Greg Nickels, Andrew Harris, Marion O. McCaw, and Bruce McCaw open 1928 and 1962 time capsules during McCaw Hall groundbreaking ceremonies; Doris Chase's *Moon Gates*; International Fountain at night; Fisher Pavilion opening celebration; VERA Project.

opposite Visitors of all ages enjoy the International Fountain's refreshing spray.

Afterword

WHEN THE 1962 WORLD'S FAIR ORGANIZERS BEGAN THEIR PLANNING, THEY ENVISIONED leaving a permanent legacy of a civic and cultural gathering place that would serve the entire community. Fifty years later, their vision lives on at Seattle Center, home to more than 30 arts and culture organizations, numerous festivals and events, and the open space and outdoor art that make this the region's premier urban park.

Seattle Center is today a cultural icon that connects our communities, drives the success of surrounding businesses and serves as the region's most popular tourist destination. While most visitors come to Seattle Center for a particular event, activity, or experience, our hope is that they will linger longer than expected because of the beauty and attractions they encounter along the way.

As the region has prospered and diversified over the past 50 years, so too has Seattle Center. Many of the buildings erected for the World's Fair now house some of the finest arts, sports and educational institutions in the nation. The concentration and quality are truly astonishing. Where else in the world can one find a world-class children's theater across the way from a top science center; and two nationally honored regional theaters adjacent to one another; and an opera and ballet the envy of their peers across the country; and so much more — all within a 74-acre area?

The City of Seattle has invested wisely in this place over the years to support capital redevelopment, campus maintenance and operations, and public programming that inspires the human spirit and brings together our rich and varied community. Its investment has been more than matched by private sector contributions. These public-private partnerships have proven to be the lifeblood of the Center.

Today we stand at a crossroads, where we look back on a place steeped in history, culture and celebration — and we look forward and envision how to maintain the cultural soul and civic relevance of Seattle Center.

The next 50 years will witness continued growth of Seattle's urban core, where green, open spaces and places to escape the bustling street life will increase even more in their intrinsic value. In this age of instant electronic communication, where individuals so often interact through a virtual world, the yearning to gather and share real, physical experiences will certainly deepen. Families will seek places for their children to play, create and learn. Those desiring cultural enrichment will continue to search out music, dance, theater and visual arts, while sports fans will continue to gather for games and competitions.

The Century 21 Master Plan provides an exciting and responsive blueprint for capital and programmatic redevelopment over the next 20 years. Incremental steps have already been taken at the perimeters of the grounds, where the Broad Street Green, Seattle Center Skatepark and Theater Commons have reshaped campus entry points. New partnerships with Seattle Opera and the Space Needle will help lead the redevelopment of multiple spaces on the campus, while major interior projects, such as redevelopment of the Memorial Stadium site and surface parking lot, await funding, which will come in time.

Seattle Center remains relevant by staying responsive to community needs and desires. As our region evolves, so will the center, in its programs and the place itself. People will continue to gather here, in the heart of our city, to discover the essence of community and the joy of human connection.

What can we do to sustain this very special place? What resources will be dedicated to its future? How best does Seattle Center continue to serve the community? What will visitors find here 50 years from now? What impressions and memories will they take away?

These are the questions with which we grapple as we approach this important milestone. As stewards of Seattle Center we carry the responsibility to continue the legacy established 50 years ago. And just like those before us we will need everyone's help to make this the best Seattle Center possible. Please help us create a center that will continue to delight and inspire future generations!

Robert Nellams Tracy Robinson
Director Executive Director
Seattle Center Seattle Center Foundation

left Leni Schwendinger's "Dreaming In Color" draws visitors to Seattle Center through Kreielsheimer Promenade under a series of glowing mesh scrims.

right Seattle Center Skatepark enlivens the western edge of the center's campus.

opposite The 2012 medallion utilizes George Tsutakawa's 1962 design on one side and *The Next Fifty* logo on the other.

Note on Sources

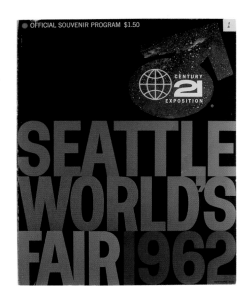

above Official Souvenir Program.

opposite Whether playing their instruments or just crossing the fairgrounds, the Official World's Fair Band attracted attention.

The Seattle World's Fair chapter in John M. Findlay's fine *Magic Lands: Western Cityscapes and American Culture After 1940* provided a wealth of thoughtful analysis regarding who participated in Century 21, and why.

Murray Morgan was the fair's official historian, and his 1963 *Century 21: The Story of the Seattle World's Fair* gave us a detailed map of how the fair came to be, from a contemporary perspective.

Don Duncan's 1992 *Meet Me At The Center: The Story of Seattle Center From The Beginnings To The 1962 World's Fair To The 21st Century* provided a wealth of anecdotes and, most importantly, captured first-person stories from many of the fair's planners who had passed on by the time we began our research.

The World's Fair chapter of Edward Carlson's memoir, *Recollections of a Lucky Fellow*, provided a wonderful view of the fair from the perspective of one of its most important players.

Contemporary publications we found helpful included Harold Mansfield and George Gulacsik's *Space Needle USA*, and *Official Guide Book Seattle World's Fair 1962*.

We were most fortunate to have the opportunity to interview a number of people who played key roles in making the fair happen. The memories they shared in those interviews were one of our most important sources, and we thank and name them in our acknowledgments. Lorraine McConahy's Ewen Dingwall oral history, Donald Schmeckle's Laurene Gandy oral history, William Street's Edward Carlson oral history, and Junius Rochester's Al Rochester oral history all provided us with key first-hand reflections from some of the fair's most important shapers.

Seattle television station KING TV was a daily presence on the fairgrounds, and existing film was a valuable resource in our project. Particularly notable are KING's "World of Tomorrow" series, KING's opening ceremonies, and KING's closing ceremonies.

KCTS 9, whose Seattle Center home stands on the site of the fair's Show Street, marked the fair's 25th anniversary celebrations with series of insightful programming that featured many interviews with key fair players. We were delighted to discover that the main reporter on this series was none other than HistoryLink.org's late co-founder, Walt Crowley. Walt's 1987 interviews, particularly those with Eddie Carlson and Georgia Gellert Penfield, provided important information, and we are charmed and honored to feel that Walt, who would have loved to have been a part of this 50th anniversary history of the fair, was thus, in a way, on the team.

As always in a project such as this, daily newspapers provide a steady path for the historian to follow. We exhaustively examined the *Seattle Post-Intelligencer*, *The Seattle Times*, *The Daily*, *The Facts*, and (for coverage of Seattle Center's growth and challenges) both the *Weekly* and *The Stranger*. Of the thousands of magazine stories that resulted from the yeoman's efforts of the amazing World's Fair public relations division, we found *LIFE*, *Sunset*, and *Progressive Architecture* particularly useful.

Secondary source material that was especially useful included James Gilbert, *Redeeming Culture: American Religion In An Age of Science*; Barbara Johns, *Paul Horiuchi East and West*; Robert S. Ellwood, *The*

Fifties Spiritual Marketplace: American Religion in a Decade of Conflict; Martin Halliwell, *American Culture in the 1950s*; David Halberstam, *The Fifties*; Tom Wolfe, *The Right Stuff*; Margaret A. Weitekamp, *Right Stuff, Wrong Sex: America's First Women In Space Program*; Paul Boyer, *By The Bomb's Early Light: American Thought and Culture at the Dawn of the Atomic Age*; Sheldon Stern, *The Week The Earth Stood Still: Inside The Secret Cuban Missile Crisis*; Seymour M. Hersh, *The Dark Side of Camelot*; and Louis Solomon, *Telstar: Communication Break-Through By Satellite*.

Finally, having written a history of the 1909 Alaska-Yukon-Pacific Exposition, for which archival materials by fair staff and planners are almost nonexistent, it was a joy to find that the exact opposite situation exists for 1962's Century 21. We utilized the extensive Seattle World's Fair records housed at the Puget Sound branch of the Washington State Archives, the Joseph Gandy materials and Ewen C. Dingwall materials held by University of Washington Special Collections, and Donald Foster's materials at the Museum of History and Industry.

Image Credits

Seattle Public Library (Werner Lenggenhager Collection).

P. 102

Ringing the Friendship Bell. Courtesy Puget Sound Regional Branch Washington State Archives, Century 21 Exposition (C9605).

Evalyn Van Vliet named the one-millionth visitor. Courtesy Puget Sound Regional Branch Washington State Archives, Century 21 Exposition (C9950).

P. 103

Bell Systems exhibit. Courtesy University of Washington Libraries, Special Collections (UW29440z).

Bell Systems cartoon. Courtesy Seattle Center.

P. 104

Fashion show. Courtesy Puget Sound Regional Branch Washington State Archives, Century 21 Exposition (CR6418).

NASA tracking station. Courtesy Puget Sound Regional Branch Washington State Archives, Century 21 Exposition, Media Photo Prints, Unprocessed Box 3 of 6.

P. 105

NASA exhibit. Courtesy Puget Sound Regional Branch Washington State Archives, Century 21 Exposition, Media Photo Prints, Unprocessed Box 3 of 6.

P. 106

The Bubbleator. Photo by Morley Studios. Courtesy Museum of History & Industry (1987.59).

P. 107

Tamar Ivask, the one-millionth Monorail passenger. Courtesy Puget Sound Regional Branch Washington State Archives, Century 21 Exposition (C10599).

Oregon Governor Mark Hatfield with members of the United Indian Tribes of Oregon. Courtesy Puget Sound Regional Branch Washington State Archives, Century 21 Exposition (CR10696).

Monorail pin. Courtesy Paula Becker.

P. 108

The Dominion Monarch. Courtesy Museum of History & Industry (2002.57).

P. 109

Bell Systems' Princess Phone. Courtesy Albert Fisher.

P. 110

The fair's south entrance gate. Courtesy University of Washington Libraries, Special Collections (UW29439z).

P. 112

HRH Prince Philip of Great Britain. Photo by Forde Photographers. Image courtesy of the Bryce Seidl Collection (4830).

Library of the Future exhibit. Photo by Morley Studios. Courtesy Museum of History & Industry (1987.59).

P. 113

Romeo and Juliet. Courtesy Museum of History & Industry (1965.3598.19.17).

Talking Storybook key. Image copyright Norman Bolotin and The History Bank, Woodinville, Washington.

P. 115

Edward E. Carlson Day. Courtesy Carlson family.

Joseph Gandy, Denver Post Publisher Palmer Hoyt, Alfred Rochester, and Ewen Dingwall. Courtesy Museum of History & Industry (1965.3598.9.2).

P. 116

Sermons from Science. Courtesy Paula Becker.

P. 117

Childcare was available in the Christian Witness Pavilion. Photo by Ken Prichard. Courtesy Ken Prichard.

Sermons from Science brochure. Courtesy Puget Sound Regional Branch Washington State Archives, Century 21 Exposition, Civic Center Development, Exhibits and Concessions Division, Box 21, Folder 233.

The stained glass window in the Christian Witness Pavilion. Courtesy Mike and Carolyn Nore.

P. 118

View of the fairgrounds from the Goodyear Blimp. Photo by Ken Prichard. Courtesy Ken Prichard.

P. 119

Model of the Science Pavilion. Courtesy Museum of History & Industry (1965.3598.9.54).

United Nations Pavilion Speaker's Ring. Courtesy Museum of History & Industry (1963.3119.65.49).

P. 120

World's fair trade dollar. Courtesy Paula Becker.

Boy Scouts with Ruth Ekman. Courtesy Puget Sound Regional Branch Washington State Archives, Century 21 Exposition, Media Photo Prints, Unprocessed Box 2 of 6.

P. 121

The Spanish Village Fiesta. Photo by Ken Prichard. Courtesy Ken Prichard.

Badge. Image copyright Norman Bolotin and The History Bank, Woodinville, Washington.

P. 122

The Official Guide Book. Courtesy Paula Becker.

Model of Jacques Cousteau's diving saucer in the Government of France exhibit. Courtesy Museum of History & Industry (1965.3598.26.3).

P. 123

The French exhibit. Courtesy Puget Sound Regional Branch Washington State Archives, Century 21 Exposition, Media Photo Prints, Box 1 of 2.

The fair's official medallion. Courtesy Paula Becker

P. 124

Les Poupées de Paris. Photo by Ken Prichard. Courtesy Ken Prichard.

P. 125

Adlai Stevenson. Courtesy Puget Sound Regional Branch Washington State Archives, Century 21 Exposition (CR12682).

Lobby of the Playhouse. Courtesy University of Washington Libraries, Special Collections (UW29438z).

Miss Indian America, Brenda Bearchum. Courtesy Puget Sound Regional Branch Washington State Archives, Century 21 Exposition (CR12654).

P. 126-127

Everett DuPen's Fountain of Creation. Courtesy Museum of History & Industry (1965.3598.25.90).

P. 128

KOMO TV cameraman films Dale Evans and Roy Rogers. Courtesy Puget Sound Regional Branch Washington State Archives, Century 21 Exposition (CR13200).

World's fair decal. Courtesy Albert Fisher.

P. 129

Seattle World's Fair Service Scouts. Photo by Ken Prichard. Courtesy Ken Prichard.

P. 130

Crowds waiting. Photo by Cary Tolman. Courtesy Seattle Center.

Alaska-Yukon-Pacific Exposition Day. Courtesy Museum of History & Industry (1986.5.2625).

Mobil driving game. Courtesy Puget Sound Regional Branch Washington State Archives, Century 21 Exposition, Media Photo Prints, Unprocessed Box 3 of 6.

P. 131

Paper fan souvenir. Courtesy Albert Fisher.

P. 132

The moon rises. Photo by Ken Prichard. Courtesy Ken Prichard.

P. 134

Thousands gather to hear Dr. Billy Graham. Courtesy Puget Sound Regional Branch Washington State Archives, Century 21 Exposition (CR13985).

Graham in Memorial Stadium. Courtesy Puget Sound Regional Branch Washington State Archives, Century 21 Exposition (CR13994).

"Gospel According to John." Courtesy Puget Sound Regional Branch Washington State Archives, Century 21 Exposition, Ephemera, Box 5.

P. 135

Art Since 1950. Courtesy Paula Becker.

Philippine fashion. Courtesy Puget Sound Regional Branch Washington State Archives, Century 21 Exposition, Media Photo Prints, Unprocessed Box 2 of 6.

P. 168

Ron Dewar. Photo by *Seattle Post-Intelligencer.* Courtesy Seattle Center.

Wenatchee Youth Circus. Courtesy Puget Sound Regional Branch Washington State Archives, Century 21 Exposition, Media Photo Prints, Box 1 of 2.

P. 169

Space Needle pens. Image copyright Norman Bolotin and The History Bank, Woodinville, Washington.

Logo coffee cup. Image copyright Norman Bolotin and The History Bank, Woodinville, Washington.

Official Century 21 mattress. Courtesy Puget Sound Regional Branch Washington State Archives, Century 21 Exposition, Ephemera, Box 5.

World's Fair luggage. Image copyright Norman Bolotin and The History Bank, Woodinville, Washington.

Contests often used the official logo. Courtesy Albert Fisher.

Portable radio. Courtesy Albert Fisher.

Postcard mobile. Courtesy Albert Fisher.

World's fair coloring set. Courtesy Albert Fisher.

Sugar packets. Courtesy Albert Fisher.

Ashtray. Image copyright Norman Bolotin and The History Bank, Woodinville, Washington.

Woman's blouse. Image copyright Norman Bolotin and The History Bank, Woodinville, Washington.

Juice glasses. Courtesy Paula Becker.

P. 170

Elvis presents a ham. Courtesy Museum of History & Industry (1986.5.40806.2).

P. 172

Bob Hope. Courtesy Puget Sound Regional Branch Washington State Archives, Century 21 Exposition (CR14659).

Georgine Camp with Elvis. Courtesy Georgine Camp.

P. 173

"I Was There" pin. Image copyright Norman Bolotin and The History Bank, Woodinville, Washington.

Elvis, members of his entourage, and fair staffer Albert Fisher. Courtesy Albert Fisher.

P. 174

World's fair poster by Irwin Caplan. Courtesy Seattle Center Foundation.

Brazilian fashion models. Photo by Ken Prichard. Courtesy Ken Prichard.

P. 175

Canadian Tattoo program. Courtesy Paula Becker.

Elvis. Photo by Ron DeRosa. Image courtesy *The Seattle Times.*

A young fairgoer and a Canadian Tattoo participant. Courtesy Museum of History & Industry (1986.5.2638).

P. 176-177

The Canadian Tattoo. Photo by *The Seattle Times.* Courtesy Seattle Center.

P. 178

Ticket to the Canadian Tattoo. Courtesy Louis Larsen.

Joseph Gandy and George Tsutakawa. Photo by Forde Photographers. Image courtesy of the Bryce Seidl Collection (1022).

P. 179

Shell lanterns. Photo by Ken Prichard. Courtesy Ken Prichard.

Crowds on closing day. Courtesy Museum of History & Industry (1986.5.2650).

P. 180

Japanese Village pearl diver. Courtesy Puget Sound Regional Branch Washington State Archives, Century 21 Exposition, Media Photo Prints, Box 2 of 2.

Maze in the IBM Pavilion's garden. Courtesy Puget Sound Regional Branch Washington State Archives, Century 21 Exposition, Media Photo Prints, Unprocessed Box 2 of 6.

P. 181

Ford Seattle-ite XXI. Courtesy University of Washington Libraries, Special Collections (UW29434z).

P. 182

Baby Diaper Service. Courtesy Puget Sound Regional Branch Washington State Archives, Century 21 Exposition (C10378).

Flight to Mars. Courtesy Puget Sound Regional Branch Washington State Archives, Century 21 Exposition, Media Photo Prints, Unprocessed Box 1 of 6.

P. 183

Vogue Magazine fashion show. Courtesy Puget Sound Regional Branch Washington State Archives, Century 21 Exposition, Media Photo Prints, Unprocessed Box 4 of 6.

Rail transport of the future. Courtesy University of Washington Libraries, Special Collections (UW29433z).

P. 184

Showgirls. Courtesy Museum of History & Industry (1965.3598.19.2).

P. 185

Carousel. Photo by Forde Photographers. Image courtesy of the Bryce Seidl Collection (6365c).

P. 186.

Closing ceremonies. Courtesy Museum of History & Industry (1986.5.2651.3).

P. 188

India Pavilion brochure. Courtesy Paula Becker.

Space Needle souvenir shop. Photo by Ken Prichard. Courtesy Ken Prichard.

P. 189

KOMO TV's Art McDonald. Courtesy Puget Sound Regional Branch Washington State Archives, Century 21 Exposition (CR16605).

P. 190

Foo-Hsing Theatre performers. Courtesy Puget Sound Regional Branch Washington State Archives, Century 21 Exposition, Media Photo Prints, Unprocessed Box 6 of 6.

P. 191

The Gayway. Courtesy Museum of History & Industry (1986.5.2768.1.1).

P. 192

Hanging fixtures at Philippines Building. Photo by Ken Prichard. Courtesy Ken Prichard.

Paula Dean. Courtesy Puget Sound Regional Branch Washington State Archives, Century 21 Exposition (CR18407).

P. 193

Logroller at the lumberjack show. Courtesy Museum of History & Industry (1986.5.2739).

Ceramic bottle of Jim Beam. Courtesy Seattle Center Foundation.

P. 194

The Wild Mouse. Photo by Ken Prichard. Courtesy Ken Prichard.

P. 195

Screaming World's Fair fun. Photo by Forde Photographers. Image courtesy of the Bryce Seidl Collection (3688c).

P. 196

Jack Gordon and Victor Rosellini. Photo by Forde Photographers. Image courtesy of the Bryce Seidl Collection (2495b).

Visitors at souvenir stands. Courtesy Museum of History & Industry (1986.5.2652).

Earl Addis. Courtesy Museum of History & Industry (1986.5.2649).

P. 197

Joseph Gandy prepares to close Century 21. Courtesy Museum of History & Industry (1986.5.2649).

P. 198-199

Plaza of the States. Photo by Art Hupy. Courtesy University of Washington Libraries, Special Collections (UW299442z).

P. 200

Fireworks were ignited. Photo by Ken Prichard. Courtesy Ken Prichard.

Mount Rainier and the Century 21 logo ignite. Courtesy Paul Dorpat.

Fair employees carried color-coded badges. Courtesy Albert Fisher.

P. 201

Young fair workers run onto the field. Courtesy Museum of History & Industry (1986.5.2649).

P. 202

Seattle World's Fair pin. Image copyright Norman Bolotin and The History Bank, Woodinville, Washington.

P. 203

The fairgrounds at night. Courtesy University of Washington Libraries, Special Collections (UW856).

Branch Washington State Archives, King County Land Use Property Records Collection, Denny's D. T. 3rd, Block 36, Lot 7.

P. 245

South Entrance. Courtesy Mike and Carolyn Nore.

Exhibition Hall and Opera House. Courtesy Mike and Carolyn Nore.

Food Circus interior. Courtesy Puget Sound Regional Branch Washington State Archives, Century 21 Exposition (CR10632).

P. 246

Gayway. Courtesy Puget Sound Regional Branch Washington State Archives, Century 21 Exposition, Printed Materials, Box 2, Folder 115.

Gas Industries Pavilion. Courtesy University of Washington Libraries, Special Collections (UW29431z).

Ford Motor Company Pavilion. Courtesy University of Washington Libraries, Special Collections (UW29448z).

General Electric Living Exhibit. Courtesy Museum of History & Industry (1963.3119.65cc).

P. 247

Home of Living Light. Photo by Art Hupy. Courtesy University of Washington Libraries, Special Collections (UW29450z).

Hydro-Electric Utilities Exhibit. Courtesy Puget Sound Regional Branch Washington State Archives, Century 21 Exposition, Media Photo Prints, Box 1 of 2.

P. 248

IBM Pavilion. Courtesy Mike and Carolyn Nore.

International Commerce and Industry Buildings surrounding the International Mall. Photo by Ken Prichard. Courtesy Ken Prichard.

United Nations Pavilion. Courtesy Alan Stein.

IBM Pavilion interior. Courtesy Puget Sound Regional Branch Washington State Archives, Century 21 Exposition, Media Photo Prints, Unprocessed Box 5 of 6.

City of Berlin Pavilion. Photo by Ken Prichard. Courtesy Ken Prichard.

P. 249

African Nations Pavilion. Photo by Ken Prichard. Courtesy Ken Prichard.

United Arab Republic Pavilion. Photo by Ken Prichard. Courtesy Ken Prichard.

P. 250

Sweden Pavilion. Courtesy Museum of History & Industry (1965.3598.26.39).

Great Britain Pavilion. Photo by Ken Prichard. Courtesy Ken Prichard.

International Fountain. Courtesy Mike and Carolyn Nore.

Republic of China Pavilion. Courtesy Museum of History & Industry (1963.3119.65.27).

Canada Pavilion. Courtesy Mike and Carolyn Nore.

P. 251

Westlake Park Monorail Terminal. Courtesy Josh Salwitz, Vintage Seattle.

Nalley's Space Age Theater (Nalley's Pavilion). Courtesy University of Washington Libraries, Special Collections (UW29446z).

Islands of Hawaii Pavilion (Polynesian Playhouse). Courtesy Paula Becker.

Japanese Village. Courtesy Puget Sound Regional Branch Washington State Archives, Century 21 Exposition, Media Photo Prints, Unprocessed Box 5 of 6.

P. 252

NASA Pavilion. Courtesy University of Washington Libraries, Special Collections (UW24660z).

Official Information Center. Courtesy Mike and Carolyn Nore.

Opera House interior. Photo by Morley Studios. Courtesy Museum of History & Industry (1987.59).

Plaza of the States. Photo by Art Hupy. Courtesy University of Washington Libraries, Special Collections (MPH083).

P. 253

Playhouse. Courtesy University of Washington Libraries, Special Collections (UW28970z).

Seattle-First International Bank. Courtesy University of Washington Libraries, Special Collections (UW29449z).

Press Building. Courtesy Museum of History & Industry (2001.78).

P. 254

Seattle Mural. Photo by Ken Prichard. Courtesy Ken Prichard.

Sermons from Science Pavilion. Photo by Werner Lenggenhager. Courtesy Seattle Public Library (Werner Lenggenhager Collection).

Gracie Hansen's Paradise International. Photo by Morley Studios. Courtesy Museum of History & Industry (1987.59).

Show Street sign. Courtesy Puget Sound Regional Branch Washington State Archives, Century 21 Exposition (C11777).

P. 255

Le Petit Theatre. Courtesy Puget Sound Regional Branch Washington State Archives, Century 21 Exposition (C7063).

Skyride. Courtesy Mike and Carolyn Nore.

Space Needle with orange roof. Courtesy Museum of History & Industry (1965.3598.26.1).

P. 256

Spanish Village Fiesta. Photo by Ken Prichard. Courtesy Ken Prichard.

Standard Oil Exhibit. Photo by Ken Prichard. Courtesy Ken Prichard.

Stadium. Photo by Frank Shaw. Courtesy Paul Dorpat.

P. 257

American Home Of The Immediate Future. Courtesy Puget Sound Regional Branch Washington State Archives, Century 21 Exposition, Media Photo Prints, Unprocessed Box 3 of 6.

Transport 21. Courtesy Puget Sound Regional Branch Washington State Archives, Century 21 Exposition, Civic Center Development, Exhibits and Concessions Division, Box 21, Folder 239.

United States Science Pavilion. Photo by Werner Lenggenhager. Courtesy Washington State Archives (AR-07809001-ph001691).

P. 258

Hofbrau Haus Restaurant. Photo by Ken Prichard. Courtesy Ken Prichard.

United States Post Office. Courtesy Puget Sound Regional Branch Washington State Archives, Century 21 Exposition, Media Photo Prints, Unprocessed Box 4 of 6.

Kobe Bell. Photo by Megan Churchwell.

P. 259

The Washington State Coliseum. Photo by Ken Prichard. Courtesy Ken Prichard.

P. 260

Space Needle construction. Courtesy Josh Salwitz, Vintage Seattle.

P. 261

Plat map of future Seattle Center site. Courtesy Paul Dorpat.

Plans for Seattle's Civic Field, Auditorium, and Ice Arena. Courtesy Seattle Center Foundation.

Opening day pass to the 1909 Alaska-Yukon-Pacific Exposition. Courtesy Museum of History & Industry (1992.1.1).

P. 262

Washington Governor Arthur B. Langlie. Courtesy University of Washington Libraries, Special Collections (UW27056z).

Aerial view of Memorial Stadium, Civic Auditorium, and Arena. Courtesy Museum of History & Industry (2004.48.2.7).

House demolition. Courtesy Puget Sound Regional Branch Washington State Archives, Century 21 Exposition, Expo Media Photo Negatives (unlogged), House Destruction 9/1/1959.

1958 Seattle city planning commissioners. Courtesy Seattle Municipal Archives (56928).

1961 Rose Bowl half-time show. Courtesy Puget Sound Regional Branch Washington State Archives, Century 21 Exposition, P. R. Division, Box 196, Folder 739.

P. 263

Senator Warren Magnuson with Century 21 Exposition, Inc., President and vice presidents. Courtesy Museum of History & Industry (1965.3598.9.47).

Century 21 logo. Courtesy Century 21 Exposition, Inc.

Promotional brochure. Courtesy Puget Sound Regional Branch Washington State Archives, Century 21 Exposition, Printed Materials, Box 3, Folder 58.

Monorail prototype. Courtesy University of Washington Libraries, Special Collections (UW29428z).

Promotional brochures. Courtesy Puget Sound Regional Branch Washington State Archives, Century 21 Exposition, P. R. Division, Box 194, Folder V 4-728.

NASA logo. Courtesy Paula Becker.

P. 264

Promoting the fair around the world. Courtesy Puget Sound Regional Branch Washington State Archives, Century 21 Exposition, P. R. Division, Box 194, Folder V 4-720.

Northwest Airlines boosted the fair. Photo by Forde Photographers. Image courtesy of the Bryce Seidl Collection (1799).

Space Needle on the drawing board. Courtesy University of Washington Libraries, Special Collections (UW14798).

Pin. Courtesy Albert Fisher.

A Night In Paradise. Courtesy Puget Sound Regional Branch Washington State Archives, Century 21 Exposition, P. R. Division, Box 194, Folder 4-728.

Seattleites predicted that these items might be extinct by the year 2000. Photo by Forde Photographers. Image courtesy of the Bryce Seidl Collection (1488).

Twenty-one 21-year-olds. Courtesy Museum of History & Industry (1965.3598.22.13).

P. 265

Coliseum construction. Courtesy Josh Salwitz, Vintage Seattle.

Rear-screen projection utilized on the cubes in the fair's theme exhibit. LIFE magazine. Image courtesy Seattle Center.

Santa atop the Space Needle. Photo by Forde Photographers. Image courtesy of the Bryce Seidl Collection (5078).

Century 21 Exposition's designated colors. Courtesy Puget Sound Regional Branch Washington State Archives, Century 21 Exposition, P.R. Division, Box 194, Folder V 4-718.

Christmas card promoting the fair. Courtesy Puget Sound Regional Branch Washington State Archives, Century 21 Exposition, P. R. Division, Box 194, Folder V 4-728.

World's Fair edition of The Seattle Times. Courtesy Paula Becker.

Monorail preview ride medallion. Image copyright Norman Bolotin and The History Bank, Woodinville, Washington.

Gold pass. Courtesy Seattle Center Foundation.

P. 266

Camp Fire Girls Day. Courtesy Puget Sound Regional Branch Washington State Archives, Century 21 Exposition, (CR7790).

World's Fair postage stamp. Courtesy Paula Becker.

Oregon's exhibit. Courtesy Puget Sound Regional Branch Washington State Archives, Century 21 Exposition, Media Photo Prints, Unprocessed Box 2 of 6.

New York promoted its upcoming world's fair. Courtesy Puget Sound Regional Branch Washington State Archives, Century 21 Exposition, Media Photo Prints, Unprocessed Box 3 of 6.

Great Britain Pavilion brochure. Courtesy Paula Becker.

Dr. Jonas Salk. Courtesy Puget Sound Regional Branch Washington State Archives, Century 21 Exposition (CR11596).

World's Fair stamp First Day Cover. Courtesy Seattle Center Foundation.

Ticket to Peaceful Uses of Space conference. Courtesy Albert Fisher.

P. 267

Citizenship ceremonies. Courtesy Puget Sound Regional Branch Washington State Archives, Century 21 Exposition (CR7144).

Logo patch. Image copyright Norman Bolotin and The History Bank, Woodinville, Washington.

Carol Channing and George Burns. Courtesy Albert Fisher.

Illinois Day. Courtesy Puget Sound Regional Branch Washington State Archives, Century 21 Exposition, Media Photo Prints, Unprocessed Box 2 of 6.

Van Cliburn. Courtesy Puget Sound Regional Branch Washington State Archives, Century 21 Exposition, Media Photo Prints, Unprocessed Box 6 of 6.

Space Wheel. Courtesy Museum of History & Industry (1986.5.2701).

P. 268

Postcard and playable recording. Courtesy Paula Becker.

Fairgrounds coaster. Courtesy Puget Sound Regional Branch Washington State Archives, Century 21 Exposition, Ephemera, Box 5.

Dr. Edward Teller. Courtesy Puget Sound Regional Branch Washington State Archives, Century 21 Exposition (C11955).

KING 5 TV cameras at the Eye of the Needle. Courtesy Puget Sound Regional Branch Washington State Archives, Century 21 Exposition (CR15030).

Coin worth $1. Courtesy Paula Becker.

Friendship 7. Photo by Morley Studios. Courtesy Museum of History & Industry (1987.59).

P. 269

Shooting the finale. Courtesy Albert Fisher.

Governor Albert Rosellini and Edward Carlson. Courtesy University of Washington Libraries, Special Collections (UW29455z).

Smith Association card. Courtesy Puget Sound Regional Branch Washington State Archives, Century 21 Exposition, Ephemera, Box 4.

Tape recorded Library of the Future. Courtesy Puget Sound Regional Branch Washington State Archives, Century 21 Exposition, Media Photo Prints, Unprocessed Box 1 of 6.

Circus Berlin aerialists. Courtesy Seattle Center Foundation.

Count Basie and His Orchestra. Courtesy Puget Sound Regional Branch Washington State Archives, Century 21 Exposition (C8334).

Joseph Gandy and Richard Nixon. Courtesy University of Washington Libraries, Special Collections (UW29453z).

Thailand's Century 21 postage stamp. Courtesy Seattle Center Foundation.

P. 270

Souvenir of the fair's closing day. Courtesy Albert Fisher.

Official medallion. Courtesy Paula Becker.

Opening of the Pacific Science Center. Courtesy Museum of History & Industry (1986.5.10058).

Festival '71. Courtesy Museum of History & Industry (1986.5.54911).

Early staffers at Seattle Repertory. Photo by Forde Photographers. Image courtesy of the Bryce Seidl Collection (8363).

Space Needle fireworks on New Year's Eve. Courtesy Seattle Center.

President Kennedy's guest pass for closing day. Courtesy Puget Sound Regional Branch Washington State Archives, Century 21 Exposition, Ephemera, Associated Items, Box 1, Folder 34.

P. 271

Seattle Children's Theatre Charlotte Martin Theatre. Courtesy Seattle Children's Theatre.

Gracie ran for governor of Oregon in 1970. Courtesy Paula Becker.

Comcast Bite of Seattle. Photo by Susana Carrillo. Courtesy Seattle Center.

KeyArena opening. Courtesy Seattle Center.

Plaque in Intiman courtyard honoring Ewen Dingwall. Photo by Megan Churchwell.

Bumbershoot. Courtesy Seattle Municipal Archives (77479).

P. 272

Opening of time capsules. Courtesy Seattle Center Foundation.

Doris Chase's Moon Gates. Courtesy Seattle Center.

VERA Project. Courtesy Seattle Center.

International Fountain at night. Courtesy Seattle Center.

Fisher Pavilion opening. Photo by Erik Stuhaug. Courtesy Seattle Municipal Archives (132742).

P. 273

International Fountain. Photo by Anne Korkikian. Courtesy Seattle Center.

P. 274

Next 50 coins. Courtesy Seattle Center Foundation.

P. 275

Leni Schwendinger's "Dreaming In Color" on Kreielsheimer Promenade. Photo by Gareth Loveridge. Courtesy Seattle Center Foundation.

Seattle Center Skatepark. Photo by Chuck Tuck. Courtesy Seattle Center.

P. 276

Official Souvenir Program. Courtesy Paula Becker.

P. 277

World's Fair Band. Courtesy Paul Dorpat.

P. 297

Champagne glass with Space Needle stem. Courtesy Seattle Center Foundation.

P. 298

Concept drawing for the Space Needle. By John Graham Associates. Courtesy University of Washington Libraries, Special Collections (UW16684).

P. 300

Poster by James Edward Peck. Courtesy Seattle Center.

BACK COVER FLAP

Author photos: Paula Becker. Courtesy Sue Lean. *Alan Stein.* Courtesy Tom Brown.

BACK COVER

The Experience Music Project. Courtesy Seattle Center Foundation.

Index

Page numbers for captions and photos are boldface.

Thank You

Many thanks to Megan Churchwell, whose keen eye and stellar organizational skills greatly benefited this project, and to our gifted designer, Nancy Kinnear. Tracy Robinson and Todd Burley at Seattle Center Foundation were wonderful to work with, as was Neal Erickson in the Seattle Center Redevelopment Office.

Many thanks to Phillippa Stairs, Greg Lange, Midori Okazaki, and Michael Saunders at the Washington State Archives, Puget Sound Regional Branch — a more pleasant place to undertake historical research could not be found. We also thank: The staff of University of Washington Special Collections, and the gracious staff of Microforms/Newspapers, whose patience and helpfulness are greatly appreciated. Carolyn Marr, Kristen Halunen, Kathleen Knies, and Howard Giske at the Museum of History and Industry. Amanda Williford, National Park Service archivist at the Golden Gate National Recreation Area, who provided a very helpful transcript of George K. Whitney Jr.'s oral history. Jodee Fenton and Bo Kinney at Seattle Public Library Seattle Room. Michael Paulus, chief archivist at Whitman College Library. Melinda Van Wingen at Everett Public Library Northwest Room. Anne Frantilla and Scott Cline at Seattle Municipal Archives. Thanks to Panda Photographic Lab for helping 50-year-old slides to sparkle.

Collector and fellow historian Norm Bolotin generously gave us access to his amazing collection of fair artifacts. Albert Fisher did the same for his extensive collection of unique fair photographs and artifacts. Thanks to collector Dan Kerlee — again! We are deeply grateful to Seattle World's Fair Assistant Special Events Director Ken Prichard, who gave us access to the beautiful slides he shot during the fair, many of which illustrate and greatly enhance this volume.

Thanks to The Rainier Club for graciously facilitating our World's Fair Reunion, and to Harriet Baskas for documenting the event. Thanks to film maker Vaun Raymond for his timely assistance with imagery, and to Marga Rose Hancock for architectural detective work. Thanks to Sue Lean for support and logistical advice; to Jean Godden, who shared memories of her husband Robert Godden's artwork for the fair; to C.R. Douglas, who gave us access to the private archives of the late Jim Douglas; and to Carver Gayton for his insights into racial issues during the fair. Thanks to Carolyn and Michael I. Nore, for providing access to William M. Kellberg's slides of pre-fair construction. Thanks also to Jess Cliffe of VintageSeattle.org and to Josh Salwitz for the wonderful photos and slides that they have collected. Alweg historian Reinhard Krischer provided insight. Mary Brazeau at Seattle Opera identified early board members. Jeff Kominski at Seattle Children's Theatre helped track down details of the Nile Temple's history. Nicole Chism Griffin and Sarah M. Berman at Seattle Art Museum did the same concerning SAM's long tenure at the Seattle Center. Many thanks to C. David Hughbanks, who read and commented on an early draft, giving this project the benefit of his long-term expertise on both the fair and Seattle Center.

As always, we thank our HistoryLink colleagues profoundly. Peter Blecha, who wrote much of our online Century 21 content, and Katherine Beck, who traveled to Palm Springs with Marie McCaffrey to interview Donald Foster, Barry Upson, and C. David Hughbanks, warrant special commendation. Thanks also to Paul Dorpat for sharing images and ideas.

Our project was deeply informed by the memories and expertise of those who made and lived the Seattle World's Fair, and we thank them from the bottom of our hearts for answering our many questions with depth and insight. These include Patricia Baillargeon, Steve Camp, Gordon Clinton and Florence Vayanger Clinton, Emily Dingwall Easton, Donald Foster, Albert Fisher, Sharon Lund Friel, Barbara Bye Goesling, C. David Hughbanks, Donnie Dingwall Jewell, Jane Langlie, Louis Larsen, Art McDonald, Bill McFarland (with extra big thanks for giving us your Last Handout), J. Ward Phillips, Ken and Nancy Prichard, Junius Rochester, Jay Rockey, Marilyn Gandy Scherrer and Leo Scherrer, Barry Upson, Marene Wilkinson, Jane Carlson Williams, Bagley Wright, and Jeff Wright.

Fair employees over the course of the exposition's seven year planning period, and the fair itself, number in the thousands. Volunteers, without whose generous help the fair could not have happened, swell that number. We commend everyone connected with the Seattle World's Fair for their tremendous efforts, and thank them for the service they did their city. We wish we could have mentioned everyone by name. Thanks also to the many people who told us their own Century 21 stories as we promoted our history of the Alaska-Yukon-Pacific Exposition. Your memories of Century 21 — *your world's fair* — inspired us.

Paula Becker thanks Barry, Hunter, Sawyer, and Lillie Brown for their ongoing support and encouragement, and David and Shirleen Becker, for the same.

Alan Stein thanks Doc Maynard Chapter 54–40, E. Clampus Vitus, for their support and camaraderie. Credo Quia Absurdum.

With gratitude,

Paula Becker and Alan J. Stein

below Crystal champagne glasses with Space Needle stems were given as party favors at the Needle's gala opening event.

above An early concept drawing for the Space
Needle by John Graham Associates.

following page James Edward Peck's stunning
poster depicts the glowing fairgrounds cradled
by sea, mountains, and the vast night sky.

Acknowledgements

Volunteerism is the voice of people put into action. These actions shape and mold the present into a future of which we can all be proud.

— HELEN DYER

We want to especially thank our key volunteers who share their wisdom and hearts with us on a daily basis helping to shape Seattle Center into the spectacular community asset it is today.

Like most projects there are a few people who deserve special recognition. Todd Burley and Neal Erickson have done a wonderful job staffing the history portion of The Next Fifty efforts. We appreciate all the hours they have spent working on the details that bring this important history to life. Special thanks and appreciation to Seattle Center staff led by Robert Nellams for their great work in stewarding the most important legacy of the 1962 World's Fair — Seattle Center.

Thank you to the amazing folks at HistoryLink — Marie McCaffrey, Tom Brown, Paula Becker, Nancy Kinnear, Alan J. Stein — you have not only made this work possible you have been wonderful fellow travelers. Your commitment to history and our community will touch many hearts and minds over the generations.

With gratitude,

Tracy Robinson
Executive Director
Seattle Center Foundation

SeattleWorld'sFair1962